Charmers and Chancers

Hugh Oram

Trafford
PUBLISHING   www.trafford.com
North America & international
toll-free: 1 888 232 4444 (USA & Canada)
fax: 812 355 4082

To all the wonderful people I've met, and often interviewed, over the past 50 years, and to the rogues, who' ve often made life that bit more entertaining, but who are best seen in a rapidly retreating rear view mirror.

Acknowledgements

I' d especially like to thank my wife Bernadette for all her help and support while I was writing this book and I' d also like to thank all the people who so generously answered all my questions. I' d also like to thank Maria Gillen in Athlone, who has given me much encouragement throughout the process of putting the book together and finally, I'd like to express my appreciation to Dean Lochner of the Bondi Group in Dublin for all his technical back- up and support.

All the contents of the book, including all the people I've included, are listed in alphabetical order.

Jeremy Addis

I knew Jeremy for over 40 years; when I first met him, he was working in publicity for Kilkenny Design. In 1976, he had launched Books Ireland magazine, which has managed to keep going, one way and another, ever since. I started doing reviews for it about 25 years ago. In the late 1980s, he and his late wife Deirdre, who died in 2010, moved to Newgrove Avenue in Sandymount. Not so long ago, at the end of 2013, it looked as if Books Ireland was going to collapse, when the Arts Council withdrew its funding, but Wordwell promptly stepped in and saved the day. Jeremy was long noted for his annual drinks party, held on January 6, Women's Christmas.

It had many spectacular occasions, perhaps none more startling than the time that the late Agnes Bernelle, the German- born actress and singer, who lived in Sandymount, clapped her hands to shut everyone up. Then she told the assembled multitude that her son was coming along; as he had trans- gender issues, he would be coming dressed as a woman. No- one batted even the hint of an eyelid.

Jeremy was very funny on occasion; in the days when my wife Bernadette and myself regularly walked the promenade at Sandymount Strand, we'd often meet Jeremy walking his dogs. Over the years, we kept in touch with his ongoing menagerie of animals, mostly dogs, but cats, too. One of his earlier dogs was an affectionate old pooch called Polly. One day, we saw her rushing to greet another dog on the strand. The two dogs, in typical doggy fashion, started sniffing each other bum holes. Jeremy said, sotte voce, with a sardonic tone in his voice, "what a good job humans don' t meet and greet the way dogs do".Jeremy Addis died on August 27,2016.

Dermot Ahern

I met up with Dermot Ahern when he was Minister for Foreign Affairs and I was writing a book on the history of Dundalk and Blackrock in Co Louth, published in 2006. I found him friendly, engaging and very down to earth; he was as keen to tell me about his youthful days of playing professional soccer in Dundalk as he was talking about the history of Blackrock, that charming seaside village just outside Dundalk, where he was brought up and where he still lives. Dermot held a whole series of Ministerial portfolios and it's a great pity that illness has forced him to retire from politics, although he still writes about it.

One person to whom he gave me an introduction was Mrs Hilda Woods, from Carlingford, with whom I had very engaging conversations when I was doing a book on the history of Omeath, Carlingford and Greenore, published in 2008. Hilda came from Liverpool and before the second world war, she had married a solicitor from Dundalk called Peter Woods, just as the second world war was starting, and had come over to Carlingford to live. Her husband ran the legal practice in Dundalk where Dermot Ahern was apprenticed and his introduction to Hilda was a wonderful opportunity. She was 95 years of age when I talked with her, and she had wonderfully crystal clear and accurate memories of what life was like in Carlingford in the old days, going right back to the 1920s. She was able to tell me who lived where and who ran which shop, going back decades, all invaluable material for the book. She herself was one of the great characters of

Carlingford, but nothing had escaped her attention and she was able to encapsulate the whole history of that historic town throughout nearly all of the 20th century. Hilda died in 2010, just three weeks after her 97th birthday.

Lord Altamont

I got on rather well with Lord Altamont of Westport, Co Mayo but any time I met him, he always insisted that I call him "Jeremy", so Jeremy it always was. Westport House and its 161 hectare estate was in the Browne family for 300 years, but sadly, in 2016, the whole estate was put up for sale, its future undecided. Jeremy, who was also the 11th Marquess of Sligo, had been born in London and was educated in the UK as well as in Dublin. Another part of his pedigree was even more distinguished; he was the 13th great grandson of Granuaile, Grace O' Malley, the pirate queen of the west.

Keeping Westport House and its estate as a going concern was always of prime concern to Jeremy. He and his wife, Lady Jennifer, initially opened the house to the public in 1960, going on to open a zoo, tea rooms and a whole host of activities within the estate, to draw in visitors and generate income. In over 50 years, up to 2016, the house and estate had attracted five million visitors, making it one of the top visitor attractions in the West of Ireland. Jeremy was a shameless publicist on behalf of his beloved house and estate; he appeared on the Late Late Show no fewer than 14 times. He died in 2014 and his death indeed proved to be the end of an era.

Eamonn Andrews

When I was researching and writing my book on Bewleys, published in 1980, I was in contact with Eamonn Andrews, who was most charming and helpful with his reminiscences on the subject. Born in Dublin in 1922, just as the new Free State was coming into being, after the Emergency period of the second world war, he began his broadcasting career as a boxing commentator on Radio Éireann. But before long, he had moved to London, where he made a stellar career for himself in television. In the 1950s, he was the host for the weekly quiz show, What's My Line, then he hosted This is Your Life, from 1955 until 1964 and then from 1969 to 1987. Although much of his career was closely connected with the BBC, he was also chairman of the RTÉ Authority from 1960 to 1964. During his time in office in Donnybrook, the Irish television service, Telefís Éireann, started up on January 1, 1962, having been officially opened by the disapproving President Eamon de Valera the night before, the last day of December, 1961.

Eamon was married to Grainne Bourke, who came from the Bourke family, renowned theatrical costumiers in Dame Street, Dublin. He and his wife had three adopted children and during the 1960s, there were many stories going the rounds over how he and Charles Haughey had come to blows in the old Jurys Hotel in Ballsbridge, when Haughey had made an alleged reference to Eamonn Andrews' "three bastards" or adopted children. Sadly, Eamonn Andrews picked up a bug that proved fatal, on a long distance flight in 1987 and died that year.

Lady Annie Arnott

Lady Annie, once of the trendy socialites of the Dublin social scene, was a most genial host. When I was researching and writing my first book on Irish newspaper history, published in 1983, I went to meet her at her grace and favour house close to the old Phoenix Park racecourse in Dublin. She had married Sir John Arnott, who was during the 1950s, the London correspondent of The Irish Times. For many years, the newspaper had been owned by the Arnott family, so it was little problem for Sir John to get a neat little number for himself. The Arnotts had many interests in Ireland; they also founded the Phoenix Park racecourse, in 1902 and it was for that reason that when I met her, Lady Arnott was living in a delightful bijou house close to the racecourse. But the days of the racecourse were coming to an end, and Lady Arnott sold it off for redevelopment.

Lady Astor

Nancy Astor was a remarkable woman, born in Virginia in the US in 1879. Later, she settled in the UK and she became the first female MP to take her seat at Westminster in November, 1919. She had come to England in 1903 and had done rather well for herself, marrying Waldorf Astor, who became an MP for Plymouth. He was first elected in 1909, but in 1919, his father died and he succeeded to his father's title. He couldn't of course continue as an MP, so his wife took over from him. She wasn't the first woman elected to Westminster; that privilege belonged to Countess Markievicz, who as a staunch supporter of Sinn Féin, refused to take her seat.

So the privilege of being the first woman to sit in the House of Commons fell to Nancy Astor. There, she got into inevitable rows with Winston Churchill. On one occasion in the House, she said to him "Winston, you are drunk", to which he replied "Madame, you are ugly, but in the morning, I shall be sober". Nancy was a keen advocate of the rights of women and children and constantly pressed these concerns in the House of Commons. She proved a very popular MP for Plymouth Sutton and was repeatedly re- elected. She lived in a fine terraced house on Plymouth Hoe.

The first major air raid on Plymouth by the Nazis came on the evening of March 20, 1941; that afternoon, King George VI and his wife, the Queen, were entertained to tea by Nancy Astor at her home on the Hoe. A total of eight major air raids were carried out on Plymouth, up to 1944. Just over 72, 000 houses were destroyed and 1, 200 civilians were killed. One of my earliest memories is of the basement in the South Devon and Cornwall Blind Institution, where I was brought up. It had been converted into an air raid shelter. Earlier in the war, before I was born, my father was in the back garden of the Institution when a bomb came down, narrowly missing him. It demolished a complete wing of the building. In the early 1950s, when it was rebuilt, I was allowed to learn some bricklaying, which I took great pride in! I also remember seeing, just after the war, the centre of Plymouth, which has been totally devastated. When a brand new city centre was built, at first, it was all white and modern and shiny all very impressive, but the last time we were in Plymouth, in 1982, it seemed dirty, litter- strewn and covered in graffiti. But one thing remains with me from those war years, the sound of the air raid siren and even today, when I hear one, it gives me the shivers.

But coming back to the 1945 general election, Nancy Astor failed to be re- elected and after 26 years as an MP, she had lost her magic touch and was unceremoniously booted out of Westminster. About a year before that election, my aunt Sheila was taking me for a walk on Plymouth Hoe. Since I was only about a year old, I was in my pram and apparently, Nancy Astor stopped, took a look inside and declared that I was the most beautiful baby she had ever seen. So from a very early age, I became aware of politicians' hyperbole!

In those days, my aunt Sheila had blonde hair and because my own hair was so fair, many people thought, incorrectly, that she was my real mother. I had been born in Devonport, just as all the German air raids on Plymouth were coming to a stop. I was brought up in the South Devon and Cornwall Institution for the Blind, where my grandfather Herbert Hammond was the superintendent. I always thought that he was the most kindly and generous grandfather any child could have and when I was just 11, I was devastated by his death. Even all these years later, I can still feel that childhood devastation. He came from Ashton under Lyne, not far from Manchester, but in his early adulthood, had lived in New York. He was keen to stay there, but his wife Elizabeth, whose background was Glaswegian, with strong Irish connections, was far from enthusiastic, so his wife's view prevailed, as usually happens. I also discovered subsequently that my other grandmother, who had links with Edinburgh, but who was brought up in India, also had a strong Irish pedigree.

When I was a child, I was quick to discover the delights of Plymouth Hoe, that vast stretch of green space between the centre of Plymouth and Plymouth Sound, that great estuary, only rivalled in this part of the world by Cork Harbour. As for Nancy Astor, who had spotted me being taken for a walk on the Hoe, she went on to retire from the world of politics; she was an often foolish and egotistical woman from a background of great wealth as well as being a lifelong teetotaller (not to be entirely recommended!) Voters eventually discovered that she had delivered far less than she had promised. She lived on for another 20 years, until her death in 1964. In the 1960s, their great house, Cliveden, became the most notorious residence in Britain, with all the partying and nude swimming at Cliveden by the whole Profumo gang, including Christine Keeler.

I lived in Plymouth until 1947, when I was four, and we then moved to a far drearier lifestyle in Birmingham. I never much liked Birmingham; all I can remember from the prep school I went to, Chigwell House- there's ostentation for you- was that the lady who was an English teacher, had been living in Tokyo in 1923 when the great earthquake struck. I can still remember her description of the houses all round her just caving in. I later went to a public school, the King Edward VI school, which I absolutely hated; the only subject I revelled in was Latin. I well remember that the then headmaster was a man called Lunt, which even in my younger days, thought was an excellent rhyme with a slang word for female genitalia.

But as for Plymouth, after we left, we still returned regularly for holidays. The last time I stayed in the Institution with my grandparents was when I was about nine. Just across the road was and still is, St Mathias church, where I was christened. It was said during the second world war that the Luftwaffe never bombed the church, because it was such a landmark, which meant that many surrounding buildings, including the Blind Institution, largely escaped. My grandfather the superintendent of the institution, was a wonderful man; to me as a young kid, all the stars in the heavens shone out of him. One of the many things that my grandparents introduced me to was the Archers, a daily serial that had just started on BBC Radio. Needless to remark, I quickly grew out of any interest in this farming 'soap'! When I knew then that I would never stay in the institution again, I spent days preparing detailed architectural drawings of the vast sprawling building, a portent perhaps of my subsequent interest in everything archival and in preserving history, especially local history.

The institution, a remarkable building, had been constructed as the blind institution in 1876 and exactly a century later, in 1976, it was taken over by the next door Plymouth High School for Girls. The last time I saw the place, from the outside, in 1982, which was the most recent occasion we've been to Plymouth, the façade hadn't changed a bit. Something else I discovered in Plymouth gave me a life-long fascination with railways. I discovered the ideal place, not far from the Blind Institution, for watching trains coming and going from North Road station. Locos were still steam in those days, so it was a formidable experience watching the long distance expresses, either arriving in Plymouth from London, or making the journey in the opposite direction. While I've never been an 'anorak' in the sense of a dedicated train spotter,

I' ve had a great interest in railway history, in Ireland and elsewhere, ever since, compounded by my second long distance Continental train journey, an overnight trip, from Paris to Rome in 1960.

Bobby Ballagh

One of Ireland' s most distinguished contemporary artists, Bobby was born in 1943 and grew up in a flat in Elgin Road, Ballsbridge. In those days, the roads around Ballsbridge were so quiet that he and his friends could play tennis in the road and complete whole games without being interrupted by traffic. He began his career in music, playing with the Chessmen, before turning to art. In his career, he has designed many theatre sets, including for Riverdance, as well as over 70 Irish stamps and the last series of Irish banknotes, before the euro was introduced in 2002.

He has also done many portraits and one of my earliest introductions to his work came one night at the Hendricks Gallery, once a fabled art venue on the west side of St Stephen' s Green, notable for its opening nights, when the great and the good invariably turned up (including the pair of us!) One particular opening night caused a real frisson; on show was a large portrait that Bobby had painted of his wife Betty descending the spiral staircase at their home, but in the nude. That wasn' t the first controversial subject he' d painted. Back in 1977, he did a painting called Oh Mona! of a man flashing at the Mona Lisa painting in the Louvre in Paris.

For two of my books the covers were designed by Bobby and as work progressed, I had detailed discussions with him; I soon found out that any conversation with Bobby soon ranged far beyond the world of art, since he has always been intensely aware politically, utterly committed in his republican and socialist views and a constant critic of the so- called establishment, whether in art or in the wider world of politics.

The first book of mine that he did the cover for was the history of advertising in Ireland, published in 1986, and the largest book I ever produced, running to close on 800 pages. I look back on that with a certain amazement, as it was created in pre- computer times, and all the copy and captions had to be typed on a portable typewriter. The second book of mine that Bobby did the cover for was the 1990 volume published to commemorate the 50th anniversary of Dublin airport. For that cover, Bobby brought together early illustrations showing sheep grazing besides the runway, as well as the iconic first terminal building.

In the years since, we have kept in touch from time to time; Bobby himself has never shied away from controversy. He is also president of the Ireland Institute of Historical and Cultural Studies, in the premises where the Pearse family once had their monumental stone business and where Pádraig Pearse, the leader of the 1916 Easter Rising, was born and brought up. One topic that's guaranteed to get Bobby going is examining the extent to which the noble principles of the 1916 Proclamation have or rather, haven't, been put into practice in the Ireland of the following 100 years. On a personal level, too, Bobby can be equally eloquent; when his beloved wife Betty died in 2011, he was very critical of the deficiencies in hospital care that led to her death.

I've always admired Bobby's undiluted integrity, whether in his artistic or political beliefs, a fearsome critic of the establishment's usual practice of saying nothing and doing that with its hand in front of its mouth.

Mary and Tania Banotti

I've met Mary Banotti on occasion; born in 1939, she's a grandniece of Michael Collins, a fearsome family heritage. She worked as a nurse for many years before going into politics and was a Fine Gael MEP from 1984 until 2004. In the

1997 presidential election contest, she came second. Mary's former husband was Italian, hence her surname. I've known her daughter, Tania, rather better. She had a long career running film and theatre organisations and in that role, I always found her exceptionally helpful. Then she made what to many people was a rather surprising choice; she went to IAPI, the organisation that represents Irish- based advertising agencies, as its chief executive, and over the past few years has put her own distinctive style of efficiency on it. Since she went to IAPI, I' ve had little or no dealings with Tania, as my work has evolved in many directions, all of them well away from the advertising history whose history I chronicled 30 years ago.

Baring family

The Baring family of the once notorious bank of the same name, have long had a connection with Ireland. In 1909, one of the family spotted an advertisement in The Field for an island up for sale. It turned out to be Lambay Island off the coast of north Co Dublin. Ever since, it' s been owned and occupied by the Baring family, which had been elevated to the peerage in 1885. The present owner is the 7th Lord Revelstoke, usually known to his friends as Alex Baring; he succeeded to the title in 2012. However, an earlier Lord Revelstoke, the fourth, met Bernadette at a reception in Iveagh House, home of the Department of External Affairs, now the Department of Foreign Affairs. His lordship made an extraordinary offer to Bernadette; he wanted her to have a set of four metre high gates from Lambay Island. But this was a present she could only politely refuse; there was no way such a set of gates could have fitted in at her suburban home, but ever since, the sheer incongruity of the offer has amused her. Out of all the Barings who have lived on Lambay, the fourth Lord Revestoke was arguably the most interesting. He lived on the island for the best part of 60 years; besides caring for the house, designed by Sir Edwin Lutyens in 1910/ 11, the groves of trees, the flower gardens designed by Gertrude Jekyll, the renowned garden designer, Lutyens' professional partner and the farm on the island, his lordship did such things as write doggerel. One visitor to the island, when he was working as press attaché at the British legation in Dublin during the second world war, was the poet John Betjeman, who declared that his lordship' s doggerel poetry was actually quite good. His lordship had another endearing habit; often in the early hours of the morning, he played chess.

Canon Noel Battye

Noel, who was ordained in the Church of Ireland in 1966, had his first parish in Dungannon, Co Tyrone, before moving to Belfast. In 1980, he was appointed rector of St Finnian' s in Cregagh in east Belfast and retired from there in 2008, after 28 years of service. Before that Belfast appointment, he had been chaplain at Pembroke College, Cambridge, between 1973 and 1978. Noel often refers to that period of his life; he had clearly enjoyed his time at Cambridge. But for the past 30 years, he has enjoyed another career, which has kept him in the public eye- and ear- as presenter of the Sounds Sacred music programme on BBC Radio Ulster. While Noel has many connections with Northern Ireland, his family background is in Kilmacthomas, Co Waterford, where his grandfather originally settled when he took up a job managing the local textile mill. Noel' s father ran a shop in the village for many years and he was also noted for the many photographs he took of the locality, during the 1950s and 1960s.

I also had a much earlier introduction to religious music, back in the early 1970s. Between the time in 1970 when Bernadette and I first met and when we married in 1972, Bernadette would often come to Belfast to spend the weekend with me. We often visited some of the lovely places around the coast in the North, including Ballycastle, Bangor, Donaghadee and Portavogie. Bernadette travelled to Belfast on a Friday evening and returned on a Sunday evening; on Sunday evenings, I' d go with her to the old station in Great Victoria Street to see her off and we' d often be serenaded in this process, as every Sunday evening, a Salvation Army band would be playing outside the station. The echoes of that brass band have followed me down through the years.

Dr Thekla Beere

Dr Beere was a remarkable woman, who did much pioneering work in equal rights for women, yet she was modesty and courtesy personified. I met her on one occasion, in the 1980s, for a book I was writing and she welcomed me to her home in Stillorgan, south Co Dublin, answering my questions most helpfully. She was then in her 80s and still very sprightly and with it; she had been born in 1901 and died in 1990 at the age of 90. A career civil servant, she achieved a remarkable breakthrough in 1959, at the age of 58, when she was made the first ever woman to became secretary (now Secretary- General) of a government department. She was promoted to secretary of the then Department of Transport & Power, covering such vital aspects of the nation' s economy as public transport, aviation, then to a large extent still in its infancy in Ireland, and energy. She played an even more important role in 1972 when she headed a commission that investigated women' s rights in Ireland. Up till then, women could no longer continue working in the public service after they had got married and soon after that commission reported, the marriage bar, ludicrously out of date, was banished into the history books.

Robin Bell

He was one of the most likeable business people I have ever met, charm personified, a great people person and very efficient in all his dealings. People couldn't help but like him and he made friends whenever he went. I got to know him in the early 1970s, because I was then editing a trade magazine for the grocery business in Northern Ireland. One of the major brands in those days was the American- owned Campbell' s Soups- it' still the biggest soup company in the world- and it turned out that the man who was its sales director in this part of the world, based at Cambell' s UK headquarters in Peterborough, was Robin Bell. Yet Robin had a remarkable ability to get on with people of all persuasions and he had as many friends in the south as in the north. He was a true master of his craft but I also remember some memorable dinners with him and his wife Vera, also from the North.

Robin left school in 1941, failed to get into Bangor Grammar School and became a telegram boy. Between 1945 and 1952, he served in the RAF in the Middle East, then with the police in Malaysia, in between working at Bangor Town Hall as an assistant entertainments and promotions officer. His first job in the grocery trade came in 1952 when he joined Scribbens Kemp selling their biscuits and slab cake in east Belfast. From there, he moved to Bird' s Custard, finally joining Campbell' s Soups, first in Belfast, then in London. By 1960, he was back in his native Northern Ireland, covering the whole of Ireland and Scotland. Then in 1965, he transferred to King' s Lynn, which is where we first met him; he was covering much of Europe, working with agents in 13 countries. He was made UK sales director in 1972.

He was a great fund of stories and perhaps the best of the ones he told me concerned a visit to Paris. He returned to his hotel late at night, put his key in the lock of his room door, went in, got ready for bed and climbed in, for a good night' s sleep. The only snag was that he had put his key into the wrong keyhole; it wasn't his room at all. When he got into bed, he found a beautiful blonde there; who was more surprised, it was hard to tell, but there the story ended, but Robin, with a big grin, flatly refused to divulge any more details. The last time that we met him, in London, where he entertained us to dinner, he was clearly unwell and a short while later, he died from a heart attack. That was 40 years ago; we still keep in touch with his wife Vera, now 90, who still lives in Bangor, Co Down.

Agnes Bernelle

An actress and a cabaret singer, she was born in Berlin in 1923; when she was 13, she and the rest of her Jewish family wisely fled Germany and settled in London. During the second world war, she broadcast much propanda material from Britain, in German, to listeners in Germany. After the war, she began her stage career in London; one of her early roles was in a production of Salome. Agnes played the lead role in the nude, which was entirely fitting for her exuberant personality. She also appeared in a number of films, 12 in all between 1945 and 1999. In 1945, she married Desmond Leslie, from the renowned Leslie family who still live at Castle Leslie in Glaslough, Co Monaghan. Agnes came to Ireland for the first time in 1963, when she was expecting their third child.

Agnes had an unpleasant surprise when she arrived in Glaslough for the first time; she found her husband's mistress sleeping in her bed. The stormy marriage to Desmond Leslie lasted until 1969; later, Agnes settled in Dublin, when she got married to Maurice Craig, the author and historian. They lived for many years at Strand Road in Sandymount, Dublin, where their house was described as being the last word in interior design decadence. Agnes continued to perform well into old age, including many outstanding contributions to the Sunday

Miscellany programme on RTÉ Radio 1. She died in 1999, aged 76, a forceful and often funny person right to the very end.

Sir John Betjeman

If anyone was a favourite poet laureate in Britain, it was Sir John Betjeman, poet, writer and broadcaster, whose appearances on television were always memorable. He was everyone's favourite grand uncle. He had an absolute love of an earlier England, especially Victorian and Edwardian and scorned much of what passed for modern architecture. He lived from 1906 until 1984 and it was one of his many eccentricities that he still had his childhood teddy bear with him when he died. During the second world war, he was seconded to the British legation, based at Merrion Square in Dublin. The man leading that legation, upgraded to embassy after the Irish Free State became a republic in 1949, was Sir John Mahaffy. Betjeman was sent to Dublin as press attaché, but he spent most of his time in Dublin getting to know the artistic community, including a young poet called Patrick Kavanagh. When I was preparing my book on the history of Bewleys, first published in 1980 then republished in 2004, I wrote to Sir John Betjeman. Although he was then in ill health, he wrote me a most charming letter saying just how much he had enjoyed his time in Dublin during the war and of course, he remembered vividly the war- time Bewley's cafés, especially the ones in Grafton Street and Westmoreland Street.

Bewley family

I had published my first book, Fishing in Ireland, in 1979, which I edited for Appletree Press in Belfast. I was comparatively later getting into books, in my mid- 30s, but when the larger than life John Murphy of Appletree asked me to edit the fishing book, I was delighted. I persuaded three of the top Irish fishing writers to contribute on their specialities, Dick Warner, Peter R Brown and Kevin Linnane and also managed to persuade Clive Gammon, then probably the best-known fishing writer cross-channel to contribute a foreword. I've never fished in my life; it' s been an ambition totally absent from all stages of my life! But I' d got roped into the Appletree book because I' d been doing an even more improbable job, editing a magazine in Belfast called the Ulster Angler. Like most forms of journalism, I found that talking to the right experts in any particular field would ensure authentic and well-informed copy. So in due course, the fishing book came out; no audience is more critical than the angling community; if you have so much as a comma out of place, you soon hear about it. The only fault found with the book was that it had mentioned a particular fishing hotel in Co Donegal, but the Irish edition of the Daily Mirror gleefully pointed out in its review that the hotel had burned down a number of years previously!

Once the fishing book was out of the way, I turned to another topic, Bewleys, which I thought would make a very interesting book, as indeed it did. Through my wife Bernadette, who knew Tom Kennedy through his film work, I got talking to Tom about doing a book on Bewleys. He proved an enthusiastic supporter of the project and I met many of the Bewley family, beginning with Victor Bewley, the patriach of the family, a great humanitarian, someone who helped the travelling community, people in prison and the Northern peace process long before they became fashionable. Victor died in 1999, aged 87. I also met his brother Alfred, who ran the bakery side of the business; the bakery was then in Long Lane. Alfred had gone to Leeds Bakery College in 1937 and there met and subsequently married Mary. She died very recently, in 2015, aged 102. Alfred and Mary had a lovely old house in Leixlip and one night we went to dinner there; Mary Bewley gaily informed us that she had picked the mushrooms for the soup in the local woods that very morning! We were very nervous, but nothing untoward happened. Rachel Bewley-Bateman was another member of the clan whom I got to know well.

There were many other members of the Bewleys family, including Patrick, still involved with the firm. In the early 1980s, Bewleys went through a tough time, then in 1986, Patrick and Veronica Campbell took it over. Eventually Patrick Campbell' s career changed into something totally different; he' s now a sculptor and artist living and working in Italy. I also met many of the staff in Bewleys, including the famous Kathleen 'Tattens' Toomey, who worked there for years as a waitress and who was known as the 'queen of Bewleys'. She and her sister Bridie both joined Bewleys on the same day in 1948. Tattens died in 2007, six years after her sister.

Tattens always had a great sense of fun and an odd sense of humour; the maiden name of one of the other waitresses was Helen Privett and Tattens always put her down on the dockets as "Miss Hedge".

In those days, Bewleys had a wonderful family atmosphere and the staff were looked after as if they were part of the family. I also found out much about the Quaker traditions that have been so meaningful to me ever since. Quakers don' t like show- off ostentation, an accumulation of material wealth, bragging about one' s accomplishments, while they are big into community spirit. Their values were the exact opposite of those that came to the fore during the notorious Celtic Tiger years that came to a shuddering halt in 2008.No bling for the Bewleys!

After getting a thorough introduction to the Bewley family and firm, the book came together without too much trouble, despite the fact that in 1977, a fire in the

Westmoreland Street café and shop had destroyed so many records. The book was modest, but was well received. Donal Foley gave it a good mention in The Irish Times and the launch, in Hodges Figgis in Dawson Street, was truly memorable, with Frankie Byrne and Noel Purcell as distinguished guests. After the launch, Bernadette and I followed an old publishing tradition by taking the publisher, Tom Kennedy and his wife Appie, to dinner in a long vanished restaurant between Dawson Street and South Frederick Street. The talk was all about Bewleys but at the end of the meal, there was one thing the restaurant didn' t have- coffee!

Birmingham

I spent 15 years of my early life in Birmingham and in many respects, it was joyless, a living hell, mostly because of the frightful public school I went to, King Edward VI, which was like an educational equivalent of a German prisoner of war camp. My first school, a prep school, was fine; I quite enjoyed that and enjoyed learning very much. By the time I was seven, I used to read the Daily Telegraph every day, so I got into the newspaper habit early. The school also had one or two notable teachers, especially one of the English teachers, who was so good that his pupils were really enticed into reading and learning about literature. He was also a very pleasant teacher, not at all given to bullying or physical punishment. I came to have great respect for him as a teacher, but then he suddenly disappeared; it was only later that I found out that he had been convicted for a substantial fraud and jailed. He was my first encounter with a chancer and it taught me that chancers can be the most glib and socially at ease people, a useful early lesson. One of the few events I can remember with great clarity from my time at the public school is what happened one day when I was having lunch with all my fellow pupils. I was about 11 at the time; all of a sudden, one of the teachers appeared by my side and told me that he sad news for me, that my beloved grandfather in Plymouth had just died. I hadn' t even known he' d been ill, so it was a tremendous shock, that burned deep into my soul. Even today, I can still feel the pain I felt then as a young boy.

I have no recollections of any of the teachers at the school, apart from the headmaster. When I was 15, I became very ill, nearly kicked it in fact; as I recovered, I made it quite clear that I had no intention of returning to the public school. Fortunately, my parents could see by then just how much I hated the place, and instead, I went to Aston Technical School and then the local College of Commerce, to do all my O and A levels, without too much problem. The subject I did best in was Latin, which is actually an excellent grounding for anyone who wants to become a writer.

In our early years in Birmingham, we lived in a bleak, terraced house in Yew Tree Road, Edgbaston. The house was quite substantial, but old. I remember vividly one hilarious episode when I still young. My father had rented out the front room as a self- contained bedsitter; one night, there was a hell of a party, which went on well into the night. The following day, many muttered imprecations followed as the clean- up was put in place and vast quantities of used condoms were picked up. Clearly, there had been a group sex party long before such things became fashionable, indeed commonplace; at the time, it seemed an excellent idea to me and I merely regretted that I was far too young to have taken part in anything like that.

We didn' t stay in that house too long. As soon as my father was earning reasonably, he opted for a brand new house on a new road that was being built in Moseley, close to the famous Edgbaston cricket ground. This was real middle class territory, but all I can remember now about the neighbours is that a Finnish couple lived next door to us, on one side, while across the road, a young Dutch boy who was training to be a pianist, practised all day long. But home living became much more comfortable. We had a lovely dog, called Netta, a female black and white fox terrier, an absolute pet. In Plymouth earlier on, my grandparents had a male dog of the same species, Bruce, who was odd in many respects. He didn' t for instance like blind people, so he never allowed any of the blind inmates at the Blind Institution in Plymouth pet him.

We also had a great family tragedy when we were living at Moorcroft Road, Moseley. My mother, Vera Annie, died at the young age of 44 from breast cancer. In those days, to be diagnosed with a disease like that was an almost certain death penalty. After my mother' s death, I started working as a teacher, without any qualifications whatsoever. I spent a year as a supply teacher in a primary school nearby, where I really enjoyed teaching the kids both English and French. I was already well familiar with France, since I had been on my first exchange visit there when I was 14. Then came university and the chance to flee Birmingham for good and go and live in Ireland, Derry in fact. My father sold the house in Birmingham and went to live in Orpington in Kent, where he eventually started married life with his second wife, my stepmother, Pat Roberts, who died four years ago. My father was working in the old Covent Garden wholesale market in London and I remember vividly him telling me one day how the famous TV comedienne, Hattie Jacques, had come round one day. It turned out, according to his description, that not only was she very big but very smelly as well!

Birmingham had however, provided some positive highlights. I used to love going into the old central library in the city centre; I' ve seen many photographs of its new replacement, but have never been into it. I also derived a tremendous amount of enjoyment from going to concerts by the City of Birmingham Symphony Orchestra, in the old Town Hall, perching in one of the cheapest seats, beside the organ. I also well remember going to a cinema that specialised in foreign films and seeing the Russian film about the Battleship Potemkin, which had a long- lasting impact. Birmingham was also the place where I saw my first ever striptease, a very modest disrobing by the standards of today, but in the late 1950s, a shocking breakdown in public morals!

In retrospect, one small trip I remembered was one I did with the rest of the family when I was quite young, probably around nine, going to visit distant relatives in the lovely countryside of Shropshire and Herefordshire. In Shropshire, I can well recall going to see an elderly woman, dressed in very old fashioned clothes, who lived in a thatched cottage that had changed little for generations. Apparently, she was of Huguenot descent, the French Protestants who fled France in the 17th and 18th century. She was related, distantly, but I never discovered what the exact connection was to the rest of the family. That same day, we went to visit other distant relatives who lived on a very old fashioned farm in Herefordshire. It was so old fashioned that in the huge kitchen, huge flitches of bacon were hung from the ceiling to cure, something I found fascinating. But I never discovered either what relations this farm family had to the rest of us. We only met these remote relatives in Shropshire and Herefordshire once and never kept in touch with them after that visit.

But of all the things I did in Birmingham, the one that had the most impact was getting involved in the Irish Centre in Digbeth and getting to know Irish people for the first time and also discovering the history of Ireland. It all had a profound influence on me and created a determination to find out more. I wasn' t to know of course at that early stage, that I was destined to meet and marry a wonderful Irishwoman and to live in Ireland permanently.

Colonel François Bonal

François was one of our great French friends; in the 1970s and 1980s, I was writing extensively about wines and alcohol generally and we found ourselves in Épernay in the heart of the Champagne district on several occasions, all expenses looked after. François was the man in charge of publicity for Champagne. We became good friends and soon got to know all about his career. He had been born in 1914, the same year that his father, a captain in the French army, was killed on the battlefield. François went to the prestigious Saint- Cyr military academy between 1933 and 1935. During the second world war, he was with the Free French army and after the war, resumed his army career in France. He retired from the French Army in 1967 and straightaway found himself a job in the Champagne region, eventually becoming head of publicity for the Champagne houses.

It was in that capacity that he looked after us so well. I well remember one visit, when we arrived at the Royal Champagne hotel just outside Épernay. On our first night, we were told to have whatever we wanted from the menu and from the selection of drinks. Three of us, my wife Bernadette, myself and a journalistic colleague from Glasgow, set to with enthusiasm. By the end of dinner that night, we had consumed nine bottles of Champagne between us, followed by half a bottle of cognac. Yet we were out in the vineyards at nine o' clock the following morning, heads totally clear.

François became a tremendous advocate for the virtues of Champagne and when he retired at the age of 65, he turned to writing about it. He wrote nearly a dozen books on the subject, some of which we still have, including a copy of his renowned Golden Book of Champagne. This is the encyclopedia on the subject, the ultimate source of information on anything to do with Champagne. François lived to a fruitful old age; until just before he died at the age of 89, he was still travelling the world, making friends with people of all faiths and none, right across the world. Besides being such a splendid host, he was also very French in another way; any time that we met up with him, he always made sure he was in just the right position to feel the contours of my wife' s bottom, a subject of much fascination to him.

Boston tea party

The one and only time that we travelled to the US was in 1980, when we spent a glorious Easter week in Boston. We saw many of the highlights of that great Irish- American city, including the Boston tea party re- enactment and the John F. Kennedy birthplace and the JFK library. But the highlight of that visit was rather unexpected. We noticed one day that a university theatrical group was staging an all- nude review in a small downtown theatre. "This looks promising", we said to each other and promptly went to the theatre that night and booked ourselves in. The group of actors, male and female, were totally nude, yet were totally unconcerned and delivered their often very funny satirical review of the current news. You could say it was the real "nudes of the world". I remember distinctly that on one side of me was a black lady, who was three times my size and she laughed so much at the antics on stage that the whole row of seats shook so violently that we feared it was going to collapse. At the end of the show came an even funnier episode. The main members of the cast came out to the foyer to talk to the audience as everyone filed out. The cast were all still totally nude and one male member of the cast, with a rather prominent member, started talking to two rather elderly ladies. They completely ignored the fact that they were within mere millimetres of a rather splendid male member. What they were really interested in was the actor's Polish name. They wanted to know which part of Poland his ancestors came from and it turned out that it was probably the same small area where their grandparents had come from. The two elderly ladies, fully dressed, really had an animated conversation with one very nude male actor, genitalia on full display, but not of the slightest interest to them, although his ancestry held them spellbound.

Gillian Bowler

In her younger days, Gillian Bowler was a real stunner, the glamour puss of the travel business. She was brought up on the Isle of Wight, off the south coast of England, but by the time she was 16, she was working for Greek Island Holidays. She came to Ireland in 1973 and two years later, set up Budget Travel, with herself as the glamorous front woman with impressive "twin peaks". I told her once that she looked even more glamorous in real life than on television, but she didn' t quite take the compliment as it had been intended! As happens with most successful indigenous companies in Ireland, eventually they are sold to international investors and that was just what happened with Budget Travel, 90 per cent of which was sold by Bowler in 1987 to the Granada Group. In 1996, it was sold on again, this time to the Thomson travel group. Subsequently, she became well- known for her high profile financial roles, but in 2010, she retired as chairperson of Irish Life and Permanent.

Michael Bowles

I got to know Michael Bowles well in the last years of his life, since he and his wife Kathleen, lived just around the corner from us, in Heytesbury Lane, Ballsbridge. If we were out for a walk in the evening, we would often meet the two of them, accompanied by their pets. Not only did they bring their dog out for walks, but inevitably, their cat came along too.

Michael was born in Co Sligo in 1901 and by 1932, he had joined the Army School of Music. Four years later, he got his degree in music from University College, Dublin. By 1941, he had joined Radio Éireann as conductor of its orchestra and a year later, in 1942, he became the station' s first full- time director of music. 1942 also saw him resigning from the Army. During the second world war, he also conducted the BBC symphony orchestra, the BBC Northern Ireland orchestra and the BBC Scottish symphony orchestra. In between all these engagements, he also started the Radio Éireann choir.

He started the tradition of public concerts by the Radio Éireann symphony orchestra, a tradition that of course continues to the present day. Michael also promoted contemporary music and composed music himself for choir, orchestra and for solo voice, the last named the compositions of which he was most proud.

However, his time with Radio Éireann was short; in 1948 he and his wife moved to New Zealand when he became conductor of that country' s national symphony orchestra. Another six years later, they moved to the US, where he became a professor at Indiana University and conductor of the Indianapolis Philharmonic Society. The Bowles stayed in the US until 1970, when they returned to Ireland to do something completely different, running a guesthouse in West Cork. From there, they moved to Wicklow, making their final residence in Heytesbury Lane. Towards the end of his life, his beloved wife Kathleen, to whom he was married for over 50 years, had to go and live in a care home. Michael was bereft living on his own; he died in 1998. The Bowles were clearly an enterprising family; later, I got to know a relative of his, also called Michael Bowles, who was the first person to run an independent media company, analysing the media for advertising clients.

Mike Brammer

One day in 1988, I got a call from the old Bord Fáilte to say that the Michelin publishing company, an offshoot of the

Michelin tyre company, was planning to produce its first green guide to the tourist attractions of Ireland. Michelin was going to organise a competition to find an Irish writer to complement the work of the staff journalist who was going to work on compiling the guide. About half a dozen well- known journalistic names competed and the task was to compile and write a Michelin- style entry for a particular location in Ireland. I was given Limerick and I set off there with little expectation that anything would come of it, but I went round all the obvious and less well- known tourist sights in the city, came back to Dublin, wrote my script and thought no more of it. Limerick had done me proud and I was delighted that some weeks later, I heard from Michelin to say that I was the Irish writer they wanted to sign up.

I had little idea of what was going to be in store. We divided the country up, so that the staff writer dealt with everything north of line from Co Wicklow to Co Galway, while I covered everthing south of that imaginary divide. I remember vividly that the first town I visited was Birr in Co Offaly. I was very fortunate that I didn' t have to do all these trips on my own; Bernadette accompanied me on all my excursions, as we drove endless miles around the southern part of the island. I particularly enjoyed exploring the delights of Co Cork, the largest county in Ireland. I was especially interested in Cork city, Youghal, Kanturk, Kinsale, Skibbereen and Bantry. It was all a wonderful relief from the tedious job I had at the time, as editor of a couple of trade magazines.

Everything had to be absolutely meticulously accurate. Michelin insisted on me being able to justify every single item of fact in the text, very wearing at the time, but something that has stood me in good stead ever since. The pay was good and so too were the expenses, but again, these had to be meticulously documented. No short cuts there, unlike the legendary story of the Fleet Street reporter who came to

Ireland and claimed vast expenses for his boat trip to Usher's Island in Dublin. He got away with it, because no-one in the accounts department of his newspaper in London had the foggiest idea that Usher's Island is anything but an island.

My editor in Michelin was a stern taskmaster, Mike Brammer, an Englishman who has lived and worked in France for decades. He often came to Ireland to see how everything was going and on a couple of occasions, we went to Paris for editorial meetings in the headquarters of the Michelin guides, in the Avenue de Breteuil in the 7th arrondissement of Paris. Michelin was very fussy about everything being absolutely accurate but the company also had a very unFrench puritanism. No alcohol was allowed on the premises and if you used the staff canteen, your choice of drinks was restricted to soft drinks only.

After the Green Guide to Ireland was published, I did no more work for Michelin, but Mike Brammer and myself became good friends. He remained with Michelin in Paris until his retirement in 2015. Not long before he retired, he and his wife Françoise, who came from Brittany, came to Ireland on holiday and we met up with them for dinner one night in Bloom's Brasserie in Upper Baggot Street, Dublin. It was a very pleasant dinner and Mike and Françoise talked of their plans for retirement. They had long had a house on the north coast of Brittany and they planned to make this their main residence; Françoise talked of how she could indulge her love of gardening. Mike had been talking of his retirement for years beforehand, yet what had been planned as a happy event soon turned to tragedy. When we had met Françoise in Dublin, she had seemed perfectly fit and able, but she was already coping with cancer and that cancer killed her in 2015, leaving my good friend, Mike Brammer, the Englishman who worked for so long on the Michelin guides, utterly bereft and distraught.

But at least the Michelin Green Guide to Ireland continues on, both in print and online. It was a truly memorable editorial experience that has stood me in very good stead ever since.

Seamus Brennan

For many years, he was one of the most popular Dáil deputies in south Dublin, although he was a Galwegian by birth and upbringing. He was first elected to the Dáil in 1981 and by the time he was 24, he was the youngest ever general secretary of Fianna Fáil, responsible for introducing many American-style promotional tactics into Irish politics. His ministerial jobs included transport; Michael O' Leary of Ryanair said that Seamus Brennan was the best ever Irish transport minister. Seamus was also a government chief whip. He was exceptionally easy to get on with, as I knew myself, and right to the end of his political career, was always very popular.

But when he launched my book on the history of Dublin Airport, in 1990, for the 50th anniversary of the airport, I was very surprised when he made some very blue jokes during his speech, most unusual for a government minister. But no- one seemed to mind!

He fought his last election in 2007, when he was already too ill with cancer to do any canvassing, but he still topped the poll in his constituency. Seamus died in 2008, aged just 60. I' ve since got to know one of his six children, Shay, who was elected a councillor for Dundrum, south Dublin, in 2014; he' s very friendly and personable, a real chip off the old block.

Basil Brindley

I got to know Basil Brindley well through his advertising work; he and his brother Donald ran Brindley Advertising for over 40 years. Basil himself was a charming host and on various occasions had entertaining lunches with him at his club, the

St Stephen's Green Club. Basil, who has a jockey's build, had been very keen on motor sports and motor cycling in his younger days- in later days, his attention turned to horses- and he first made his name as a sports journalist. He opened his ad agency in two rooms at Lincoln's Inn at the back of Trinity College, Dublin, in 1956 and subsequently moved to Upper Mount Street. Coincidentally, this was just a couple of doors away from where I had a bedsit in the mid- 1960s, at Number 20 Upper Mount Street. The rent was a very affordable £2 10 sh a week! The family who owned and lived in the rest of the house were the Keatings; he was an architect, a very pleasant fellow, but utterly disillusioned by the lack of opportunities in Ireland. In due course, the Keatings went to live and work in London.

Basil's ad agency thrived over the years, especially through all his connections with the newspaper business and the agency generated other 'characters', like Eileen Byrne, Basil's right- hand woman for many years. I also got to know one of Basil's daughters, Bernice, who made a name for herself as a feature writer in the media. Sadly, another of the Brindley daughters, Sarah, died in 2011. In 1978, Basil had bought the grandiose Killeen Castle in south Co Meath but it was destroyed in an arson attack during 1981. Subsequently refurbished at enormous expense, it is now a luxury hotel, complete with its own golf course. Basil's family home is now in Dunshaughlin, where he also runs the Rathbeggan Horse Stud.

When Basil's ad agency was in its heyday, practically the entire advertising industry in Ireland was indigenous, whereas these days, it's nearly all multinationally owned. When the industry in Dublin was locally owned, it gave rise to a succession of wonderful 'characters', each unique in his or her own way. Basil was one of the leaders of the pack. But these days, the key figure in any international advertising agency is the head accountant based in some far flung head of empire, like New York or London. The local 'characters' have been replaced by number crunchers. Basil himself contributed to this trend when he sold his agency in 2005 to the UK- based Aegis group for €12 million.

John Broderick

I once interviewed John Broderick, an odd son of Athlone, not only a bakery owner but a writer of some renown besides being someone of ambiguous sexual tastes. I found him rather strange, a curious combination of hometown business mores and literary ambition. His parents owned a local business, Broderick' s Sunshine Bakery, already thriving in the 1920s but by the 1940s so popular that a popular children' s rhyme in Athlone went: "Broderick' s bread would kill a man stone dead".

Broderick left college in Ballinasloe, Co Galway, in 1941, without his Leaving Cert, but with the certainty that it was his lot in life to take over the family business. In the early 1950s, Broderick lived in Paris, where he met such expat writers as Gore Vidal and Trumane Capote. Then in 1956, The Irish Times published a travel article by him, followed that same year by his first book review. He managed to make himself thoroughly unpopular in the literary establishment by dismissing the works of such acclaimed writers as Heinrich Böll, who had a long time relationship with Achill in Co Mayo, Seamus Heaney and Edna O' Brien. Time has judged his criticisms of these and many other writers to have been seriously flawed. In 1961, he published the first of more than a dozen novels; when The Pilgrimage appeared that year, it was promptly banned. Much later, in 2004, The Times Literary Supplement summed up Broderick succinctly when it ran a feature on him with the headline: "The baking, banning and bisexuality of John Broderick".

He lived most of his life in Athlone and his home town has well recognised him, including naming a street John Broderick Street. His father had died when he was three, but his mother married again in 1936, when Broderick was 12. Her second husband was the bakery manager. In later years, Broderick lived with his mother in Athlone, until her death in 1974. He then lived alone until he moved to Bath in southwest England in 1981, dying there in 1989. He was a strange, unnerving, waspish kind of man, rather unsettling, so the one time I interviewed him was quite enough.

Garech Browne

In the days when we were regulars for lunch at the Roundwood Inn, run for more than 30 years by German- born Jürgen Schwalm and his Irish wife Áine, we often met Garech Browne, one of the Guinness family, who lives at Luggala, near Roundwood, deep in the hills of Co Wicklow. The bearded Garech, renowned for wearing his hair in a pigtail and better known by his Irish name, Garech de Brún, was born in 1939. As both his parents were married three times, he has had two stepmothers, two stepfathers and a number of half siblings older than himself. His only full brother, the Hon Tara Browne, was killed at the age of 21 in a car crash in London. In 1981, Garech married an Indian princess, Purna, so as a result of his marriage, he spends part of each year in India. Over the years, Garech has taken a keen interest in the arts, including the formation of Claddagh Records in 1959. Garech was also instrumental in the setting up of the Chieftains, one of the best- known of traditional Irish folk groups. One of the players in the new group was Paddy Moloney, famed uileann piper, whom we also met on occasion at Roundwood.

Vincent Browne

The legendary Vincent Browne, known as one of the few journalists in Dublin who'll ask all the right questions, was born in Broadford, Co Limerick, in 1944. In 1968, he was in Prague while Czechoslovakia was being invaded by the Soviet Union, while I was also in Prague until a few days before the invasion. He and I were the only two representatives of the Irish media when it was all happening; these days of course, there would have been Irish TV crews everywhere. Vincent covered Prague in 1968 for The Irish Times and in 1970, became the Northern news editor with the old Irish Press group. But Vincent was always a man to do his own thing and in 1977, he launched Magill magazine, which became hugely influential. Vincent was also the editor of the Sunday Tribune for many years; that newspaper was founded in 1980 and managed to last until 2011. While Vincent was running the Sunday Tribune, running verbal battles with the staff were commonplace. Often, at weekends, members of the staff were fired in brutal fashion by Vincent, but most of them took the seasoned advice of older colleagues; they came back to work the following Tuesday only to find that Vincent had forgotten and forgiven. He made a huge mistake by launching the Dublin Tribune, a freesheet, which promptly collapsed with huge debts. He did the same again in 2004 when he launched The Village magazine, which again created massive debts for him.

From 1996 to 2007, he had a nightly radio show during weekdays on RTÉ Radio 1, but after a bust- up with the radio station, he went to TV3 to do a nightly TV show show, which he has been doing ever since. The difficulties of working with Vincent are legendary in the media business, but fellow scribes respect him as being often the only journalist willing to ask the hard, incisive questions of politicians and others. I' ve had several dealings with Vincent over the years and he has always been helpful, but while he' s a good person to interview, he' s also someone I'd much rather not work for.

Éamon de Buitléar

Éamon was the son the military aide de camp to the first President of Ireland, Douglas Hyde, a keen Irish speaker.

Éamon himself grew up in a house of Irish speakers in Co Wicklow and he began his working life in Dublin selling fishing gear and shotguns. Starting in the 1960s, he made many television series on wildlife, for long working with his Dutch film making partner, Gerrit Van Gelderen. One of their best- known series was Am Uigh Faoin Speir (Out Under the Sky). Éamon was also closely involved with Seán Ó Riada, the composer, and was involved in the formation of the traditional music group, Ceoltóiri Chualann. Éamon' s wife, Lailí, was the daughter of the landscape painter Charles Lambe. Éamon' s family home was for many years at Kilquade, Co Wicklow. The last time that I saw him in person was at the Hungry Monk restaurant in Greystones, where he cut a lonely figure having dinner by himself. He died in 2013 at the age of 83.

Turtle Bunbury

Turtle is a most engaging character, great company but with a ferocious work ethic. He was born in 1972, which makes him considerably younger than me, but we' ve always got on well together. He was brought up in comfortable circumstances on the family estate in Co Carlow, but in 1996, he went to Hong Kong, where he spent several years working for a number of Asian media outlets, including the South China Morning Post. Turtle came back to Ireland just before the start of the present century and in the years since, he has become one of the most prolific writers and performers, in newspapers and books and on radio and TV. In 2006, he married Ally Moore from Clones, Co Monaghan; since 2007, they and their family have been living on the family estate in Co Carlow. Turtle's books, over a dozen in all, have featured everything from the landed gentry and artistocracy of counties Kildare and Wicklow, to the older people of a fast vanishing Ireland. When I was working on the book about the history of Flahavans, the Co Waterford oat millers, Turtle helped considerably, and most efficiently, by carrying out a wide range of interviews, but we are still waiting for the book to appear in print.

David Burke

David has long been editor of the Tuam Herald in Co Galway, one of the most respected of the regional newspapers. We go back a long way; when I was an editor in the deadly dull world of trade magazines in the 1970s and 1980s, I often used to commission stories from the young David in Tuam. His father, Jarlath, was one of the best regional newspaper editors and David has followed most ably in his footsteps. The paper itself goes back a long way, to 1837, when it was founded by a 27 year old Co Galway businessman, Richard Kelly. The paper was sold to the Burkes in the 1930s. The Tuam Herald also has a good reputation as the training ground of journalists who went on to garner national renown. Jim Fahy, who for years was RTÉ's western editor, based in Galway, and who retired in 2012, began as the first reporter outside the Burke family on the Tuam Herald. Gerry O' Regan, a former editor of the Irish Independent, began his media career in Tuam and so too did Kevin O' Sullivan, the current editor of The Irish Times.

John Butler

John worked for many years on The Irish Times, where I got to know him well. In 1982, after having done many travel features for Cara, the inflight magazine of Aer Lingus, I rang up John one evening and offered my services as a travel writer. He was then in charge of the weekly travel articles in the Saturday edition and in 1982, my first Irish Times travel article appeared in the paper, on the subject of Normandy and our stay in the fascinating seaside town of Trouville. It's a much more interesting and atmospheric place than its next door neighbour, Deauville, which is so snobbish and disdainful of the lower orders, and lives in the thin atmosphere of the aristocracy. Trouville is also the place where we stayed in the Hotel St James. The woman who ran the hotel loved her cats even more than her customers and it's the only hotel we've stayed in where we've had to share the breakfast table with half a dozen cats, all of whom needless to remark made excellent early morning companions.

Soon after John had recruited me to The Irish Times, we were invited to the grand launch of The Irish Times weekend supplement, at New Ireland House in London. There, we met up with such luminaries as Maeve Binchy, a lovely person to talk to and so down to earth and full of fun. That day, after the reception was over, John Butler took Bernadette and myself to a most enjoyable vinous lunch. Bernadette revealed her poetry writing skills and she too was soon appearing in the paper.

John, who lived in Greystones, was a very pleasant and agreeable section editor to deal with, all very efficient and no histrionics. But I remember the time he wrote a huge article on travel in Egypt and his prose was really turgid. He was a great organiser and diplomat, for instance bearing the wrath of staff journalist, who considered that she was far better equipped than I to write a travel feature on snow holidays in the Austrian mountains. When my piece appeared, John had to use all diplomatic powers to restore a semblance of tranquillity. In latter years, I had moved on from doing travel pieces in the weekend magazine and lost contact with John but when he died in April, 2013, Bernadette and myself mourned the passing of a really decent and honourable guy.

Alfie Byrne

Needless to remark, Alfie Byrne, nine times the Lord Mayor of Dublin, was before my time, although I did on one occasion meet one of his sons, Paddy. Alfie was born in 1882 and bettered himself very quickly, becoming a publican at an early age. He was eight times Lord Mayor of his native city during the 1930s and had a reputation for being everywhere and knowing everyone. When Bernadette was a young girl at school, he visited one day and had presents for all the kids; she remembered it vividly. He met so many people on his peregrinations through the city that he became known as the 'Shaking Hand of Dublin'. When I was doing my book on the history of the Bewley cafés and family, published in 1980, I felt it was almost obligatory to include a photo of Alfie Byrne. He was Dublin for so long, managing a final session in the Mansion House in the early 1950s. His feat of mayoral longevity has never been repeated; he died in 1956.

Frankie Byrne

She was Ireland' s first agony aunt, for years presenting a show on RTÉ Radio sponsored by Jacobs Biscuits. The 'Dear Frankie' show ran from 1963 to 1985, when RTÉ abandoned sponsored radio. The show was renowned for its coy letters written in by comely maidens up and down the country. On one occasion, Frankie got very annoyed when it was suggested that she had written some of the letters herself. Frankie had started her public relations career working for McConnells Advertising, then in Pearse Street, before setting up her own public relations agency in 1963. Herself and Gordon Lambert, then managing director of Jacobs Biscuits, were great friends and they hatched and ran the Jacob's Awards for TV and radio, for many years. Frankie's father was Mick Byrne, who was a well- sports journalist and Frankie herself had a gilded introduction to the world of work, before she went to McConnell's ad agency. She had started her career working in the Brazilian Embassy in Dublin and living in the Gresham Hotel, so that she got an instant entrée to Dublin's high society of the time.

In the 1950s, she began a long affair with Frank Hall of Hall's Pictorial Weekly fame. Her daughter, Valerie McLoughlin, was born in 1956 and given away for adoption. At Frankie's funeral, at the Sacred Heart church in Donnybrook, Dublin, in December, 1993, we were introduced to Valerie. After the affair with Frank Hall ended, Frankie continued to live with her sister Esther, a glamorous blonde who worked in production in RTÉ television, at a bungalow called Dunbur, just off the foot of Eglinton Road in Donnybrook. The inside of the bungalow was chaotic and in her later years, Frankie, who had slimmed down her once enormous figure, became addicted to alcohol. After the two sisters died, their bungalow was eventually demolished and an apartment development built on the site, called Dunbur, after the name of the bungalow.

Gay Byrne

Gay Byrne has had a truly remarkable radio and television career and now that he's in his early 80s, he is still broadcasting as fluently and tellingly as ever. Born in Rialto in 1934, he was brought up in that working clas district of south Dublin; his father worked in Guinness. After an early career as a clerk, he managed to break into television and was lucky to have come along just as Telefís Eireann was starting in 1962. At that stage, he had already had four years experience working for Radio Éireann, then based at the top of the GPO in central Dublin. But for the summer of 1962, he proposed a temporary filler programme that would run for just a few weeks, The Late Late Show; 54 years later, it is still running, but hosted by Ryan Tubridy. Side by side with his presenting and producing the Late Late Show, what started as the Gay Byrne Hour and became the Gay Byrne Show ran on Radio 1 from 1972 to 1999. Gay has done many other things, too, such as chairing the Road Safety Authority. But throughout his career, he has also pioneered new ideas and formats; as recently as 2009, he began his RTÉ TV series, the Meaning of Life while in recent years he has also been doing a Sunday afternoon show on Lyric FM.

He married Kathleen Watkins, the daughter of a vet from Saggart, Co Dublin, in 1957. For many years, they lived at Howth, but in recent years, they have moved much closer to the city centre; home is now a luxury apartment in Sandymount Avenue, Sandymount. I've known Gay quite well over the years, although he has never interviewed me on any of his programmes. I've also enjoyed his wry sense of humour, too, such as the time when I was researching my 1986 book on the history of advertising in Ireland. The phone rang one day; I answered it and the person on the other end of the line said simply: "Byrne here". The voice of course was an absolute giveaway; there can't be anyone in Ireland who doesn't recognise the voice. He's also very patient; once, at a Publicity Club Christmas lunch in the old Jury's Hotel in Ballsbridge, I had to give a rather long speech, with two of the guests at the top table being Gay and Kathleen.

Gay has also had his traumas, especially the Russell Murphy saga. Murphy was Gaybo's accountant, while he also did, or should I say, cooked the books of Hugh Leonard, the playwright and columnist. When Russell Murphy died in 1988, Gay found that Murphy had swindled him out of most of his savings. But since then, Gaybo has managed to more than restore his finances, including through many sensible property investments. And Russell Murphy has an entirely honourable and honest grandson, whom I know, Eoghan Murphy, a Fine Gael TD for the constituency we live in.

As for Gaybo, despite some recent illnesses, he still keeps going, undoubtedly Ireland' s greatest broadcaster, someone who did more than anyone else to help change the nature of Irish society. In his early days in television, he was also doing a lot of work for Granada television in Manchester, but for one reason or another, he never made his long term career in British television and radio, unlike the late Sir Terry Wogan. For that, Ireland' s TV viewers and radio listeners have much to be thankful.

Des Cahill

Des is a very genial fellow and a great authority on everything sporting, as one of RTÉ' s leading sports presenters and commentators. He started as a print journalist, working with the old Irish Press, then the Kerryman and the Carlow Nationalist, before moving into broadcasting with RTÉ in 1984. In the 32 years he has been with the station, he' s become one of the stalwarts in the sports department, and in 2015 and 2016, he was named the most influential Irish journalist on Twitter. On one occasion, about 10 years ago, he was doing a morning summer show on RTÉ Radio 1.

I had just had one of my tourism books published and I got a call to come into the Radio Centre and have a quick chat with Des about the book. He' s such an easy going character to get on with that we ended up talking about this, that and the other and it turned out to be the longest live broadcast I've ever done, running for the best part of half an hour. I was pleasantly surprised to get feedback from friends all over the country, who' d heard the epic!

Fr Tom Cahill, SVD

I've known some remarkable people who' ve served their respective churches well; however, although I' m a great believer in the powers of St Anthony, I've never in my life had much time for organised religion. When I was a young child, I had to go to Sunday services in the local Anglican church in Edgbaston, Birmingham, where we lived at the time, and I absolutely hated those excursions. They did little for me except instill in me a lifelong loathing of all religions, even after I had started becoming much more sympathethic to the main religion in this part of Ireland, Catholicism. I still find the Anglican persuasion, although perhaps more morally honest, a fundamentally cold and inhuman version of religion; I much prefer the much warmer, more human, tones of the Catholic church.

Having said all that, one priest with whom I was exceptionally friendly was the late Fr Tom Cahill, SVD, of the Divine Word Missionaries. Life can take many peculiar turns and by one of those strange coincidences, I found myself being invited to contribute to the Order' s general interest magazine, The Word. It raised many an eyebrow among some of my more secular friends. I remember in particular that genial journalist on The Irish Times, its motoring editor for many years, Andrew Hamilton, found it rather hard to take that I should be writing for The Word. However, they paid well and Fr Tom had such an eclectic view of life that he was happy to commission non- religious articles on a wide variety of topics. The cheques, too, always arrived promptly after publication. Fr Tom was a very well- informed and generous editor, so that it became a pleasure to work for him and the magazine for a number of years.

The Word, not to be confused with a UK publication of the same name, had started in 1936, but was suspended for the duration of the second world war. It didn' t resume publication until 1953. It hit its highest point in 1970, when it was selling 250, 000 copies a month, an incredible amount. But by the time it closed down in 2008, it was selling a mere 17, 000 copies a month, a powerful indication of how the sweeping advances of the Internet and online publishing have made so many print publications irrelevant.

But as for Fr Tom, after the magazine was closed down by his superiors, he went to Rome for a number of years, and from there, I often heard from him as he tried to master the intricacies of Italian as he wrote online. He had come from a farming background in Co Limerick and in his younger days in the Divine Word Missionaries, he had spent much time in Asia, which he clearly loved. When he died in 2012, both Bernadette and I felt as if we had lost a very dear friend.

John Callan

John Callan and us go back a long way, to Drogheda in the 1970s when we were living in that delightful and historically fascinating Boyneside town. We had moved to Drogheda in 1974, having 'escaped' from Belfast in the middle of a big loyalist strike. Altogether, we lived in Drogheda for just three years; we might still be there if the commuter train service to and from Dublin had been better then. But one of the first places we got to know in Drogheda was John Callan' s restaurant and crafts shop in Narrow West Street, which was just across the road from the then Garda station. The Callan family had been in business in the street, a continuation of West Street, the now forlorn Main Street of Drogheda, since 1890, when they opened a saddle and harness making business. John Callan, who subsequently married Jane, a nurse, ran a very successful place in the mid- 1970s and it was always a great pleasure to have lunch there and find some worthwhile fashion or craft item to buy. John went on to establish Callan Computers in 1983, although it was subsequently sold in 2003 to Don Hammond, the manager. John remains the generous, open hearted person he always was, despite the ravages of the recession that struck in 2008. We keep in touch with John and Jane, as I do with another, more recent friend from Drogheda, Brendan Matthews, the Drogheda historian, a walking repository of information on the town's history and a long time contributor to the Drogheda Independent.

Noelle Campbell- Sharp

One of the great characters of Irish publishing in recent decades, I've been friendly for many years with Noelle, who at one time ran a magazine empire of considerable range, 11 titles at its peak. Noelle was born in 1943 and grew up in Wexford with the family who adopted her. She had been given away the day after she was born, first fostered and then adopted. As she has noted, in those days, society was so ruined by the male- dominated Catholic religion that it was a savage country. She began her working life at 15 as a clerk/ typist in Pierce's, the foundry and agricultural machinery company in Wexford. Even in those days, Noelle had a rebellious attitude to life. She soon moved to Dublin and became a journalist there, ending up as Ireland's first female large scale magazine publisher.

It all came unstuck in 1991 when she sold her publishing company to the UK media mogul Robert Maxwell. Soon after the deal was inked, Maxwell died or was murdered; the Maxwell empire collapsed, owing a large amount of money to Noelle. About a year later, the love of her life, musician Niall McGuinness, brother of Paul McGuinness, the U2 manager, died. Niall was only 39 when he died from a heart attack. Before her relationship with Niall, Noelle had been married to an English fashion photographer, Neil Campbell- Sharp.

But despite this tragedy and the amount of money she was left owing from the Maxwell deal, Noelle persevered; she's a brave woman who never gives up. In 1992, she started the Cill Rialaig artists' retreat on the Iveragh peninsula in Co Kerry. In the years since, over 3, 000 artists have stayed there, many world-famous. Noelle is also the owner of the Origin Art Gallery in Upper Fitzwilliam Street, Dublin. She is a remarkable lady and it was no surprise when years ago, when I went out to her fabulous house in Killiney, to interview her, that she confessed that her great hero was Napoleon.

Ray Carroll

Ray Carroll has had a remarkable career in the hospitality industry; he spent many years managing some of the top hotels in London's West End, then came home to Ireland, where he took over the Cashel Palace Hotel in Cashel, Co Tipperary, turning it into a superb small luxury hotel. Around 30 years ago, Michael Smurfit began to seek out his advice for the luxury hotel and golf resort he was planning in Co Kildare, which became the K Club. When it opened, 25 years ago, Ray was the first chief executive and I had many dealings with him there, as the K Club in its first years, commissioned me to write an elaborate book on the history of the place and its gestation as a top class golfing venue. It was published in 1996. He retired from that job in 2005, after more than a decade in charge, but he has continued to work as a hotel consultant. He and his wife now live in retirement, close to the town of Dundalk, which is the home town of both of them.

Dr Francis X Carty

Francis Carty and myself have been friends for many years; at one stage, he was running his own agricultural publication, while he also lectured in media studies, especially in public relations, at the Dublin Institute of Technology. He wrote a famous book on the subject, Farewell to Hype, published in 1992. In 2010, Francis wrote another book, the history of a very controversial Catholic archbishop of Dublin, John Charles McQuaid. Francis comes from a family well- known in the media. His father was first an editor of the old Irish Press newspaper, before becoming editor of the old Sunday Press. Jane, the sister of Francis, worked in classical music programming in RTÉ for many years, while his brother, Ciaran, was for many years, the film critic on the old Sunday Tribune. Few if any film critics had such an ell- embracing knowledge of the film business as Ciaran. Francis still lives in the old family house in Sandymount and when I was putting together my recent book on Sandymount, he was an enormous help, especially on one of his favourite interests, Irish cricket, something I'd previously known little about. Sandymount is one of its strongholds.

Christopher Casson

An old theatrical hand, whose parents were steeped in the theatre, he lived in Sandymount for many years. For some years before he died in 1996, whenever Bernadette and I went to Sandymount' s front for a walk, we would invaraiably bump into Christopher, who lived just on the far side of Strand Road. He was always the very epitome of old- fashioned charm and good manners, a most delightful man to know.

He was born in Lancashire in 1912, the son of very well- known actor parents, Sybil Thorndike and Lewis Casson. Chrisopher made his stage debut at the tender age of three, with a walk- on part in Julius Caesar at the Old Vic in London. He toured the world as an actor during the 1930s, then in 1938, he joined the company run by Micheál Mac Liammóir and Hilton Edwards at the Gate Theatre in

Dublin. Three years later, he married an Irish stage designer and artist, Kay O' Connell. Christopher went on to work for Longford Productions, also at the Gate Theatre, before becoming freelance in 1950. He went on to play a vast number of theatrical and film roles, but he didn' t become nationally famous until he was cast as the Church of Ireland rector in the RTÉ television soap, The Riordans. Ironically, Christopher had long before converted to Catholicism.

Bob Chalker

Bob, who died in 2003, aged 88, was an American who was a long- time resident in Ireland, where he had established himself as a great character. He was born in Alabama in 1914 and spent most of his career in the US foreign service. It was while he was serving in the US Embassy in London in 1946 that he married his first wife, Edna Wood, who died in 1985. He was eventually transferred to the US Embassy in Ballsbridge, Dublin, and was on the staff there when it opened in 1964. Bob was responsible for buying the fine house in Mespil Road that became the residence of whoever is the number two person in the US Embassy in Dublin. After four years service there, he retired, straightaway becoming executive director of the American Chamber of Commerce in Ireland, a job he held from 1968 until 1995.

He became a very familiar figure in the business community and always very approachable. He was also noted for the vintage Mercedes he drove. His passionate interest in music and theatre led him to meeting Louise Studley, a leading lady in the Rathmines & Rathgar Musical Society, which has been on the go for the past 103 years. Louise became Bob' s second wife in 1990. In subsequent years, Louise' s daughter, Melanie Ryan, and her grand daughter Rebecca Winckworth, have also had a close connection with the R & R, continuing a family musical tradition.

Charlie Chawke

Charlie is a remarkable man in two ways. A native of Adare in Co Limerick, he has built up an 'empire' of pubs in Dublin, beginning with the Goat Grill in Goatstown, that has been remarkably successful in the face of the devastating recession that began in 2008. One of his more recent acquisitions has been Searson' s in Upper Baggot Street, which he has made into one of the most successful pubs in the area. Another of Charlie' s pubs with which I'm very familiar is the Dropping Well in Milltown. That particular pub goes back a long away, around 150 years, to the dreadful days of the famine, when the building that became the pub was used as a morgue.

But Charlie was lucky to survive an attack outside the Goat Inn in 2003; one day, he was driving to the bank with takings he was going to lodge, when he was attacked by two armed men. Charlie had about €50, 000 in cash and a lot of cheques with him. After he was stopped, one of the men shot Charlie in the right leg. He was rushed to St Vincent' s Hospital, where massive blood transfusions saved him. He lost his right leg above the knee, but subsequently has never let that dreadful incident from deterring him. So a very brave man on two counts, as well as being a very genial host.

Rita Childers

Born in 1915, she was the second wife of Erskine Childers, the fourth president of Ireland, who was in office for less than two years when he collapsed and died in November, 1974. The night when he died, Bernadette and I were walking home to our then home on the outskirts of Drogheda. The night was very clear and in true Shakespearean style, it was laden with shooting stars, often a portent of momentous happenings.

Rita had been working as a press attaché in the British Embassy in Dublin when she met Erskine; they married in

1952. Subsequently, he was a Fianna Fáil government minister before eventually being elected president. After Erskine' s death, she tried to run for the presidency, but found she was blocked at every turn by former Fianna Fáil colleagues of her husband; she became very critical of them. But when I approached her with some queries for book research, I found her very helpful and charming. The Childers' daughter, Nessa, first entered politics when she became a local councillor in Dún Laoghaire- Rathdown in 2004, standing for the Green Party. In 2009, she became a Member of the European Parliament, although she resigned from the Labour Party in 2013. Her mother, Rita, died in 2010.

Brian Cleeve

A tall messianic figure who had the words "Servant of God" carved on his tombstone, lived near us, in Heytesbury Lane, for many years, so I got to know him quite well. He was born in England in 1921; he was one of the family that owned the renowned Cleeeves toffee factory in Limerick. In 1948, Brian Cleeve and his wife emigrated to South Africa, where they set up a shop selling perfumes. But he soon became highly critical of the apartheid regime in South Africa and the pair of them were ordered out of South Africa in 1954 because of their criticisms of the apartheid regime. Settling in Ireland, Brian turned his attention to writing, producing over 100 short stories and 21 novels. When the new Irish television service started in 1962, Telefís Éireann, Brian joined as a presenter. He soon became one of the interviewers on the Broadsheet programme, the first current affairs series, then in 1966, started with the 7 Days series. Eventually, Brian left Heytesbury Lane, where his house no longer exists, as the site has been redeveloped; after his wife Veronica died in 1999, he moved to Shankill. He married his second wife, Patricia, in 2001, but he died two years later, in 2003.

Dick Cochrane

Dick was a Scottish baker who spent most of his career working in Dublin, at the Kylemore Bakery, which had been founded in 1887 and which was taken over by the Hogan family in 1920. For many years, Dick was the master craftsman in charge of the bakery' s confectionery production. Despite problems at the family home in Clontarf, where his wife was an invalid for many years, Dick remained a very congenial and generous character. After his wife' s death, he travelled widely and he was an early visitor to Bangkok, which he thoroughly enjoyed, for all the wrong reasons.

When I was editing a bakery trade magazine, I well remember being at a bakery trade meeting in the Boyne Valley Hotel in Drogheda in the 1970s. Dick was there, too, and afterwards, when the bakery owners and managers came out of the meeting in a shell- shocked state, I asked Dick what had happened. He told me that instead of discussing boring old business matters among themselves, he had decided to liven things up by giving a blow- by- blow account of the goings- on in the Bangkok sex show he had attended. His description of the women who performed in the show by shooting balls out of their vaginas had the bakers' eyes out on sticks. The way Dick told it was absolutely hilarious. He was a big man with a shock of white hair and he looked very much like Colonel Sanders of Kentucky Fried Chicken fame. He was also a very generous man and from time to time took Bernadette and myself to dinner in Dublin, on occasion going on the old Barbarella' s night club, where he was a regular. He was a brilliant baker and an equally brilliant social host, who sadly died 30 years ago.

Pan Collins

I was very fond of Pan Collins, a lady who' d tell it like it was and always with a humorous twist. Her husband Kevin had been art director at The Irish Times in the 1940s. Pan had joined the staff of what is now RTÉ in 1961, just before the new television service started. The Late Late Show had started in the summer of 1962 as a brief summer filler- it's still going strong- and in 1966, Pan joined it as a researcher. She stayed in the job for a remarkable 22 years and in 1972, won a Jacob' s Award for her research work. For nearly quarter of a century, she was responsible for finding an endless stream of interesting guests for the programme. I also well remember her, later in her life, and long after her husband had died, telling how she was happy to downsize in her apartment and to throw out all the memorabilia when she was going to her new flat, clearly a woman who wasn' t too sentimental. Pan, a great character in the world of television, died in 1992 at the age of 78.

Tony Collins

Tony is a most likeable character, now in his late 70s, who owns and runs Uncle Tom' s Cabin, one of Dundrum' s most noted pubs. The pub has been going since 1842 when it was started by a man called John Murphy; in those far off days, it was mainly a grocery shop, with a small bar, as was typical for the time. Later in the 19th century, its name was changed to the Cyclists' Rest and Tea Gardens; cycling was a then brand new hobby and sport and the pub was well placed for cyclists going on excursions to Enniskerry. In 1888, James Collins, grandfather of Tony, who was already well- established in the Dublin pub trade, wanted to buy another property. He went to an auction with the intention of bidding for the Horse Shoe House in Ballsbridge, but was late arriving, and ended up by the pub in Dundrum. It was an example of a purely chance happening changing the whole history of a family.

James Collins was unsure of what to call his newly acquired pub, but one day, his wife had a brilliant idea; James was engrossed in a book and said "let's call the pub Uncle Tom' s Cabin after the book you' re reading". It's been that way ever since. Tony' s father Edward was born in 1901 and Tony himself started working in the pub in 1953 as a young lad. In the years since, he' s seen many improvements to the place and a host of well- known names as customers, including the broadcaster the late Eamonn Andrews, who often dropped in during the 1960s and 1970s. Tony, the ever genial host, is also a fund of stories, like what happened when Guinness dropped their horse- drawn drays in favour of lorries around 65 years ago. The men driving the lorries found that if when doing their rounds, they put their bacon and eggs on the bonnets of their lorries, by the time meal break time came around, they' d have a perfectly cooked breakfast!

Marcus Connaughton

Marcus, the presenter and producer of the Seascapes programme on RTÉ Radio 1, is a veteran of the Irish music industry. First of all, he worked for the old Bord Fáilte, and then he worked for Polydor and others in the Irish music industry, building up a fund of knowledge and expertise. He has long been deeply interested in the life and times of Rory Gallagher, an icon of rock music, and had his encyclopedic book on him published in 2014. But the music industry provided an uncertain living for Marcus, who in the late 1980s joined RTÉ Radio 1 as a producer. He went on to produce many music programmes for the station; most of his career has been spent with RTÉ in Cork and for many years, he produced the Seascapes programme when Tom MacSweeney was the presenter. When Tom reached retirement age five years, he handed over the programme to Marcus, who ever since has combined the dual roles of presenter and producer. Marcus is married to Helen, who had a completely different career profile, as a hospital theatre sister.

Liam Cosgrave

It' s not often that one can become friendly with someone whose family connections go back to the foundation of the State in 1922, but that' s the case with Liam Cosgrave. His father was the first president of the Executive Council, a post he held for a decade. It was de Valera who turned the office into that of the Taoiseach under the 1937 constitution. Liam took up the Fine Gael political mantle at an early age, not finally retiring from the Dáil until 1981. Liam had himself been Taoiseach, in the coalition government between 1973 and 1977. Liam always had a public perception of being a rather aloof and serious public figure, but in private, he' s someone with a great sense of humour, still passionately interested in horse racing. Now aged 96, he also has a truly remarkable memory of people and events and still makes public appearances. I knew his daughter, Mary, better, in the days when she worked in publicity for the old Bord Fáilte.

Lucinda Creighton

Lucinda is a remarkable and feisty political person, a native of Claremorris, Co Mayo, where she was born in 1980. Trained as a barrister, she first came to public notice in 2004 when was elected to Dublin City Council for the Pembroke area of south Dublin. When she was elected to the Dáil on her first attempt, in 2007, she was the youngest member of the House. Subsequently, when the 2011 government came to office, she was made Minister of State for European affairs. She was a lively, committed and efficient minister, traits which her constituents in Dublin South- East were also quick to notice. But in the summer of 2011, she was expelled from the Fine Gael parliamentary party for voting against the Protection of Life During Pregnancy Bill. She then sat as an independent TD until March, 2011, when she launched her Renua Ireland party, with the aim of cleaning up government and bringing reforms to the business and other sectors. In the 2016 general election, she lost her seat in the Dáil after nine years while her new party also failed to gain any seats. She and her husband, Senator Paul Bradford, who was also in Fine Gael, live in Sandymount and have a two year old daughter, Gwendolyn Nicola. After the election, Lucinda said her main immediate aim was to find a job for herself; whether she will go back to politics remains to be seen.

Michael Cullen

I've known Michael for over 30 years; I first knew him when he was working for a Dublin magazine called Marketing Opinion. He then went to Australia for three years and when he returned, he didn' t want to return to a publication that was ailing, so he made the brave step of starting his own publication, Marketing, in 1990. Marketing has been going strong ever since, as the 'bible' of the advertising and media industries, with Michael in charge of editorial and his wife Jenny in charge of advertising sales and the commercial side. In 2009, the magazine was rebranded as marketing.ie, its website was revamped and its blogs were launched. As Michael says, digital has not only changed the way publications operate, but even more crucially, how people consume the media.

Michael also started writing a weekly column of advertising for what was then the Evening Herald, five years ago, and just before that all began, I wrote a profile of the Herald for Marketing magazine and met, for the first time, the

Herald's then editor, Stephen Rae, now in overall editorial control at Independent News & Media. In late 2014, Michael's column on the advertising business was transferred to the Irish Independent and he's been doing it ever since. For Michael to have done what he's achieved, writing incisively and freshly about advertising, without a break, for close on 30 years, is quite a publishing achievement. I'm glad that from time to time, I'm still contributing to marketing.ie, as it's an invaluable forum.

Aisling Curley

Aisling is a most charming young woman, whom I got to know in recent years, purely by chance. She is currently working on her PhD at Trinity College, Dublin, and a couple of years ago, she contacted me to see if I could help with some contacts. She's already read my tome of nearly 800 pages on the history of Irish advertising, published in 1986. I met up with her and gave her some introductions in the advertising business, who all proved very useful. Since then, we have met up from time to time, for coffee or lunch, and she is always the most polite and considerate companion, good fun to have for company. She's never short of tales and stories to tell, since she and her husband David are inveterate world travellers; just within the past six months, they've done a tour in China as well as visiting the American west coast.

She was born in 1971, the youngest of five children and she says that her wonderful parents are Brendan and Margaret, while she has been happily married to David Clarke since 2005. Aisling says that most of her childhood was spent day dreaming, but that she has achieved one of her childhood dreams, to have enough money to buy as much Cadbury's Dairy milk chocolate as she wanted. But other ambitions are still outstanding, such as being given a present of detachable fairy wings. She began working with

Irish Life in 1989, in investments, before going on to work for Bank of America Merrill Lynch. Her Trinity PhD is on the interaction of industry evolution and digital information and communications technology.

Trevor Danker

Trevor was the epitome of the smooth social columnist, a role he performed with distinction for close on 40 years at the Sunday Independent in Dublin. He knew everyone, especially in the world of entertainment. Born in Belfast to Jewish parents who had emigrated from eastern Europe, his first major work experience was on the Belfast Telegraph, before he moved to London to work on such titles as the Daily Express and the Daily Mail. His wife, Carmel Concagh, died in 2007 and Trevor died in Brighton in 2013, aged 74. He had no connection with another Danker- Rodney Danker, the book enthusiast who was renowned for keeping over a million books at his home in Terenure, Dublin.

Jack and Margot Davis

I was very friendly for many years with Jack and Margot Davis, then of the Meath Chronicle in Navan, always the epitome of helpfulness and friendliness. I also remember that in 1990, when we were involved in a car crash, due to the reckless driving of another driver, near Navan, they were the first to ask how we were. The newspaper for which I was then freelancing and for whom I was doing a story when the crash happened, never bothered to make any effort to see how my wife Bernadette and I were getting on. Jack was connected with the Meath Chronicle for 50 years and was managing director for many years. His wife Margot ran a newspaper called Modern Woman. In 2002, they retired from the paper when it was bought out for over €30 million. A cousin of Jack's, Ken Davis, is still the editor.

Mary Davis

Mary is one of the most dynamic business people I've ever met. Born in 1954, she was educated as a sports teacher, but soon found herself teaching people with special needs. From that grew her involvement in the Special Olympics movement. Prior to the Special Olympics world summer games being staged in Dublin in 2003, Mary had spearheaded the presentation on Ireland. For her, I wrote a detailed presentation on all the delights of Ireland as a tourist delegation. She has had many other responsibilities, including being on the Council of State and a director of the trust of The Irish Times and in 2011, made an unsuccessful attempt to be elected President of Ireland. Just recently, she was made the global ceo of the Special Olympics movement, the first time a non- American has held the post.

Treasa Davison

She was a long time presenter on RTÉ Radio 1. A native of Galway, where she learned her acting skills, she got married and emigrated to Canada. But after her husband was killed in a plane crash there in the early 1960s, she returned to Ireland with her young children and began her radio career. She was famous for presenting the Playback programme as well as requests for Irish troops on UN duties in the Lebanon. She retired from RTÉ in 1999, because her voice was too feeble. A short while after that, when I was going through the grounds of RTÉ one day, I spotted Treasa wandering around, looking like a totally demented and lost soul. She died a short while later, in 2001.

Ronnie Delany

Ronnie is Ireland' s first modern sports super star. Born in Arklow in 1935, he lived for most of his younger life, up until the time he got married, in St John' s Road in Sandymount. His family had moved to Sandymount when he was just six years of age. He had most of his early athletics training at Vilanova University in the US and it stood him in good stead for the 1956 Olympics, staged in Melbourne, where he won his gold medal in the 1500 metres race. He retired from competitive running six years later, in 1962.

He then went on to spend 21 years of his working life with the old B + I shipping line, where he became assistant chief executive. In 1988, he set up his own marketing consultancy. He also chaired the Sports Council for 12 years, while in 2013, he became an Ambassador for Friends of the Elderly. He now lives in Carrickmines, south Co Dublin. When he was running his own marketing company, based at the Mespil Flats complex in Dublin, I had quite a lot of dealings with him and found a very efficient and congenial person to work with.

Michael Dell

Michael Dell is one of the giants of the computer business and I've met him a couple of times. He was born in Houston, Texas, in 1965, got his first computer at the age of 15, an Apple II, which he took to pieces to see how it worked. He started his own company, Dell Computers, when he was 19, to sell PCs direct to consumers, thus making them much cheaper.

I was in at the start of Dell in Ireland. They set up in Limerick in 1991 in an old video games factory. The man in charge of the operation was Buddy Griffin, a Tipperary man, who had been working for Dell in Asia. He had no doubts that Dell was going to become a big name in Ireland, as indeed it did, with its main manufacturing operation for Europe based in Limerick. It lasted until 2009, when the Limerick plant was closed down, but Dell remains a big employer in Ireland. As for Michael Dell himself, he is friendly and personable, if laden with all the technical jargon commonplace and necessary in the computer industry. These days, his personal fortune is worth around $20 billion; he had started his company in 1984 with just $1, 000. He took Dell private in 2013, in the world' s biggest management buyout since the great recession started in 2008. Then in 2015, Dell paid $67 billion to take over the EMC company, the biggest ever technology merger. I found Michael Dell himself quite a modest man but behind the almost ordinary exterior, there lies a true genius in the world of computers, a genius at thinking ahead in computer technology as well as well as in business.

Éamon de Valera

Undoubtedly, the best- known Irish politician of the last century, he was born in New York in 1882- his mother was Irish and his father was Cuban Spanish. He was brought up in Bruree, Co Limerick, by his grandmother but when in his early teens, got into Blackrock College in Dublin. In 1904, when he was 22, he graduated from what is now University College, Dublin, with a degree in maths. It was then part of the Royal University of Ireland. In later life, working out mathematical equations was a great hobby for him. He became teacher and he met his wife, Sinéad Ní Fhlannagáin, who had been born at Balbriggan, north Co Dublin in 1878, when she taught him Irish at the Leinster College of the Gaelic League, in Parnell Square, Dublin. She went on to write 31 books for children in Irish and English. She was an old lady when President Kennedy visited Ireland in 1963, but he too fell for her charms as such a charming and delightful person.

De Valera first came to public notice when he was in charge of the revolutionaries who occupied Boland' s bakery and mill in south central Dublin. He managed to escape the fate of the 1916 leaders, it is often said because of his American connections. By the time the Anglo- Irish Treaty was signed in 1921, he found himself on the opposite side to Michael Collins. De Valera went on to found the Fianna Fáil party in 1926, then in 1931, he set up the Irish Press newspaper. From 1932 until 1959, he ruled the political roost, having been Taoiseach on successive occasions during that long period. He became president in 1959. In his later years, he suffered considerable problems with his sight. My wife Bernadette who was then working in the Department of External Affairs, often found herself at State functions with the task of guiding round de Valera, who at that stage could hardly see, so she got to know both Eamon and Sinéad very well.

The couple had their own tragedies; in 1936, their son Brian was killed in a horse riding accident. Sinéad herself died in 1975 at the age of 96, the day before her 65th wedding anniversary; her husband died eight months later. Their eldest son was Vivion, who was a Major in the Army during the second world war 'Emergency'. He also went into politics, but in a much more minor way than his father; Vivion was a TD. His most notable achievement was as managing director of the Irish Press group from 1952 until his death in 1982. He was also a great personal friend of Bernadette and they had innumerable discussions together.

As for Éamon, he was a political colossus, the best- known and most powerful politician of 20th century Ireland, in many ways, Ireland' s equivalent of General de Gaulle, but he was also a divisive figure; many people adored him and what he stood for, while many others took an entirely different view. Once, the party he founded was able to enjoy sizeable majorities in the Dáil, as after the 1977 general election, but these days, although the party has recovered much, it and its opposite number, Fine Gael, are much diminished numerically in the Dáil, as independents and Sinn Féin have come to the fore.

Candy Devine

The only time I met Candy Devine was when she was the host for a long running afternoon chat show on Downtown Radio in the North. In the early 1980s, one of the many tourist guides to Ireland that I did for Appletree Press in Belfast, was launched in Belfast. Bernadette and I had a lot of trouble getting to Belfast that day, because of security delays on the rail line, but eventually we arrived and Peter Carr, who then worked for Appletree, took us to a splendid lunch in the Europa Hotel. By the time it was finished, I was well under the influence! We took a taxi out to the Downtown Radio studios in Newtownards. The delightful Candy Devine, with whom I established an immediate rapport, chatted to me for 20 minutes about the book. Fortunately, I didn' t put my foot in it and the alcohol had one strange effect. At one stage, Candy asked me what price the book was selling for; no- one had told me, but somewhere in the recesses of my brain, I came up with the right answer, a true miracle. Bernadette was sitting in reception listening to the broadcast and expecting every minute that I would make some dreadful howler, which I didn't, but she did remark that Candy and I sounded as if we got on so well that we were playing footsy under the table!

Candy, whose real name is Faye Ann Guivarra, was born in Australia; she had a multicultural background, including Sri Lankan, Filipino and Torres Straits backgrounds. She began her media career on television in Australia, then came to Ireland in 1969 on what was planned to be a short visit. Instead, she married her booking agent, Donald McLeod, in Dublin in 1970 and spent the next five years working in cabaret on the Dublin nightclub scene. In 1976, she began her long career with Downtown Radio and managed to get an MBE in 2014. But her husband died in 2012 and the following year, she moved back to Australia, where she is still going strong, based in Brisbane. She certainly made an impact on me; she was very friendly, personable and generous, a delightful radio host who brought out the best in me, despite my inebriation! But I learned a lesson; after that incident, I never again had a drop to drink before I did a radio show.

Joe Dolan

The only time I saw Joe Dolan in action was one day at Heuston Station, Dublin; Bernadette and I were returning from a trip down the country. When we got off the train, we spotted Joe Dolan huddled in a corner with a group of friends, all busy swigging from cans of beer and clearly having a great time. But I have long admired his music; he had his first Irish hit in 1964 and his last in 2008, just after he had died, a total of 57 Irish hits. He was a big star, too, in many other countries around the world, including Russia. He had started his working career on the production side of the Westmeath Examiner in his native Mullingar before breaking into the pop music business. Although his private life was kept a closely guarded secret, he met up with Isabella Fogarty in 1977, started dating her in the early 1980s, before they began living together. She was with him during his last, brief, illness, when he was taken ill on Christmas Day, 2007. Of all the innumerable artistes that the showband era produced in the 1960s, including two other greats, Dickie Rock and Brendan Bowyer, probably none can compare with Joe Dolan, a true great of pop music, commemorated by a fine statue in his native Mullingar.

Catherine Donnelly

She was one of the finest advertising copywriters the ad agency business in Ireland has ever produced, with a sardonic personal style, cigarette in hand, that gave rise to much memorable copy. For long, she worked at the old McConnell's ad agency and that was where I got to know her when I was researching my 1986 history of advertising in Ireland. Her copy helped then fledgling brands such as Ballygowan water and Ryanair get airborne. In the case of Ballygowan, she created a brilliant series of ads that parodied the Table for Two restaurant series of the time in The Irish Times. From McConnell's, she moved to Irish International Advertising; out of all her work, probably the most memorable and certainly the longest lasting was the Christmas commercial she wrote for Barry's tea. She also wrote a novel, The State of Grace, in 2003. Her long time partner, whom she eventually married, was Frank Sheerin, another advertising genius. Catherine died much too young, in October, 2014, at the age of 66. I was fortunate to get to know both of them well.

Noel Dorr

For many years, he was a colleague of my wife Bernadette in what became the Department of Foreign Affairs. Noel rose to ambassador level and he held many posts with great success, including Irish Ambassador to the UN and Irish Ambassador in London. Born in Limerick in 1933, he joined the Irish diplomatic service in 1960. But when I met him on various occasions, despite his high diplomatic status, he was always totally down to earth, friendly and charming. Bernadette met him at one funeral service involving the diplomatic corps and was amused to see Noel there, bringing his work home with him. He had not one but two bulging briefcases, surely a first in the Irish diplomatic service! He became secretary of the

Department and long after his retirement, continued as an often consulted expert on diplomatic issues, both for RTÉ and for The Irish Times, with which he had a close involvement, as a member of The Irish Times Trust. He has also long had an intimate connection with the Royal Irish Academy, where he chairs its committee on international affairs. The Royal Irish Academy, incidentally, has one of the best libraries in Dublin.

Gerry Downey

Gerry has been a personal friend for many years and he also has what is a nearly complete collection of all my books over nearly 40 years. It' s been a long tradition that whenever I bring a new book out, I sign a copy for Gerry. He has always been a great pal and a very decent person to know. For many years, we had a great friend in common, the late Cathal O' Shannon. Gerry was born and brought up in a house at Ballsbridge Terrace, which is now Kite' s Chinese restaurant, and on occasion, has dined in the upstairs dining room at Kite' s, a room that was once Gerry' s bedroom. He has been in the gents' hairdressing business for something like 50 years, enough to make him a legend in his own lifetime, known to many of the great and the good in politics and business. For years, his hairdressing business was in the old Berkeley Court Hotel, but in recent years, he has been based in what was once the old Jury's Hotel in Ballsbridge, now known as the Ballsbridge Hotel, where he runs his hairdressing business with his son Gerard. Gerry' s wife is Marie.

Paul Drury

Paul was one of my great friends in the media business and writing this a year after he died at the age of 57 I still find a great sense of loss. He had a very iconoclastic and sardonic view of life, something that sometimes got him into trouble, but despite or perhaps because of all that, he was a great editor and an even better writer. The columns that he wrote for the Friday editions of the Irish Daily Mail, almost up to his death, were masterpieces of style and wisdom.

He had an unusual background, his father, Maurice, was a psychiatrist of great renown but by the time Paul came along, he was 50. Paul began his career with the then Independent Newspapers, becoming deputy editor of the Irish Independent under the equally legendary Vinnie Doyle. Then he became editor of the Evening Herald and the first time I met him there, I was amazed to find such a young man carrying off the task of editing the paper with such panache and élan. From there, he moved as editor to the Irish Daily Star, launched in 1988. From that paper, he went to Ireland on Sunday which eventually became the Irish Mail on Sunday. From that, he became the first editor of the Irish Daily Mail, launched in 2006, the same year that Ireland on Sunday, which had been bought by Associated Newspapers in 2001, was rebranded as the Irish Mail on Sunday. It was Paul who got me into feature writing for both papers, newspapers that brought a new professionalism to Irish journalism and publishing.

After all, the Daily Mail had been founded in 1896 by Harold Harmsworth, later the 1st Viscount Northcliffe, and his brother, Alfred, the 1st Viscount Northcliffe. Alfred was born in Chapelizod, Dublin, in 1865 and brought up there.

As for Paul himself, he was an interesting and agreeable character in so many ways, always with his own take on life. A member of the Church of Ireland, he was a total Gaelgoir and indeed in a previous media existence, had edited an Irish language publication. He was also exceptionally devoted to the West of Ireland, where his own family had long connections. His widow, Áine Ní Fheinne, comes from Connemara; her own professional background is as a journalist in RTÉ. They had three children, Niamh, Oisin and Éanna and the family home is in Rathmichael, south Co Dublin. Paul's funeral service in March, 2015, was at the Church of Ireland in Rathmichael and rarely has there been such a vast turnout of journalists to mourn a much revered colleague.

Gordon Duffield

As a seasoned journalist, I've always been a little wary of public relations people-their agenda shouldn't be the same as that of journalists- although I do make exceptions for some exceptional people in that craft, such as Don Hall, who runs his own pr company in Dublin and Pauline McAlester of Murray Consultants. But someone else in the business for whom I had a huge amount of time was Gordon Duffield. He was the most genial and generous of people and indeed on more than one occasion at one of his events in Dublin, I came home by rail, clinging on to the railings along Upper Leeson Street!

Gordon started his career with the Belfast Telegraph, then when Ulster Television started up in 1959, he became its head of publicity, going on to found his own firm, IPR (Irish Public Relations), which started in Belfast and expanded to Dublin. When we were living in Belfast in the early 1970s, Gordon's company ran something called the Monday Club in the Wellington Park Hotel. It was a great meeting place for the journalists in the city, representing both local and cross-channel publications. On one famous occasion, when I had asked Bernadette to go in my place because I was involved with something else that day, she came home to tell what I had missed. For a press launch Gordon had organised that day, he had brought in a real, live topless mermaid and dang it, I'd managed to miss the occasion! Two people we often met at the Monday club were the delightful Rosenfield sisters, Judith and Ray, both journalists, who were so polite that sometimes they told Gordon that they had no right to be there that particular day, and there was nothing happening they could write up. Gordon, as ever the genial host, waved aside such nonsense.

Gordon also had an interesting array of young women working for him; one was Harriet Duffin, who later went to work in public relations in Dublin and for years was the partner of that late lamented great journalist, Con Houlihan, who always referred to her as his "friend girl".

Seán Duignan

Born in Galway in 1936, he started work with the Connacht Tribune in that city, joined RTÉ in 1963 to work in the newsroom. He went on to front many news programmes such as This Week and the News at 1. 30pm, in the days when the lunchtime news went out at that time, rather than its present 1 pm. He became RTÉ' s political correspondent in 1976 and then co- anchor of the Six One television news in 1988, together with Eileen Dunne when that programme first aired. Then came a complete change of direction, from 1992 to 1995, when he was government press secretary during Albert Reynolds' time as Taoiseach. Seán produced his memoirs, One Spin on the Merry- Go- Round, in 1995. He called Albert Reynolds a "born gambler". After his time working for the government, Seán returned to RTÉ and presented the Week in Politics on television from 1995 until 2003. Seán is a legendary storyteller, with few his equal in the media.

Peter Dunne

Peter Dunne and Mitchells the wine merchants he works for, and myself go back a long way. Mitchells itself dates back to 1805, making it Ireland' s oldest wine and spirit merchants. It began operating from Kildare Street in 1886 and stayed there until 2008, when it moved headquarters to the chq building, near the IFSC. The Mitchell family also once had a legendary café business in Grafton Street, where McDonalds is now located.

As for the Mitchell firm, I was long friendly with Bobbie Mitchell when he was managing director; he was the grandson of Robert Mitchell, the founder of the firm. Bobbie was eventually succeeded by his son, Jonathan, still there today, while in 1995, Jonathan's son Robert joined the company.

It was at Mitchells in Kildare Street, which had a legendary shop, cellars, where it once bottled many of the products it sold, and a basement restaurant, that I met with another legendary character in the firm, Peter Dunne, always a most generous host. Peter joined the firm in 1970 and became a director in 1986. Peter is an absolute expert on the wines that Mitchells sells and has long led wine trips abroad as well as appearing on radio and television talking about his favourite subject, fine wines. Peter and his family live in Herbert Park, Ballsbridge, so they are also near neighbours. For three of my recent book launches, Peter and Mitchells have been their usual generous self, providing the wine for the launches to make sure that each volume was suitably launched on an unsuspecting world.

Alan English

Alan English has been editor of the Limerick Leader newspaper in 2007 and the paper has done a better job than many other regional newspapers in surviving in the face of the recent economic recession and the unrelenting switch to digital. He comes from Castleconnell, just outside Limerick city; his father, Tom, was a former manager of the Savoy Theatre in Limerick. Alan began as a junior reporter with the Limerick Leader in 1988, then three years later, moved to the Western Morning News in Plymouth, the city where I was born and grew up as a young child. In Plymouth, Alan's great interest began in writing about sport, and from Plymouth, he moved to London, where he spent a decade. In 2005, he returned to Ireland, where he became sports editor of The Sunday Times Irish edition. Then eight years ago, he returned to the newspaper where he had started, this time as editor. During his tenure, the Limerick Leader has continued its strong news and features agenda and Alan hasn' t been shy about running controversial stories, as with the allegations made against the University of Limerick by two suspended employees. He has also written a number of rugby books, including Brian O' Driscoll' s autobiography, published in the autumn of 2014.

First visit to Dublin

I made my first visit to Dublin when I was 15, at the end of the 1950s. We' d left Plymouth, a place I've always had a great affection for, to go and live in Birmingham in 1947. I spent 15 years in Birmingham, until I went to university in Derry in 1962. I always found it hard to find anything positive about Birmingham, which I usually thought of as a miserable bloody place, somewhere to make things, like cars, and where finer interests, like culture came way down the line. My father did well in his job, in the wholesale fruit and vegetable business, for the family to be able to move from the tall, gloomy, terraced house at Yew Tree Road in Edgbaston for a brand new house in a new road, Moorcroft Road, that was developed in Moseley in the mid- 1950s. We had become middle class with a vengeance, but it was a desolate environment. One of the few personal consolations I found was in writing nature poetry, which I did in abundance when I was in my mid- teens. We had a very long back garden, that had to be created from scratch, and it went uphill to a copse of trees at the end of the garden. Those trees, and the way in which their leaves changed in keeping with the changing seasons, inspired a lot of the poetry I wrote in those days.

The other consolation was the Irish Centre in Digbeth; I can' t remember how and why I first started going there, but as soon as I started chatting with some of the Irish immigrants there, I was in another world, a kindlier, more informal one than the social setting I was used to. Meeting them soon got me curious about Irish history and before long, it struck me that the history of Ireland had been totally erased from all the history books I studied at first and second level. Irish history simply didn' t exist; it' s as though Britain had a very guilty conscience about the way it had behaved in Ireland over the centuries, a sensible enough explanation. To cut a long story short, I decided to go and see for myself. One weekend, I set off for Dublin, to spend a couple of days there by myself; I was 15 at the time. To raise the money for the train and ferry fare, I pawned my camera, so I couldn' t take any photographs of Dublin.

When I got to Dublin, I found a very inexpensive b & b place just off Sean McDermott Street and close to Amiens Street. It was comfortable and I was well looked after and during the two days I was in Dublin, I had a good look round the city centre, seeing the GPO and hearing all about the 1916 Easter Rising for the first time. I soon became a real rebel at heart, identifying closely with those who had wanted to throw off the yoke of British imperialism. There must have been many psychological reasons for such identification! I may well have climbed to the top of Nelson' s Pillar on that occasion - I can' t remember - although I have very clear memories of subsequent ascents. But during that first trip to Dublin, two things struck me immediately. Firstly, the place looked very poor and run- down- in the subsequent nearly 60 years, the city has improved enormously in many ways. The second thing that struck me was how little traffic there was; the roads and streets, even O' Connell Street, were noticeable for their absence of traffic. I remember well the old green CIE buses, but in those days, few people had their own cars. O' Connell Street was also remarkably peaceful and safe in those far- off days, not a junkie in sight.

But those two days set the style for the rest of my life. I decided then that I would be much happier living in Ireland, somewhere I felt at peace with myself, rather than staying in England. It also turned out subsequently that I would also find writing in Ireland much easier; the words have always flowed with ease, whereas any subsequent time I was in England, I always found myself literarily constipated. Very strange! Within a year or two of my first trip to Dublin, it became obvious that the best way to come to Ireland was at university. I had applied to a couple of English universities, Brighton and Exeter, without much enthusiasm and with no success. Then I tried Trinity College, Dublin, and University College, Cork, again without success. The admission paperwork for UCC had largely baffled me, since so much was in Irish. But in the end, I got a place on a Trinity College course at Magee in Derry and even though the academic life turned out to have zero appeal for me, at least it had got me landed in Ireland.

Dr John Fleetwood

For many years, he was one of the best- known contributors to RTÉ Radio 1, on such programmes as Sunday Miscellany, while he was also a frequent guest on the Late Late Show on television. John was born in Edinburgh in 1917, into a prominent Scottish medical family. From there, he and his family moved to Plymouth, then when John was in his early teens, he and his family moved again, this time to Ireland. He went first to Presentation College in Bray, then to Blackrock College, before going to study medicine at UCD. In 1938, when he was 21, Radio Éireann produced a programme for the college rag week- it would never do anything similar nowadays- and John was paid the grand sum of four guineas for hosting a 30 minute show. He became hooked on broadcasting, although his early ambition to become the station's cricket correspondent never came to anything.

He graduated in 1941 and held a number of positions during the second world war Emergency, including that of assistant master at the Coombe maternity hospital in Dublin. Then from 1944 to 1947, he worked with Dr O'Grady's GP practice in Donnybrook, before starting his own practice, at Proby Square in Blackrock. It's still there, run these days by one of John's four children, John junior. In the early days of his own practice, if the daily round of patients went anywhere near Sandycove, John would strip off and go for a swim in the altogether at the Forty Foot. If he happened to have a male medical student with him, John would ask the student if he'd care to join him for a dip in the nip. In those far-off days, medical students were nearly all male.

For many years, he continued to contribute to radio and television and indeed on several occasions, I met him at the RTÉ Radio Centre, where he was always his avuncular and good-natured self, remarkably laid back. He also appeared many times on the Late Late Show, demonstrating the Heimlich manoevre, which stops people choking to death if something they've swallowed has gone down the wrong way. Even recently, Gay Byrne, the programme's host, told me that he still gets people coming up to himself and his wife, Kathleen Watkins, saying how grateful they were to Dr Fleetwood and his advice on television, advice that had saved a relative or a friend's life.

John also had a great sense of humour and one of his most memorable pieces on Sunday Miscellany concerned a holiday the family once spent in a self-catering house in Normandy. The drainage system got blocked and John found a local man who falsely claimed to have plumbing skills. When he tackled the blockage, he managed to blow up the whole system and the walls and ceiling were absolutely splattered with merde. I've seen the original script, which is in his archives kept in the library of the Royal College of Physicians of Ireland, in Kildare Street, Dublin. It's absolutely hilarious and when I was reading it, I couldn't help but burst out laughing. How he read the script in studio with a totally straight face, I do not know.

He was also a great traveller and liked to shoot 8mm colour film wherever he went. During the early 1960s he and his wife did an extensive trip through the then USSR, a travel plan that was entirely novel for its time. At one stage, RTÉ One television made a complete documentary, about 10 years ago, from all the film that John had shot on his travels. He was a remarkable man, with a twin career in medicine and broadcasting, and a wonderful character to boot. He died in his 91st year, a good innings indeed.

Margot Fleming

I got to know Margot well in the early 1960s, when I was doing my best not to pay too much attention to my studies at Magee College in Derry, where the curricula were then laid down by Trinity College in Dublin. I found most of my studies utterly boring and pointless- me and academia never gelled- but I did get to know Margot well. She was an assistant librarian and we became great friends. She had a cosy little flat in College Terrace, a cul de sac off the Rock Road in Derry, and I spent many a happy evening there, talking about everything under the sun. It was a remarkably chaste relationship; I don't think I ever even kissed her. But we spent a lot of time together and even went to Rome together on holiday on one memorable occasion. She was the daughter of a Garda superintendent and her family lived at Oak Road in Donnycarney, on Dublin's northside. It was Margot who introduced me to one of her friends who worked in the newspaper business, Catherine Rynne, who was then a feature writer with the old Evening Press in Dublin. It was the first time that I became close friends with someone working in the newspaper business; it must have inspired me. I lost touch with Margot, a gentle and kindly soul, the best part of 50 years ago, and the last I heard of her was that she was working as a teacher in Gorey, Co Wexford. She may not have known it at the time, but she had a big influence on me and my ambitions to get involved in the media world.

Pádraig Flynn

'Pee' Flynn was one of the most boastful politicians I have ever met; I have rarely, if ever, met another who was so full of himself. Born in Co Mayo in 1939, he was first elected to the Dáil in 1977 and went on to hold various Ministerial portfolios, including that of Environment, which he headed from 1987 and 91. He went on to become a European Commissioner, between 1993 and 1999.

I interviewed him at the EU' s Dublin headquarters when he was a Commissioner, about his time as Environment Minister in charge of housing. At the time, I was writing a history of the old First National Building Society- the planned book was never published, but all the archival material I had excavated was placed in the archives at UCD. But the day I met 'Pee' Flynn to talk to him about his housing record while Environment Minister was hilarious. Not only did he try and suggest the questions I should ask him, but he formed the answers to reflect his view of himself. It was one of the most unproductive and bombastic interviews I ever conducted, even though he was very friendly, and when I came to type up my notes afterwards, there was precious little material I could safely use. In January, 1999, he engineered his own political downfall, in one of Gay Byrne' s classic interviews. 'Pee' Flynn explained to Gaybo how difficult it was to manage the various houses he had to maintain on the mere salary of an EU Commissioner. Flynn also had an equally controversial TD daughter, Beverly, but in his case, he was truly the architect of his own political downfall and ended up having to resign from the Fianna Fáil party before he was expelled.

Flynn has long since retired to his native county, where in recent years, he has been active as a landscape painter. The local wags sometimes refer to him as 'Pee Casso'. Most politicians are full of themselves, but I have never, ever met one who was so over the top in self- praise as Mr Flynn.

Brian Farrell

I got to know Brian Farrell, one of RTÉ' s most legendary political interviewers, late in his life; any time we bumped into each other, he was unfailingly polite, the epitome of good manners. But those good manners disguised a forensic skill at analysing politicians and what they were saying and promising; he had an uncanny ability to coat the deadliest of questions with perfect manners. He was born in Manchester to an Irish family, who returned to Dublin during the second world war. Brian was educated at Coláiste Mhuire in Dublin, UCD and at Harvard.

He went on to have a long academic career at UCD, all the while developing his second career, in the media. He began by writing on politics for the Irish Independent and the old Irish Press, before joining Radio Éireann as an interviewer in the1950s. When the new Irish television service started up in 1962, he was there from the very beginning, becoming a star interviewer on such programmes as Broadsheet and Today Tonight. He retired from UCD in the mid- 1990s, but kept his broadcasting career going until 2004, when he was 75. He was married to Marie- Therese Dillon, whose uncle was James Dillon, leader of the Fine Gael party from 1959 to 1965, so politics was in the very air Brian breathed, both at work and at home. He died in 2014, aged 85.

Conor Faughnan

When I was writing quite often for The Irish Times motoring supplement, I used to have quite a lot of dealings with Conor, an engaging spokesperson for the AA. He began his career as a presenter for AA Roadwatch, reading out details on radio of traffic holdups around the country; these days, he is director of consumer affairs at the AA but is still seen from time to time on television. Married with three teenage children, he and his family live in Knocklyon, south Dublin.

Michael Fewer

Michael is an engaging writer, much interested in the outdoors and in walking. Once, after I'd written a favourable review of one of his many books in Books Ireland, he rang me up and suggested we go for a coffee. We've been doing that at regular intervals ever since, usually in the delightful surroundings of the Dunne & Crescenzi restaurant in South Frederick Street, Dublin, which has a very authentic Italian atmosphere. Michael started off as an architect, but since 1988, he has written many excellent books on such subjects as walking and travel. One of the recent books in which he was much involved was the 2013 study of T. J. Byrne, the architect who had such an influence on the emerging Ireland of the 1920s and 1930s. Michael was born and brought up in Waterford and he was as fascinated as I was recently, when I discovered that I had a great- great- grandmother called Mary Whelan, also born in Waterford, but in 1790 and brought up there. Michael, whose wife is Teresa, is a most convivial person with a fund of stories about his native city and county-I always look forward to the next coffee drinking session with him!

Arthur Fields

Who didn' t know Arthur Fields? He was the photographer who stood on O' Connell Bridge for over 50 years, day in, day out, even Christmas Day. During that time, he took over 180, 000 photographs, which his wife developed in a nearby studio. His father was a Ukrainian Jew who fled from Kiev to Dublin, where Arthur was born in 1901. Anyone coming up from the country, usually for a GAA match in Croke Park, knew Arthur Fields, as we did from all the times we used to be in the city centre in the 1970s and early 1980s. He' d pretend to take people' s photographs and if they stopped, he' d really take their photo, and give them a ticket so that they could collect their prints a short while later. Arthur had begun this unusual job in the 1930s and he carried on until he finally retired, in 1985.

Mary Finan

I've long known Mary Finan, from Co Roscommon, a most charming but equally determined woman who was for long the managing director of Wilson Hartnell public relations, now part of Ogilivy and WPP. When she started in pr in the 1970s, it was very much a business entirely dominated by men; these days, it has its fair share of equally able women and Mary was one of the pioneers. In the late 1960s, she had worked on a bilingual quiz on RTÉ television. Having made the transition to the pr business, she remained the md of Wilson Hartnell pr until 2003; other positions she held included as first woman president of the Dublin Chamber of Commerce and chair of the RTÉ Authority. She also has a very keen interest in opera and the theatre, very involved with such organisations as Opera Ireland and the Gate Theatre in Dublin. In 2015, she was given a lifetime achievement award by Image magazine.

In 1970, she married Dr Geoffrey MacKechnie, who went on to become head of the department of business studies at Trinity College; they had a daughter called Victoria. When I had a lot of dealings with Mary, the public relations company she headed was in Leeson Park and her home was directly opposite, a very handy state of affairs. Her husband died in 2008, aged 67.

John J. Finegan

John was the most knowledgable person on the Dublin theatre, the doyen of Dublin theatre critics. He had a remarkable career, as the theatre critic of the Evening Herald, now The Herald. In his long career, stretching over more than 50 years, it was rare indeed for him to miss a first night. He knew all the greats in the theatre business, whether these were Irish stars or visiting actors from the UK and beyond. When I was preparing my Paper Tiger series about the newspaper business in 1992, first a radio series, then a book, John was most helpful. He had seen his first theatre show in 1913 and he retired in 1990 from the Evening Herald. He wrote a total of 2, 145 pieces of criticism for that paper and always said that the most memorable first night he attended was in 1960, when Micheál MacLiammoir opened in The Importance of Being Oscar. A former colleague of his, Des Rushe, who was a former theatre critic on sister paper, the Irish Independent, described John as being kind, gentle, loveable, awesomely knowledgeable, an institution of princely uniqueness, which is exactly how I found him.

Fortunately, much of John' s work is preserved in the Irish Theatre Archives, which are part of the Dublin city archives.

Michael 'Fingers' Fingleton

For years, he ran the Irish Nationwide Building Society, and became a legend among money men. Born in Tubbercurry, Co Sligo, in 1938, he became a chartered accountant, working for Concern, the aid organisation, in the late 1960s, when he was closely involved in organising food supplies to Biafra, trying to break away from Nigeria. Eventually, he became chairman of Concern. But by 1971, he had moved into an entirely different field, when he was made secretary of the Irish Industrial Building Society, founded in 1873 in Upper Camden Street. Michael Fingleton was also called to the Bar in 1973, but he never practised as a barrister. Instead, what had been a tiny building society soon started developing fast under a new name, the Irish Nationwide with Michael Fingleton in charge.

I have two abiding memories of him; at a New Year's Eve Ball in the old Burlington Hotel, he was busy doing the 'Birdie' dance, a sight to behold. On another occasion, we spotted him and his wife busy sniffing all the cheeses in the Donnybrook Fair shop in Donnybrook. In the mid- 1990s, when I was in the throes of researching the abortive book on the history of the old First National Building Society, I went to interview Michael Fingleton in his office in Camden Street- that was before they made the grandiloquent move to the old Carroll's building on Grand Parade. I asked him about the history of the building society he was running and he was fairly forthcoming. But when I suggested that perhaps they should follow the First National example and do a book of their own history, I saw a horrified expression cross his face. It wasn't until years later when the true story of Irish Nationwide came to be told and taxpayers were lumbered with a bill running into billions of euros, that it became clear why Michael Fingleton didn't want the inside story told of 'his' building society. When he was in charge, he was always very generous in ensuring home loans for people working in the media; unsurprisingly, investigative copy never appeared, until years later, when it was too late.

Theodora Fitzgibbon

Theodora was a legendary writer about food and that was quite apart from the legendary story of her life, a remarkable lady. Born in London in 1916, she had a very bohemian upbringing, including time in Paris, before the second world war. She was perfectly happy to do such things as work as a nude model. She married an Irish- American writer called Constantine Fitzgibbon in 1944, but the marriage proved very troublesome, partly because of her husband' s addiction to drink. It lasted 15 years. In 1960, she married again, this time to George Morrison, a most amiable and talented film maker, who was born in Tramore, Co Waterford, in 1922. This time, it was a happy marriage that lasted until Theodora' s death in 1991.

George made a number of very striking films, including Mise Éire, which was created from a compilation of newsreel films from the 1916 era, with music by Seán Ó Riada. It was a most dramatic film with an enormous emotional influence; I well remember the first time I saw the film, when it was shown at Magee College in Derry, where it had an enormous impact on the audience. George went on to make several other documentary type films in similar genres.

But Theodora and George always had a rather unsettled existence; I remember vividly going to interview Theodora in the elegant house that they were living in at Dalkey in south Co Dublin and it turned out that they were living in a 'grace and favour' apartment that depended especially on Theodora doing chores for the woman who owned the house. Towards the end of her life, Theodora sold a cherished Henry Moore statue that she owned and it made enough money for herself and George to buy a house for themselves. Theodora didn' t live long to enjoy her good fortune; she died a couple of years later. Never get what you wish for!

Theodora was a fine writer and for years she was the restaurant critic for The Irish Times. Her critiques were always memorable and the reading public fell avidly upon her literary crumbs. But Theodora, brought up in a bohemian lifestyle, always had a nose for sniffing out life- saving deals. I remember well the night we came out of a reception in Mitchell' s in Kildare Street, together with Theodora and George. She said to her husband, "which restaurant shall we go to tonight?" It was quite common for restaurants to offer the couple free meals so that night, as ever, they had a splendid choice of establishments, any one of which was more than happy to welcome the couple. She also had a very open and pointed sense of humour, as we found in the Isle of Man. We were staying there in 1972, just after we had got married in what was then St German' s Anglican church in Peel- it' s now a cathedral- when we met up with Theodora and George. They were on the island as George was attending a film festival. They met us in the small hotel we were staying in on the promenade in Peel and the pair of them waltzed in, full of hugs and kisses, Theodora totally over the top as usual. The other residents in the hotel had their eyes out on sticks. Theodora and George had a rented Mini car and we all managed to squeeze in, but a little further down the road, Theodora said out loud in her most commanding voice: "George, stop the car at this instant or I shall wee wee in the back seat". A great couple, the life and soul of any party!

George married again, to a Scottish lady called Janet and even though George suffered from a stroke in 2005, he has carried on with his film making work well into old age.

Dr Garret FitzGerald

Garret was a remarkable academic who also managed to become Taoiseach. Born in Dublin in 1926, he was the son of Desmond Fitzgerald, the first Minister for External Affairs in the Irish Free State. Garret's brother, also Desmond, made a remarkable contribution to public life as an architect; it was he who designed the first terminal at Dublin Airport, which opened in 1940. That remarkable Art Deco building is still there, one of Ireland's iconic modern buildings.

Trained as an economist, Garret worked for many years for Aer Lingus, until 1959, where he created the timetables, a particular passion of his. He also lectured on economics at UCD and worked for The Economist and The Irish Times. He was Taoiseach on two occasions, when Fine Gael led coalitons in 1981- 82 and from 1982 to 1987. He had also been leader of Fine Gael from 1977 until 1987. Earlier on, he had emulated his father by being Minister for Foreign Affairs from 1973 until 1977. Garret had a remarkable grasp of economic theory and he sometimes used to say of any pet theory: "it may well work well in practice, but does it work in theory?"

He was married to Joan O' Farrell, often regarded as the eminence grise behind the throne in Fine Gael, but Joan grew progressively more debilitated the older she got. But she managed to get around, often with Garret by her side, her ever devoted husband. On one occasion, when Garret was Taoiseach and had travelled to Waterford for official engagements, he had Joan with him. 'Smokey Joe' Walsh, then editor and owner of the Munster Express newspaper in Waterford, created national outrage when he went on Morning Ireland on RTÉ Radio 1 to denounce Garret for bringing his wife with him on his trip to the city; she was in a wheelchair and 'Smokey Joe' thought this was unbefitting for the leader of the country. Joan died in 1999 and Garret died in 2011; a son, Mark, has in recent decades, become a big name in the property business in Ireland. I found Garret a very decent person, ever willing to help, but he always had a strong element of academia about him, which I found less appealing. His personality and approach to life was radically different to that of the politician who was his great opponent, Charles Haughey, likewise a former student of UCD.

John Flahavan

I got to know the Flahavan family well after they decided to commission a book from me on the history of their remarkable oat milling firm, based in Kilmacthomas, Co Waterford, which has an extraordinary history going back well over 200 years, to the late 18th century. John Flahavan, the present managing director, is the great- great- great grandson of Thomas Dunn, who took over the mill in 1785. John' s son James now works in the family business, making him the seventh generation in the family business, which mills about 120 tonnes of oats a day. During my trips down to west Waterford to research the history of the firm and the family, I discovered many fascinating nuggets of history and a remarkable story of how a family owned and run firm has managed to keep going for so long without selling out to a multinational. I also had some very memorable meals at the Flahavan family home, right across the road from the mill and met other people who play key roles in the firm, such as John Noonan, the sales and marketing director. I bowed out of the project a couple of years ago when it was clear that it wasn' t going anywhere very fast, despite the help that other writers such as Turtle Bunbury and Regina Sexton from UCC had given in interviewing many key members of staff. All in all, we managed to produce a remarkable archive of oral history. A & A Farmar, the Ranelagh, Dublin, publishers of renowned historical books, took over the project and even though the Flahavans say they are still committed to the project, at the time of writing, there was still no sign of this gargantuan scheme finally appearing in print.

Donal Foley

He was a legendary figure in The Irish Times, news editor there when Douglas Gageby was editor first time round. They were a sensational combination and did much to make the paper what it is today.

Donal was born in Ring, Co Waterford and grew up in Ferrybank. He had been London editor of the old Irish Press before being recruited to The Irish Times. He recruited many of the remarkable women who joined the paper in the 1970s as journalists. He also wrote a famous satirical column, Man Bites Dog, from 1971 until shortly before his death in 1981. I owe him a great debt of gratitude, because when my book on the history of the Bewley' s cafés and family was published in 1980, he gave it a great write- up in The Irish Times, something that was a great encouragement to my bookish ambitions.

Ever since, I' ve been very friendly with his niece Catherine Foley, who was a journalist with The Irish Times, where she often wrote in Irish. She continues to contribute to the paper. Catherine, too, lives in Ring and she often appears on TG4, the Irish language station. She and her sister, RoseAnn, have made many documentaries for the station, including a memorable one on their uncle, Donal, back in 2007.

France

I made my first trip to France in 1958, when I was a young and gauche teenager; I was hooked immediately and have never lost my enthusiasm for the country since. It helps of course that we had Huguenot ancestry in our family and I think that all these genes from three and four centuries ago have resurfaced in me.

When I did that first trip, I travelled to France by myself and remember well confronting such primitive technology then as the jetons that you had to use in the public payphones. I also remember that the trip from the Gare de Lyon in Paris to Lyon took something like eight hours in a steam powered train; these days, the trip takes a couple of hours by TGV. I was staying with a family in a small village to the north of Lyon and not far from Mâcon. The family I was staying with was large; at dinner every night, a dozen people sat at the vast table. None of them could speak English and I couldn' t speak a word of French, but by the end of that trip, I was fluent in French, much to my own astonishment and that of my school friends. I also brought home a large amount of Gauloises cigarettes, but after trying them for a fortnight, I gave up in disgust and from that day to this, have never smoked again! The date of that trip is indelibly imprinted on my mind; while I was in France, the most serious, but unsuccessful, attempt was made to assassinate General de Gaulle, by rebels who wanted to keep Algeria French. I have the most vivid recollections of going to the village cinema and seeing a black and white newsreel depicting the assassination attempt.

In the many years after that 1958 trip, I made many more trips to France, from 1971 onwards making them with Bernadette, who has always had similar enthusiasm to my own for everything and everyone French. We often used to stay in the 7th arrondissement in Paris, where we could observe the many civil servants who work in that district, lingering over lunch until 3 pm or 3. 30pm, and enjoying copious wine. They then returned to their offices for a small amount of work before departing for home. I always thought that was a tremendously civilised way of doing things! But I've never, ever been tempted to live in France. The French have a peculiar love affair with bureaucracy and in France, it' s like some totally obtuse thicket that you can' t find your way into, or your way out of. After all, it was a Frenchman who invented VAT and this love of bureaucracy and form filling in France has extended into every corner of the EU.

But out of all the numerous trips we' ve done to France, in our time, visiting every single one of the old departments, our favourite was in 1986 to the seaside town of Collioure in the far south- west, near the frontier with Spain and not too far from Barcelona. In the early 20th century, the town was home to numerous painters and much more recently, Patrick O' Brian, the maritime author, who wrote the Aubrey- Maturin series of novels about the Napoleonic wars. He has been acknowledged as one of the greatest of maritime novelists and while most of his life, he was considered Irish, because of his nom de plume, he wasn't anything of the sort. He was English through and through but had lived with his wife in Collioure for many years. After he died in the Fitzwilliam Hotel in Dublin in 2000, he was buried in Collioure.

We loved our time in the town, with its quaysides, castle, beaches and quaint church beside the sea; the place has remained almost entirely unspoiled; if it had been in Ireland, large parts would have been demolished and either concreted over or filled with revolting 1970s style office buildings totally devoid of any architectural merit. France has a very good, but not perfect, record, of preserving its architectural patrimony- just look what they did to Les Halles, the old wholesale fruit and vegetable market in Paris!

At Collioure, we also managed to have a narrow escape on a boating trip.

One sunny afternoon in Collioure, we went to a small jetty some way from the town and found a boat loading up with scuba divers. We asked if we could go along for the ride and the skippper was friendly and inviting. But we had no sooner got out into the open sea than a tremendous storm blew up. The waves almost turned the boat over; since we were wearing light summer clothes, we were both soaked to the skin. Even the well- clad scuba divers were getting very nervous, but we eventually managed to return to land. We staggered to the nearest bar, ordered two double cognacs and promptly had two more, all to insulate against the effects of the sudden cold and wet. For many reasons, Collioure has remained our favourite holiday trip in France, but such is the intensity of culture, art and history in France that it is almost impossible to go anywhere without finding something of interest. And we have always been fortunate in getting on so well with French people, who tend to see people from Ireland as wild, disaffected cousins.

We had a splendid example of this one time in Cherbourg. We were returning from a trip to Normandy and had gone to Cherbourg to get the ferry home. We had managed to be very late and would have missed the sailing, except that a local man, driving past, stopped and asked if he could help. We told him our predicament and he promptly drove us to the ship so that we made it on time. He had assumed that we were from the Home Counties of south- east England, so he made polite conversation about all the rugby games he played in against English teams and how the English were always perfectly gentlemen. We disabused him and told him we were in fact from Dublin and were going home there. In an instant, his whole demeanour changed and he became very voluble and friendly and shouted out at the top of his voice: "Voilà, les Anglais", adding in English, they're a lot of bastards. Sadly, in the last year or two, France and everything French have lost a lot of their appeal and as things stand, I doubt I'll ever revisit the country.

Catherine Fulvio

Catherine may be a celebrity super chef, but she's thoroughly down to earth, chatty, homely and always totally positive. I' ve always found her more than willing to help and very easy to deal with; if only more super stars from the telly were so down to earth! She was brought up on a farm at Ballyknocken, near Glenealy in Co Wicklow and the farmhouse is now Catherine's lovely guesthouse, where guests from all the world enjoy all home comforts. Right next door is her cookery school. She started off working at Tinakilly House Hotel, just outside Wicklow town, but she's long been a celebrity chef, first on TV3 and now with RTÉ, as well as making guest appearances on channels all over the world.

She also has a strong connection with Sicily- her husband is from Palermo there, so Italian cuisine has had a huge effect on her work, resulting in such TV series as Catherine's Italian Kitchen, and the inspiration for some of her cook books.

Douglas Gageby

One of the most remarkable newspapers editors in 20th century Ireland, Douglas Gageby was editor, twice, at The Irish Times, during which periods, the paper made a remarkable transformation from a national publication with a modest circulation into a vital component of the mainstream media in Ireland.

Born in Belfast in 1918, he brought a strong sense of Northern ethics and down- to- earth thinking to his job as a newspaper editor. A graduate of Trinity College, Dublin, during the second world war Emergency, he worked in Army intelligence, where his knowledge of German stood him in good stead. After the war, he went to work for the Irish Press group, working on the Sunday Press after it was launched in 1949. When the Evening Press was launched in 1954, it brought a whole new dynamic to the newspaper business, competing with two existing evening newspapers in Dublin, the Evening Herald and the Dublin Evening Mail. Douglas was the first editor of the Evening Press and he did a remarkable job, aided by an equally remarkable editorial team, in producing an evening broadsheet that was soon selling around 200, 000 copies a night, an absolute 'must' for Dublin readers, not only for its editorial content, but for its small ads.

It's hard to think now that in the late 1950s, the three Dublin evening newspapers were selling close on half a million copies a night between them. But the Dublin Evening Mail closed down in 1962, tellingly the year that Irish television started. These days, The Herald is an all- day newspaper, as is the Belfast Telegraph, so that these days, Ireland has just one true evening paper left, the Evening Echo in Cork, which sells about 12, 000 copies a night.

From the Evening Press, Douglas Gageby moved to The Irish Times, first in an executive role, becoming editor in 1963. During the following decade, he totally transformed the fortunes of the paper, helped by Donal Foley, the news editor, who recruited many of the women journalists who graced the pages of the paper in decades to come. Douglas retired in 1974 and was succeeded by Fergus Pyle, an able but uninspiring editor. He lasted just three years and when Douglas Gageby returned as editor in 1977, many of the editorial staff regarded it as akin to the second coming. He finally retired in 1986. When I was working on my Paper Tigers RTÉ radio series about Irish newspapers, in 1992, I got to know Douglas well and found him immensely helpful. I loved visiting his home in Rathgar, where his appreciation of nature and wildlife was evident, as we recorded the taped interviews for the series.

His wife Dorothy was the daughter of Seán Lester, another North of Ireland man, who became the last head of the League of Nations. The Gagebys' son, Patrick, is a well-known barrister, while their daughter, Susan Denham, is the Chief Justice of the Supreme Court.

Galway, 2012

An invitation to Galway in 2012 turned out to have all kinds of pleasurable ramifications. At that stage, I knew Galway quite well, having often visited the city, to interview people like Des Kenny the bookseller and Jack Fitzgerald, a former editor of the Connacht Tribune. He had been appointed the Tribune's Clifden correspondent in 1933 and eventually became editor in 1950, a job he held for the best part of 30 years. He was a genial and slow- moving man, but very sharp as an editor. Outside the office, everyone knew him as very amiable, but inside, he often had spectacular rows with Bill King, then then news editor, who had a completely different type of personality.

I also knew other places well in Co Galway, especially Clifden, which was a delightful old style town on the edge of the Atlantic, always with the smell of turf smoke in the air and in the water, before it was so developed as a tourist mecca. But the invitation to Galway in 2012 was different. When I was doing my book on Achill, published in 2012, I had had some correspondence with a lady living in Caherlistrane, not far from Tuam, Mary J. Murphy, who was an expert on Eva O' Flaherty, who had run Achill's famous knitting industry.

Out of the blue that summer, I had an invitation from Mary to come to Galway and do the launch in the city of her new book on the life and times of Eva. Mary was a most generous host and ensured I was well looked after for the night at The House Hotel close to the quays in Galway and just round the corner from Charlie Byrne's, the famed Galway bookstore. On Friday, September 14, 2012, I made a speech to a large crowd in the bookshop, to launch Mary's book; everyone gave the speech a kind reception. Eventually, we retired for drinks to The House Hotel, where I was able to chat with such delightful people as Bernadette, Mary's mother, a most charming lady, who died towards the end of 2015. This was the beginning of what has become a very dear friendship with Mary. And that night, during drinks at The House Hotel, I spotted a young woman, a great friend of Mary's; she had a very enquiring attitude towards everything and I discovered that her name was Maria Gillen, from Athlone. She too has become a very dear friend; I was so lucky during that trip to Galway to have met two women with whom I have been able to share many interests and in the years since, I have been much enhanced and enriched by their friendship.

Declan Ganley

A remarkable entrepreneur, he was born in England in 1968, to Irish parents, but he and they returned to Co Galway when he was 13. While he was still at school, he was busy trading in stocks and shares, an early indication of his entrepreneurial skills. He went on to earn a vast fortune from forestry in what had been the USSR. He owned the largest private forestry operation there, before selling out in 1997. Then he went on found broadband, cable TV and wireless networks in western, central and eastern Europe as well as making many telecom inventions. I had direct dealings with him, on behalf of The Irish Times, when he started up a limousine service for business people. I found him very easy and straightforward to deal with, no messing, no bullshit, always getting to the heart of the matter very quickly. He also went on to become very active in politics, successfully helping to campaign for a 'No' vote in the Treaty of Lisbon referendum, the first one. More recently, his interest in politics has become more subdued. He and his family live in considerable splendour in a mansion near Tuam, Co Galway; his is a story of a local boy made good, very good.

Lynn Geldof

In the 1980s, we used to bump into Lynn Geldof, an elder sister of Sir Bob Geldof, at press receptions in Dublin. She was always a bit of a hipster in the way she dressed and carried on, but she was good company and a good writer, too. Then, she was writing for such publications as In Dublin and the RTÉ Guide. When we knew her, she had been the first person we knew who had been to communist Cuba and seen it all for herself; in those days, Cuba was very unknown territory. Lynn went on to write extensively about Cuba, including a renowned book in 1992, and she was always very sympathetic towards the island. These days, she' s still a writer, as well as being a Unicef campaigner.

Maureen Gelletie

Maureen was a formidable hotelier, who ran Hunter' s Hotel at Rathnew, Co Wicklow, for many years. For a number of years, we used to go there for lunch quite often and got to know her well. She came from Cootehill, Co Cavan, where she was born Maureen Murtagh. At the start of the second world war, she took up a job at an hotel in Redcross, Co Wicklow, but soon afterwards, in 1940, she started a new job, at Hunter' s Hotel, on the reception desk. It' s a remarkable place, tracing its history back to around 1650. By the early 18th century, it was trading as the Newry Bridge Inn; the Hunter family took it over in 1825. Years ago, Thomas Gelletie set up and ran a watch making and jewellery business in Wicklow town- the Gelletie shop is still there- and in due course, the Gelletie and the Hunter families got together through marriage. Maureen married Michael Cecil Gelletie in 1944; their marriage lasted for 20 years, until his death in 1964. But in the subsequent decades, Maureen kept going as the woman behind this lovely, comfortable, family- run hotel. She was a lovely lady, but a formidable business woman who ensured that the hotel continued to trade very successfully. She died in 2010, aged 91.

Maria Gillen

I met Maria for the first time at a memorable event in my life, on September 14, 2012. Mary J. Murphy had asked me to do the Galway launch of her book on Eva O' Flaherty of Achill fame, at Charlie Byrne' s bookshop in Galway. There was a great crowd at it and everyone seemed to like my speech. I was staying at a nearby hotel and after the launch, Mary entertained all the guests; a great night was had by all. I was introduced to Maria at the launch- she is a great friend of Mary's - and happily, we've been great friends ever since. She has a very original way of looking at life, often through cats' eyes, which I find very appealing, and she has a razor- sharp appreciation of Irish history and heritage, something else that means a lot to me.

Her mother's family lived on Achill Island for many generations and her father' s family were seafarers. That gave her a lifelong love of stories and travel and there' s nothing she likes better than combining the two. Many years ago, an elderly neighbour called Mary Kilcoyne McNamara told her about a woman who lived on Achill when she, Mary, was a young woman. The story of Emily Weddall' s life immediately caught Maria' s interest and she had been researching her life and work, promoting it and writing a regular blog ever since. Emily Weddall was the daughter of a Church of Ireland rector and the wife of a sea captain and she became a leading light in the artistic and crafts revival on Achill in the early years of the 20th century, playing a key role in the foundation of Scoil Acla, the oldest summer school in Ireland, still going strong. Emily, a great friend of the Pearse brothers, also managed to get herself imprisoned during Easter Week, 1916, but she went on to play her part in the struggle for Irish independence.

Later, she moved to Dublin, where she died in 1952. Emily M. Weddall had a momentous life and Maria' s extensive research has turned up many fascinating aspects, previously hidden from view. Maria, who has lived in Athlone for some years now, also enjoys hanging out with animals in her spare time, while she also spends time when she can in India. Maria and myself meet up reasonably often for lunch; she' s a most delightful and companionable companion and we always find that we end up talking about every subject under the sun, plus a few more! We' ve also met up on occasions in recent years in Athlone and she has given me a great understanding of the town' s remarkable history. Maria has also given me tremendous encouragement for my own work, especially my books, over the past few years.

Larry Gogan

A larger than life character and a very engaging person to meet, Larry is an absolute fund of information about the pop music industry since the year dot. He was born in 1938 and when he was a teenager working in his father' s news agency shop in Fairview, Dublin, he got to know one of the customers well; she was Maura Fox, who worked for McConnell' s, then the biggest ad agency in Dublin. It was Maura who gave young Larry the necessary introductions into the world of pop music and broadcasting. When he was young, Larry spent a mere six months working for CIE, the State- owned transport company, but it was clearly not for him. He had always wanted to work in radio and to be a DJ, so he was able to start fulfilling his life' s ambitions early on, starting off as a presenter on some of the numerous sponsored programmes that Radio Éireann then broadcast. When Radio 2, now 2FM, went on air for the first time in 1979, in response to the wave of pirate radio stations around the country, Larry played the first disc. Now, 37 years later, he is still broadcasting on 2FM, regaling listeners with his quizzes. It has produced many bloopers, such as "which famous star is followed by travellers?" Answer: Joe Dolan.

At the beginning of 2014, he started a new two hour weekend show on 2FM and during his time in broadcasting, he has also hosted a variety of television shows. He also did the television commentary for RTÉ on the Eurovision Song Content on four occasions.

Larry met his wife Florrie when she was 16, working in her father' s newsagent' s shop in Parnell Street, Dublin, and they married six years later. They went on to have five children, but sadly, Florrie died in 2002 at the age of 60, leaving Larry bereft. But in true show biz style, he has carried on pop picking ever since.

Jacqueline Gold

I interviewed Jacqueline Gold once, one time she was in Dublin. We met up one Sunday afternoon at the Fitzwilliam Hotel on St Stephen's Green but if I had any expectations that it would be full of titillation, given her job as head of the Ann Summers sex shops, I was sadly mistaken. The interview was full of management speak in which vibrators and home marketing parties for the Ann Summers range became the subject of some very boring conversation, not remotely exciting. Until then, I hadn' t realised that the wonderful subject of sex could become in fact, a mere tool of successful management and about as exciting as rows of figures on a balance sheet, spreadsheets rather than spread legs. By the end of the interview, I was bored out of my mind and later, I struggled to turn my notes into reasonably interesting copy.

But there was no doubt about Jacqueline' s ability to turn her work experience into a vast personal fortune. She is now estimated to be worth over £500 million sterling. Her father David ran a publishing business that introduced the concept of sex magazines to High Street newsagents in Britain. She grew up in a wealthy family home in Kent, funded by porn publishing, but her parents separated when she was 12. Her father bought the then four shops in the Ann Summers chain in 1972 and in 1979, he gave Jacqueline, then 19, summer work experience for less pay than the tea lady earned. Over the years, she has transformed the Gold Group International into a vast enterprise, embracing Ann Summers and Knickerbox. She had become chief executive in 1987 and since then, the group has gone from strength to strength. The controversy 20 years ago when the first Irish Ann Summers shop opened in O' Connell Street, Dublin, directly opposite the hallowed GPO, has long been forgotten. By 2016, Jacqueline had been bestowed with the CBE for her work in services to entrepreneurship, women in business and social enterprise.

Noele Gordon

She was the first soap superstar in this part of the world and she was very nearly my mother. Noele Gordon, born in London in 1919, went into acting at an early age. While many of her early appearances were on the London stage, she also appeared frequently at some of Birmingham' s top theatres, especially the Alexandra. My father was a young man then, addicted to fast cars and he also had a taste for fast theatrical ladies; the latter is something I' ve inherited! My father met up with Noele Gordon in Birmingham and they did a line for a while, so if they had persisted, she could have ended up as my mother.

When the new commercial TV station in Birmingham went on air for the first time in 1956, Noele was back in Birmingham helping to set it up. She started as an executive, the first female executive in British television, but quickly moved into programme presentation and her first show, Tea with Noele Gordon, was the first chat show on TV. This soon evolved into a daily daytime entertainment show called Lunchbox and when it came to an end in 1964, after more than 2, 000 episodes, ATV replaced it with a soap set in a motel, called Crossroads. Noele played Meg Richardson, the motel owner. She stayed with the show until 1981, making her the first soap superstar in these islands. The script for the series was corny and the sets always wobbled when they appeared on screen, but despite that, it was a ratings winner.

In 1961, Noele hosted an early presentation of colour television at the ATV studios in Birmingham and I was lucky enough to get an invite. It was the first time I'd seen colour TV.

Noele never married; she died, from cancer, in 1985.

Princess Grace of Monaco

Meeting her and her husband, Prince Rainier, was a great experience for Bernadette, who was then working in the Department of External Affairs, now the Department of Foreign Affairs. In 1968, the pair of them made an official visit to Ireland and Bernadette went to great lengths to greet them in style, learning how to curtsey and how to greet them in French, both accomplishments she carried out perfectly, in the Gresham Hotel in Dublin. It wasn' t Princess Grace' s first visit to Ireland; she had been here in 1961, keenly aware of her family' s Irish roots and visiting her grandfather's old homestead in Co Mayo.

She went into the film business and as Grace Kelly was remarkably successful but at the age of 26, she retired from films in order to marry Prince Rainier and settle in Monaco, the tiny principality he ruled over. She had had an illustrious film career, but later, many stories began to circulate about her promiscuity. But her years in Monaco turned her into a demure royal mother; one of her children now rules Monaco as Albert II. Grace was killed in a car crash in Provence in 1982;

afterwards, there were many inaccurate stories that the car was being driven not by her, but by her daughter Stephanie. But in more recent times, it has also been suggested that she was murdered because she knew too much about Italian gangs that wanted to rob the riches of Monaco. The weekend the car crash happened, we were staying in the Greville Arms Hotel in Mullingar. The Westmeath Examiner had a big function there on the Friday night to celebrate the centenary of the paper, it was a most enjoyable do, led by the then editor, Nicholas Nally. But at Saturday lunchtime, when we were quietly recovering, we turned on the television news in the hotel only to hear the shocking news that Princess Grace had just been killed in a car crash. It was a dramatic and horrifying end to a fairytale marriage, although Prince Rainier, as a widower, lived on until 2005.

Robert Greacen

I got to know Robert Greacen, the poet, rather well in his later years, when he was living in Sandymount, Dublin. He and I were both writing plenty of reviews at the time for Books Ireland and any time that I went to the home of Jeremy Addis to collect books for review, Robert was usually there, doing exactly the same, but using the occasion to enter into long and detailed discussions with Jeremy about minute comings and goings in the literary world. Robert had been born in Derry in 1920, but he grew up in Co Monaghan, before going to Methodist College, Belfast- at that stage, his father had a newsagent's shop on the Newtownards Road in Belfast- and Trinity College, Dublin. After he graduated, he spent many years working and living in London, where he came to notice as a poet of note as early as 1941, when he was 21. He returned to Dublin in 1989; his marriage to Patricia Hutchins, also a writer, had ended in 1966; she died in 1985. They had a daughter, Arethusa, who still lives in Ireland.

Greece

One of the most memorable trips we did was in October, 1978, when we spent a week based in Athens. The flights there and back from Luton in southern England were basic to say the least-they were with Thomson Holidays. The Athens hotel we stayed in was also fairly basic, but if sufficed. It all worked reasonably well except for the day we wanted to go to the island of Hydra, about 40 km from Piraeus. We had ordered a taxi to take us from the hotel to the hydrofoil at Piraeas, but the member of the hotel staff who had made the taxi booking made a complete cock- up of it and the taxi never arrived, so we missed the boat, literally.

We had one other experience in the hotel which was rather spooky. The last night we spent there saw Bernadette waking up in the middle of the night and declaring that she had seen the ghost of a woman, like a theatre performer, sitting at the dressing table, looking into the mirror doing her make- up. There was no question but that it was a ghost, who remained in Bernadette' s vision for quite a while, although by the time she had woken me up, the ghostly apparition had disappeared. Maybe there had once been a theatre on the site of the hotel, or perhaps it was a ghost from the second world war, a troubled period indeed in Greek history, when the Nazis overran the country. Then as the war was ending, the communists appeared to be on the brink of gaining control and a fierce civil war ensued. By the time we had got to Athens in 1978, the country had only just returned to democracy, after the overthrow of the neo- fascist colonels four years previously. The colonels were bad, but they were nothing compared to the travails that Greece has gone through in the past few years, as its economy has virtually collapsed, while the Germans demanded fiscal adherence to frightening austerity measures as part of Greece' s price of remaining in the EU.

We found the Greeks to be generally charming and helpful, with a definite dash of rebellion. We had an excellent example of this. In Athens, we had found it difficult to locate restaurants where we could have dinner in the evenings and enjoy a reasonable meal. In the end, we went to one of the posh hotels in Athens, the Grande Bretagne, right in the centre, near the parliament. The food was excellent and not too expensive. But one night when we were leaving after dinner, we got talking to one of the concierges, who thought that we were from somewhere deep in the Home Counties of England. He was very polite, but also very disclined to talk. No, we told him, we are from Ireland and he literally jumped for joy and shouted out the name of De Valera. He was very well informed about Irish history and in line with so many of his compatriots, saw many parallels between Irish and Greek history. He became positively effusive and we ended up having a great chat with him.

Something else that happened one afternoon in Athens also made an impression, an almighty downpour, which ended with the gutters being turned into miniature rivers, carrying tables and chairs from cafés downstream on the raging waters. Yet generally speaking during that week, we had excellent weather and on several occasions, took a hydrofoil to nearby islands. We went to Aegina a couple of times and enjoyed it very much; the best part of that island was being taken for a trip round the island in a horse- drawn tourist cart. The elderly driver had little or no English, but was most friendly, and we enjoyed seeing all the unspoiled orchards and other parts of the landscape. We also visited the island of Poros, about 30 km from Piraeus. There, on the heights above the main village, we found a very bedraggled cat, but the poor creature was in such a bad state that when we gave it some food, it simply sicked it up.

On the island of Salamina, which is very close to Athens and Piraeus, we saw someone beating the bejasus out of an octupus on the quayside, to make it ready for the cooking pot, all very stomach churning. Other sights we saw included the Corinth Canal, an extraordinary feat of engineering. All in all, it was a most interesting trip and it endeared Greece and the Greek people to us and over the past few years, through all their troubles, we have felt much sympathy for them.

Bernadette Greevy

She was a mezzo soprano of wonderful talent, who began in a humble way, working in the old Clery's department store in Dublin. Born in Dublin in 1940, by the time she was in her mid- 20s, she was winning great acclaim for her performances, both in Ireland and around the world. She had real star quality, but she was also very temperamental, especially if she felt she wasn't being given proper respect for her talents. Quite right! She was devastated when her husband, Peter Tattan, died in 1983. They had one son, Hugh, who worked for a time in the Sullivan Bluth cartoon studios after it was set up in Dublin in 1979. In the late 1980s, we often had dinner at Kilmartin's, a wonderful bistro- type restaurant in Upper Baggot Street, where one was always guaranteed to meet someone interesting. It was there that we met up with Bernadette Greevy on several occasions and found her to be most likeable and charming, not a bit like the grand diva she had been depicted as. She died in 2008.

Victor Griffin

A wonderful character, for long a Church of Ireland minister. He comes from Carnew, Co Wicklow, where he was born in 1924. He was ordained into the Church of Ireland in 1948 and went on to serve at churches in Derry from the late 1950s until 1969. I first met him when I was a useless student at

Magee College in Derry, struggling fruitlessly to make sense of the Trinity College curricula I was supposed to be following. Victor lectured in philosophy at Magee College and I must admit, his lectures were among the most interesting I attended. I can still hear him talking about the philosophical greats and what they had achieved. In 1969, just as the troubles were getting under way in a big way in the North, Victor and his family left Derry and moved to Dublin, where he remained Dean of St Patrick's Cathedral until 1991. In his years there, I often followed his remarks about contemporary political life- he was always very liberal in his views. Now retired, he lives in Limavady in the North of Ireland and we still keep in occasional touch. He is, I am glad to say, still as jaunty and engaging as ever.

Dennis Griffiths

I first became acquainted with Dennis Griffiths, regarded as the most punctilious historian of London newspaper history, in the very early 1990s. Dennis was born in Swansea and soon followed his father into the newspaper business at the South Wales Evening Post. His father was both the chief compositor and the chief reporter. Eventually, in 1968, Dennis got a job at the Evening Standard in London and soon became its production director. After the Evening Standard changed hands, Dennis became research and development director with Express Newspapers and was involved with the launch of the Daily Star in 1978. A decade later, in 1988, the Irish Daily Star was launched as a co- venture between Independent Newspapers and the Daily Express group. But eventually, Dennis became disillusioned with the Express group and left in 1986.

He then wrote the definitive history of the Evening Standard and the former owner of the paper, Viscount Rothermere, praised Dennis for his scholarship and said that he had shown there were almost as many stories about the Standard as there are stories in it. From 1999 to 2002, Dennis was the very active chairman of the London Press Club when he helped organise events for the 300th anniversary of the Daily Courant, the first daily newspaper in the UK. The next step for Dennis was researching and writing the Encyclopedia of the British Press, 1422- 1992, which occupied five years of his life.

Dennis got in touch with me and asked me to contribute. I found him meticulous to work with and equally diligent about ensuring that payments from the publishers reached me when they were due. The title of the book is an anomaly, because it also contains a reasonable amount of Irish newspaper history, North and South, material that I contributed. Dennis was very generous in his description of my first book, The Newspaper Book, a history of Irish newspapers from 1649 to 1983, which he described as the seminal work on Irish newspapers.

After the launch of this vast encyclopedia in 1992, Dennis set his sights on an even more ambitious target: he wanted to produce an encylopedia of the world' s press. Even though many correspondents were lined up for it around the world, including myself, the project became bogged down with the publishers in London. Eventually, it end up with a publisher in New York, where the whole project ran into the sand and simply petered out. As for Dennis himself, he died on Christmas Eve, 2015, just after his 82nd birthday. He is survived by his wife of 55 years, Liz, their daughter Jane and son Mark. Dennis was a remarkable historian of the printed word and a delightful and utterly painstakingly careful person to have worked with.

Christina Grimmie

Atrocities of one kind and another seem almost endless these days, but one recent tragedy really got to me, the slaying of 22 year old singer Christina Grimmie in Orlando, Florida. After she had given a concert there on the evening of June 10, 2016, she was signing autographs when a crazed gunman came up to her and shot her dead. Christina, who came from New Jersey, had immense musical talent, that she developed through her appearances on The Voice and on You Tube. Yet when she was a small child, making her first appearance on stage, she was too shy to sing and ran off the stage! She was also a remarkably generous and loving person and it was typical of her that when she saw the gunman approaching her, before she realised what was happening, she greeted him with open arms to give him a hug. She was also a great animal lover. It's truly awful that her life was snuffed out at the start of her career and I was so devastated by the news that I sent sympathies to Heather Weiss, her Los Angeles- based publicist.

Frank Hall

One of the stars of RTÉ television in the 1960s and 1970s, I got to know him quite well over the years. Born in Newry in 1921, where he was brought up by an aunt, he started work at 12 in a local shop, later becoming a waiter in London. On his return to Ireland, he managed to get a job in the art department of Independent Newspapers, before graduating to a job on the Evening Herald, where he wrote about show bands. He soon moved on, to RTÉ, where he spent the rest of his career. He started off working in the newsroom and from 1964 until 1971, he presented Newsbeat, a regional news programme. During the 1964 season of the Late Late Show, which had started in 1962, he stood in as presenter for Gay Byrne, who was then busy with his commitments at Granada television in Manchester. But Frank Hall was a disaster on the Late Late Show and Gaybo soon came home to take up the programme's reins again.

But after Newsbeat ended, Frank Hall started a new programme, the defining one of his career, Hall's Pictorial Weekly, in which he poked fun at a wide variety of targets in public life, creating a mythical county council at a place called Ballymagash. By the time the 1977 general election came round, the programme's satirical digs at the Coalition government, including all the budget cuts of then finance minister Richie Ryan, were widely credited with helping the Fine Gael/ Labour coalition lose the election. By the time the show finished in 1980, over 250 episodes had been broadcast and many are still fondly remembered today. When he had finished his broadcasting career, he became the national film censor, an unlikely role, and finally, an even more unlikely role in charge of the RTÉ credit union. He was a great character, always coming up with the most unlikely anecdote, often anchored in his early days in Newry. He died in 1995, while his wife Aideen, who came from Camlough, not far from Newry, died in 2014. The family home for years was in Santry, Dublin. But for a long time, he had an affair with Frankie Byrne of radio agony aunt fame and at Frankie's funeral, we met her daughter from that liaison. In recent years, I've become friendly with Frank's son, Don, who has long run his own pr company in Dublin.

Andrew Hamilton

Andrew, who died a decade ago, in March, 2006, was the long-time motoring editor of The Irish Times. He began his career in journalism at the Impartial Reporter in Enniskillen, where he developed one of his legendary skills, remembering car registration numbers. It was said that he never forgot one. He then moved to The Irish Times, where he was a reporter in the news room, before graduating to motoring correspondent, a job he held for 35 years. He was long regarded as the doyen of motoring correspondents and knew everyone in the business. He was also a very convivial and generous person, a true gentleman. But I have to say that in the days when I had to input copy at The Irish Times office, sometimes I had to use the keyboard on his desk; in all my years in journalism, and I'm bad enough myself in this respect, I never met anyone else who had such a messy desk! Andrew, who never married, lived in Monkstown, Co Dublin, while he had a close affinity with West Cork; in March, 2006, he was visiting his sister in the North when he collapsed from a heart attack. He was rushed to Craigavon hospital, but died a short time later, a short while before his 65th birthday. A great procession of friends and colleagues made their way to his funeral and burial in Newtownstewart, Co Tyrone.

David Hammond

I met David Hammond through the BBC in Belfast and Bernadette knew him better, through all her film work at the Department of Foreign Affairs. He was an extraordinary musician and film maker, born in Belfast in 1928. He began as a teacher; one of his pupils was a young lad who became Van Morrison. In the early 1960s, David became a producer for the schools' department in the BBC in Belfast and he worked at the BBC for more than 20 years. He was also a founding member of the Field Day theatre company in 1980. But he was chiefly known for his skills as a traditional music maker, great friends of the likes of Pete Seeger and the Clancy Brothers and Tommy Makem. He had a vast repertoire of traditional Irish tunes. When he left the BBC in 1986, he set up his film making company, Flying Fox Films, and made really outstanding films about such people as Stephane Grappelli, Seamus Heaney, Brian Keenan, the Beirut hostage, and

Yehudi Menuhin. David, better known by his friends as Davy, died in 2008 aged 79.

Richard Hannaford

The partner of Norah Casey, he died in 2011. He had married Norah in 1996 at the University Church on St Stephen' s Green and that was where his funeral was held. The two of them had met at a press dinner in London in 1992; he was health correspondent with the BBC while Norah who had trained as a nurse, had gone into publishing. At the time they met, Richard was just 30. Although he worked for the BBC for 17 years, eventually, he came to live in Dublin and he ran the Harmonia publishing company in tandem with his wife. I subsequently met him on a few occasions just after Harmonia had taken over Ireland of the Welcomes from the old Bord Fáilte. He was a great character in his own right and in due course, he got well used to all the local variables in the Irish publishing industry. Norah herself has had an equally stellar career, including as a Dragon on Dragon' s Den.

Gretta Hannon

She came from Headford, Co Galway, where she was buried in January, 2016. I never knew her during the years she worked in The Irish Times accounts department, but got to know her long after she had retired, as she lived in Raglan Road in our district, and I often bumped into her when out walking. She always used to tell me that she loved every day of her job there and after The Irish Times moved to its new and present building in Tara Street a decade ago, she kept the key to the old works entrance on Fleet Street.

Dan Harrington

I got to know Dan very well during the 1990s, when we' d often meet up in Murphy' s old news agency on Upper Baggot Street, now Donnybrook Fair, or elsewhere in the district. Dan was a great character, a real countryman with a great stock of expressions about the weather and a good deal else. From West Cork, he had worked in the construction business in England for many years before returning home. In retirement, he and his wife lived in a flat on Pembroke Road, close to the junction with Waterloo Road. She predeceased him and Dan died in 2002, aged in his late 90s. I still remember him vividly and the delightful conversations we used to have.

Harrison family

I got to know the present generation of the Harrison family when I was researching Ballsbridge Then & Now, published in 2012. What had once been a coach house in Pembroke Lane, in the days when many houses in the district had a coach house for the horses that drew their carriages, was turned into a shop in 1920. By that time, the advent of motor cars over the previous two decades had rendered these coach houses redundant. That shop was taken over in 1941 by John Harrison and for nearly five succeeding decades, he and his wife, Mary Catherine, ran what became known as the Wee Stores. The shop was renowned in the district for selling all kinds of groceries, as well as coal and peat briquettes, but the arrival of supermarkets in the district in the 1960s was a big blow.

John died in 1987, his wife in 1991. Eventually, the shop was let to other firms, including Sheridans the cheesemongers and also to a Frenchwoman who ran a boutique shop there. Then about five years ago, it reopened as First Editions, an excellent antiquarian bookshop. I got to know well Anthony, son of the original Harrisons, and Carmel, their daughter, who is married to Allan Gregory, the man who runs the bookshop. In his professional life, he was an engineer, but now he is engrossed in what really interests him- literature. He is closely involved with the Irish Byron Society and a host of other literary outlets, as well of course, with his excellent bookshop.

Billy Hastings

Billy Hastings has become known as the quintessential hotel owner in Northern Ireland, always a very pleasant, down to earth but forthright person to deal with. He began with a small hotel in Ballymena back in 1967 and his hotel empire grew to six prime hotel properties in the North, including the Europa Hotel in Belfast, the Culloden just outside Belfast and the Slieve Donard in Newcastle, Co Down. He also has a 50 per cent stake in the equally successful Merrion Hotel in central Dublin. In 2009, he became Sir Billy Hastings for his services to the hospitality industry in the North.

Charles Haughey

A remarkable politician and the most controversial Taoiseach of all time. His admirers have long praised him for his contributions to the arts, the creation of the International Financial Services Centre and for such measures as the introduction of free travel for pensioners. His detractors condemn him with equal vehemence for his large scale corruption. Born in 1925, he went to UCD before going into accountancy and then into politics; in 1951, when he was 26, he made a very shrewd move by marrying Maureen, daughter of Seán Lemass, long time Minister and eventually Taoiseach himself. But that didn' t stop him having a 27 year long affair with Terry Keane, a journalist on the Sunday Independent.

Haughey made a great personal move in the mid- 1960s when he sold the comparatively modest house, with much land, that he and his family owned at Raheny, and bought the magnificent house of Abbeville, at Kinsealy, just north of Dublin, where he had a residence that matched his Napoleonic like ambitions. He was always controversial, including during the 1970 Arms Trial, but eventually, he took over as Taoiseach from Jack Lynch in 1979, creating a bitterly divided Fianna Fáil party. He was Taoiseach on three occasions, from 1979 to 1981,in 1982, then for the longest spell, from 1987 until 1992. I knew him quite well and always found him very personable and encouraging. After my book on Bewleys was published in 1980, even though he was up to his tonsils in one of of his frequent political crises, he sent me a most charming letter congratulating me on the book and wishing me well for my future endeavours. Bernadette, through her work in the Department of Foreign Affairs, got to know him even better than I did, and they often met at State functions. At the end of every such occasion, he always went out of his way to ensure that the staff on duty that night were all properly looked after and even though it would be a very non- u term these days, he often called Bernadette "his little pet".

Jarlath Hayes

One of my greatest friends in the media was designer Jarlath Hayes, who designed two of my books, the one on Newspaper history published in 1983 and my book on the history of Dublin airport in 1990; he also gave me a lot of help with my book on the history of advertising in Ireland in 1986. Born and brought up in Dublin, Jarlath began working in the advertising business in 1945 and for years, he worked in a long defunct agency called O' Keeffes in Fitzwilliam Square. He also lectured on the subject of advertising design. But his real love was type and book design. In 1970, he went freelance, working with his daughter Susan, who has gone on to become a noted designer and publisher herself. The first time I met Jarlath, it was to interview him at his then studio at 38 Percy Place, Ballsbridge. But he soon found the overheads unrealistic and in 1979, started operating from his own studio at his home just off the main road in Stillorgan. During the 1970s and 1980s, he worked on many books projects, for publishers as diverse as Gill & Macmillan, Four Courts Press and the Lilliput Press. He also designed his own typeface, Tuam Uncial, which was used for the credits on the Glenroe soap opera on RTÉ television and on many regional shopfronts. His other great love was of timber and he often made tables, chairs and other wooden items for family and friends. Besides being a brilliant book designer, Jarlath was also wonderful company, highly irreverent and sacriligious. He was the first person I heard mention the property supplements that were then starting to blossom in the Dublin newspapers in the early 1980s; Jarlath said to me that they would be the ruination of the economy, because they would encourage the wrong kind of people to invest in property. How right he was, more than 20 years before the big property- led crash started, in 2008. He loved coming up with the most scurrilous stories, many of them about the bosses he had known in the advertising industry. He was also known for a succession of black terrier type dogs, each one of whom was called Murphy. Jarlath's wife was Oonagh, a long suffering woman who often had to cook meals for publishers who managed to drop in at the most inconvenient times. Jarlath died in 2001; Oonagh survived until 2012.

Seamus Heaney

Seamus Heaney, a world class poet, who lived from 1939 to 2013, lived for many years on the Strand Road at Merrion in Dublin 4; strangely enough, I never met him, although I heard many interesting stories about him. When I was researching my book on Old Newcastle in Co Down, published in 2007, I discovered that a young Seamus Heaney, then a student at Queen's University, Belfast, had a summer job as a waiter in a restaurant in the town. But even though I never knew Seamus personally, both Bernadette and myself know his wife Marie Devlin quite well. We often used to bump into her at shops in Ballsbridge and have a chat and when one of the Sunday Miscellany anthologies was compiled by her, it included one of my contributions. Seamus came from Co Derry, while Marie was from Ardboe, Co Tyrone, one of six beautiful and clever sisters. One of her sisters is Polly Devlin, the writer.

Denis Heffernan

Denis has been a great friend of Bernadette and myself ever since we got to know him at the old Cashel Palace Hotel in Cashel, Co Tipperary. He was the head barman there and a more congenial man in charge of a bar you would be hard put to find. Denis also has a fine singing voice and he launched a CD of his singing in 2011. He has great stories about some of the legendary figures who stayed at the hotel in the old days, including Richard Burton and Elizabeth Taylor, Andrew Lloyd Webber, Trevor Howard and a 10 year girl called Lady Diana Spencer, who went on to become the famed Lady Di. By the time that the 70th birthday of Denis came round in 2013, he had worked at the hotel for 47 years, having joined in 1967. I was also fortunate to have met, on one of my trips to Cashel, Josephine, mother of Denis; she sadly died in 2011, in her 93rd year.

Donald Helme

He is one of the very few people I' ve kept in touch with since we were both students at Magee College in Derry and that was back in the early 1960s. Donald, although English, made his career in advertising in Dublin, working for some of the big ad agencies in years gone by, such as Arks and Youngs. He set up his own agency in 1986 and it went through mergers with other agencies, such O' Connor O' Sullivan, until eventually, the Helme Partnership was bought out by Grey Advertising in 2004. He eventually cut all his ties with the business. But in recent years, he built up a great following on Lyric FM as the station' s resident jazz expert. However, his programme hours got whittled down, until the last of his shows was dropped in 2015. Much public protest followed, all to no avail. He and his wife, Dale Parry, spend part of their time in Italy, a far cry from those long ago days in Derry.

Arran Henderson

Arran is a near neighbour of mine; he works out of Heytesbury Lane, in the house that was once occupied by his grandmother, Patricia Vial and her second husband, Viv. He has all sorts of qualifications, including a degree in fine art from the National College of Art & Design in Dublin and a Masters from the Dublin Institute of Technology. He knows his subjects inside out, art and history in Ireland and the history of Dublin, but has a great knack of making all this information very accessible. He' s the founder of Dublin Decoded.

He is a most charming and genial person, who teaches as well as doing lots of guided tours. In recent times, I helped him with the construction of his 1916 walking tour of Ballsbridge. He also runs a popular blog, arranqhenderson. com Arran always seems to be in a whirlwind of activity, doing this, that and the other, or going for a trip somewhere, with the energy and enthusiasm of younger people; he' s a lot younger than me and has a lot more energy! He also has a most charming and delightful partner, Una Butler, whom I' ve met briefly.

Brum Henderson

He was the managing director when Ulster Television went on the air in 1959, opened by Sir Laurence Olivier, and he remained managing director until 1983, when he found himself pushed upstairs to the chairman' s office. He stayed with the company until 1990. I knew him well when he was running UTV and he was a great character in an industry that produces so many. He was a real extrovert and a fund of stories about how the fledgling station had got on the air in the first place and how it was built up to become such a firm favourite with viewers both in Northern Ireland and across the border, where people north of a line from Dublin to Galway put up huge aerials to receive the station, long before cable television came along. Incidentally, Brum was an abbreviation of his middle name, Brummell. Brum came from a newspaper family; his father, Bill, was for long the managing director of the Belfast News Letter, then as now a staunchly Unionist publication. Brum' s brother, the equally famous but more dour Captain O. W. J. Henderson took over as md of the News Letter. Brum himself was educated at Trinity College, Dublin, and when he was running UTV, he had a very inclusive format for appealing to viewers of both persuasions in the North. In its early days, Brum used to call UTV the "fun" factory and certainly the staff there had a lot of fun, including in their social life outside work. I heard entertaining tales of much bed- hopping! But after the troubles started in 1969, the station had to go into hard news overdrive. Brum was a great host and on the odd occasion he invited me to lunch in Havelock House, UTV's headquarters, I could be guaranteed an hour or two of wonderful anecdotes and stories.

Brum wrote his autobiography in 2003, for the Appletree Press, but sadly, he died in 2005, a showman to the very end. These days of course, the locally owned UTV no longer exists; the channel is now owned by ITV and the original owners are now known as the Wireless Group, having sold out their television interests. Now,in turn,the Wireless Group has been sold to Sky.

Paul Henderson

One of the brightest of bright sparks in the media business, he is the managing director of what is now called DMG Media Ireland, publishers of the Irish Daily Mail and the Irish Mail on Sunday, which have developed such brand innovations as evoke. ie, as part of the group' s digital transformation. Paul had previously worked with the Irish Daily Star and TV3 before joining the Daily Mail group in Ireland in 2008. He' s a very lively character, always fizzing with new ideas and new strategies, that have put the two newspapers he' s in charge of at the forefront of media innovation in Ireland. Paul is always full of new ideas and innovations that will drive the business forward. I well remember his unalloyed excitement when the group opened its own studio at its Embassy House premises in Ballsbridge, so that they could shoot their own TV commercials and carry out other audio- visual creativity.

The man he succeeeded was John Thompson, another legendary figure in Irish publishing. John had been the launch managing director of the Irish Daily Star, a joint venture between Independent Newspapers and the Express group in London. I always remember the memorable launch of the Star, in 1988, in the Powerscourt Townhouse Centre. Before the Star, John had worked with the Irish Farmers' Journal, had been the launch managing director of U magazine and had worked for the Sunday World, where he coined the famous slogan for that paper, "are you getting it every Sunday?"

John stayed at the Star until 2001, when Associated Newspapers, publishers of the Daily Mail, bought Ireland on Sunday from Scottish Radio Holdings, eventually transforming it into the Irish Mail on Sunday. When John left the Star, he was succeeded by Paul Cooke, someone I often interviewed; he is now ceo and joint owner of the Sunday Business Post.

But as for John, he was struck down in his late 50s with cancer, but he refused to give in. I quite often met him for an early morning coffee in the Upper Baggot Street area, at a time when I was writing a lot about the media industry. Very often, John had just been for his latest session of cancer treatment, then when we had finished coffee, he' d head for the office. A remarkable man, who was just 63 when he died in 2006.

P. J. Hennelly

P. J. was a legend in his own lifetime in the newspaper business and it' s fair to say that most people in Co Mayo and beyond, knew him or knew of him. The Connaught Telegraph in Castlebar is by far the oldest newspaper in Co Mayo, founded in 1828, which makes it 55 years older than the Western People in Ballina. The founder was Lord Cavendish, then it fell into the ownership of James Daly, who was very involved with the Land League, before it was taken over the Gillespie family. I met P. J. in 1992 when I was recording my RTÉ Radio 1 series, Paper Tigers, when one of the episodes was all about the newspapers of Co Mayo. P. J. was an ideal interviewee, genial, good natured and full of fascinating anecdotes reflecting his lifelong career with the paper, where he was the general manager in charge of the commercial side. The funny thing is that very modestly, he didn' t mention his own long involvement in the development of camogie in the county. He was a delightful person to interview and the tape yielded some fine radio. In April, 1996, the newspaper had its new building in Castlebar opened by the then President, Mary Robinson, herself a native of Ballina, but sadly, a mere four months later, P. J. passed to his eternal rest. For so many of the years that the warm- hearted P. J. was running the commercial side, an equally legendary character, Tom Courell, was the editor. Eventually, like practically all the regional newspapers, once family owned, the Connaught Telegraph was taken over by the Celtic Media Group in 2014 and promptly changed from broadsheet to tabloid format. What P. J. would have made of that, I' m not quite sure!

Pat Herbert

In recent years, I've got to know Pat Herbert of the Hurdy Gurdy Vintage Radio Museum in the old Martello tower at Howth, very well. Pat has always been most helpful in my book researches. He opened his radio museum in 2003, as a reflection of his lifelong interest in the medium. Pat grew up in Co Mayo and listening to the wireless there in the late 1940s spurred a lifelong interest in the subject, which means he has accumulated a vast collection of radios, material relating to radio broadcasting and gramophones. The museum itself is absolutely fascinating and of course Pat has long been intrigued by the early connections that Marconi had when he was developing wireless communications. Among the many notable events commemorated in Pat' s museum is the opening of the Athlone radio transmitter on June 26, 1932, in time for the Eucharistic Congress in Dublin that year. Pat and his assistant at the museum, Joe Guilfoyle, have turned the museum almost into a travelling radio show and they are constantly promoting it at events around the country. Not long ago, the BBC' s Radio 3 gave a good mention to the museum.

George Hetherington

I first got to know George, who became joint managing director of The Irish Times, in the early 1980s, when I was researching my first book on newspaper history. Little did I think then, as we sat talking in the lobby of the old Burlington Hotel, that one day, he and his wife Christine would one day become close neighbours. When we moved to Wellington Lane, Ballsbridge, in 1988, we soon discovered that they were living just round the corner, in Heytesbury Lane. For my newspaper research, George was most cordial and helpful, filling me in on the intricacies of the shareholders who bought out the interests of the Arnotts in the paper. As a result of that changeover, George became a shareholder himself in The Irish Times in 1954. For long, George was the owner and managing director of Hely Thoms, the printers in Dublin. He was a joint managing director in The Irish Times through the 1950s, but gave up the job when Douglas Gageby was made managing director, before he went on to become editor. However, George retained his connections with the paper until he retired in 1973. George was also a poet of note. He married Christine Foster, from Derry, who had been the first wife of Dr Conor Cruise O' Brien; they had had three children. The youngest of them, and George' s youngest step child, was Kate, who had a brilliant literary career and who died, tragically, from a brain haemorrhage, in 1988, when she was just 49. George himself died in December, 2001, when he was in his 90s. I remember vividly in January of that year, talking to George, who told me he was off to see the Turner water colours and drawings in the National Gallery of Ireland, which are only exhibited during January of each year, because the natural light is then so weak it won' t damage them. George said to me: "I'm going in to see the Turner works and I know that it will be the last time I see them". His wife Christine died five years later.

Rev Stephen Hilliard

I didn' t know him personally; the nearest I came to that was when we donated to Dick Ahlstrom, long- serving science editor of The Irish Times, when he took part in a running race, just after Stephen' s tragic death in 1990, to raise funds for his family. Stephen came from an interesting family background; his uncle Robert, was a Church of Ireland cleric who was known as the 'Boxing Parson' in his native Killarney. He also supported the Republican side in the Spanish civil war and he was killed in Spain in February, 1937. Stephen became a journalist at The Irish Times, before being ordained into the Church of Ireland in 1986. He and his family had only moved into the vicarage at Rathnew, Co Wicklow, three weeks before he was brutally murdered, stabbed during a robbery at the vicarage. Someone else at The Irish Times also became a Church of Ireland cleric, creating something of a tradition at the paper. Patrick Comerford became a journalist at the paper in 1974 and after toiling there for 19 years, was made foreign desk editor in 1994, a job he held for eight years. He then became a Church of Ireland priest and has remained so ever since, all the while producing some notable writings on people and places both in Ireland and internationally.

Susan Hinchcliffe

She was my first serious girlfriend and what a young lady she was!I met her when we were both attending a technical college in the centre of Birmingham. She came from a conservative, middle class family in Solihull, a dormitory town just outside Birmingham. Despite the fact that she was doing a serious line with a guy at the college who came from the Middle East, Susan and I got to know each other very well, until we too started doing a line. She was very outgoing, with a lovely figure; very often, when she knew her parents were going to be out for the day, she would invite me to her home in Solihull, where we spent endless time in kissing proximity. In those days, people didn't usually go much further and nice girls certainly didn' t do it. If we had known each other now, of course, we' d have been shagging each other silly, in the best rabbit tradition. She was an extremely sexy young woman and I thoroughly enjoyed my time with her. One particular occasion I remember with her was in 1961; one Sunday, on a bright summer' s day, we went to the country for a picnic and romps in a field. It was only when we got back to Birmingham that we heard the news, that the East Germans, helped by the Russians, had just started building the Berlin Wall. I still remember vividly the evening we broke up; we had arranged to meet in Birmingham city centre and when we met up, she simply told me that she had met up with someone else and didn' t want to continue our relationship. At the time, it was devastating news, but as with everything else when you' re young, you get over it pretty quickly. When you' re young, time seems to stretch out for ever, but of course, as you get older, it contracts at an ever faster pace. I' ve never heard any more about big busted Susan- no doubt she went on to become an uber respectable middle class housewife, following in her parents' footsteps.

John Holohan

Over the past few years, I' ve got to know John Holohan extremely well, in his capacity as chairman of the Ballsbridge, Donnybrook and Sandymount Historical Society. Passionate about local history, when I writing about Ballsbridge especially, he was a mine of information and always most helpful, always able to put his finger exactly on any piece of information or photograph that was needed. His society has always worked closely with the library in Anglesea Road and it was there, at John's behest, that I gave a lecture on

Ballsbridge during 2015. John was born and brought up in Clyde Road; what was once the family home is now Raglan Hall luxury apartments. His grandfather, William Davy, took over Searson's pub in Upper Baggot Street in 1884. John is a former estate manager, but in retirement he has found a whole new lease of life with the local historical society. I've also got to know his wife Jacqueline well. From Dundalk, she is a most accomplished artist, producing wonderful paintings and drawings of landscapes. One of her best known paintings is of a very simple subject, a Georgian door in Dublin. For two of the books I did on the history of Ballsbridge and Dundrum, Jacqueline did absolutely splendid drawings that enhanced the texts no end.

Con Houlihan

One of the greats of newspaper journalism, he had a totally unique way with words. A native of Castleisland, Co Kerry, where he was born in 1925, he worked for many years for the old Irish Press group. Much of his work there was for the old Evening Press, where his sports column, in which he mixed many musings on Irish and world events, was legendary and mandatory reading for anyone interested in sports or simply good journalism. His way of working was strange; he used to start at 4 am every morning and write all his copy by hand, one paragraph to the page. Deciphering his handwriting needed special skills among the compositors at the Irish Press. After the group shamefully closed down in 1995, Con took his wordsmithing skills elsewhere, to the Sunday World and the Evening Herald. He was considered by many other journalists as the father of modern sports writing in Ireland. He was lucky in his later life, because he had a partner in Harriet Duffin, who had come from working in public relations in Belfast to doing the same in Dublin. They were a devoted couple; in his later life, Con was plagued by ill health, but continued to write. He spent the last year of his life in St James's Hospital and died in 2012.

Emily Hourican

I got to know Emily well in her early days as the editor of Hospitality Ireland magazine; she has also long contributed to the Sunday Independent. Very recently, since late 2015, she has been writing for that newspaper about her battle with cancer. She's a brave and courageous lady and everyone hopes that for her sake and that of her family, that she will win this particular battle.

She was born in Belfast, where her remarkable father, Liam Hourican, was the RTÉ correspondent in the early 1970s. He then went on to become a member of the cabinet of Richard Burke, then Ireland's EU commissioner, who died in March, 2016. This meant that Emily was brought up in Brussels, where she became fluent in Eurospeak. In 1976, Liam came back to Ireland and in 1981, became press secretary to Garret FitzGerald's government. But that government lasted no length of time, collapsing the following year, putting Liam out of a job. He was subsequently found a job as inspector of the EU's overseas offices, which suited him to a T. Liam died at Cahirciveen, Co Kerry, in 1993, when he was just 49. He had been a remarkable journalist and writer and his tradition is well continued by Emily.

Con Howard

He was a remarkable Irish diplomat of the traditional variety, but often very undiplomatic in his behaviour. He worked for more than 40 years with the Department of Foreign Affairs, but even though he was Irish consul in London, Boston and New York, and also for a time the Irish representative on the

Council of Europe, he was never made an ambassador. It's not hard to see why.

Con, who came from Co Clare, was a hard drinker and a great man for a party. But he also liked women, in a way that's totally unacceptable today. At Iveagh House, the headquarters of the Department, if he saw an attractive young woman rushing in first thing in the morning to sign the book, his reaction was to say to them "I'd just love to put my hand between your thighs". On one occasion, at the UN, he did just that, putting his hand up the skirt of the French ambassador's wife; to avoid a diplomatic incident, he was promptly sent home. But he had many positive achievements to his name and when he wasn' too drunk, he was great company. It was he who opened the doors of the White House to the Irish and in later years, in the early 1980s, he helped revive the Wren Boys' tradition on St Stephen's Day in Sandymount. He was also very involved in the British Irish Association and he was also the founder of Cumann Merriman in his native county. After he died in 2009, aged 84, the late Seamus Heaney said that on the anniversary of Con's death every year, the true meaning of pandemonium should be debated.

Someone else who indulged in hanky-panky in the Department was a former ambassador, who's still alive, in his late 90s, and these days, an ardent Catholic. I don't want to embarrass him by saying who he was, but the story about him is hilarious. And you thought that government departments were always the model of correct behaviour! This former ambassador, when he was home and working in Iveagh House, struck up a relationship with a sultry looking woman who worked in the typing pool; she was allegedly a hot shot at languages, so every lunchtime at 1pm, she would go up to the ambassador's office, he would lock the door for an hour and he would undergo allegedly intense language tuition. It sounds a likely story!

Another story from the Department, during the 1960s, is equally hilarious but perfectly clean! President Sukharno of Indonesia had played a major part in wresting Indonesian independence from the Dutch at the end of the second world war. He was the independent country' s first president, for more than 20 years, up to 1967, came to Dublin on an official visit just before the end of his autocratic rule. An excellent lunch was organised in the best traditions of Iveagh House, but after the lunch, his personal bodyguard was nowhere to be seen. Eventually, he was found behind a curtain, fast asleep!

Miroslav Hudec

He was the Czechoslovak trade representative in Ireland during the mid- 1960s and as a symbol of the growing trade links between the two countries, in those days, many a farmer was the proud owner of a Zetor tractor. Miroslav and his family lived in Foxfield Avenue, Raheny, and I got to know him well because at the time, I was working with Business & Finance magazine. He and his family were very friendly and hospitable and the idea grew of producing a business supplement on Czechoslovakia. For me, it was a great opportunity, as it was the first time I had been sent abroad to work. Mind you, I almost managed to miss my connection at Heathrow- that was long before direct flights between Dublin and Prague. The Czechoslovak Airlines plane I got at Heathrow was quite an experience; naturally, the plane was Soviet- built and all the wording on the interior of the plane was in Russian, which was meaningless to me. Eventually, the plane landed at Prague airport and I found a taxi to take me to my lodgings. The taxi driver told me that in a previous life, he had been a university professor but had fallen foul of the regime. My lodgings in Prague were amazing, a large room all to myself in an apartment on Národni, the Prague equivalent of O' Connell Street, Dublin, right in the centre of

Prague. The woman who lived in the apartment had little or no English, but we got on well together and once I'd had my breakfast every day, I left for the day. I had to go round a whole series of government agencies to organise all the editorial copy for the supplement and everything was so efficiently organised that I ended up with most of my time in Prague to myself. So I saw most of the main tourist sights in and around the city, including the Charles Bridge and the cathedral, as well as the famous Child of Prague statue, then so popular in so many Irish households. I saw many bizarre sights, such as the man changing money on a street corner; between deals, he practised his skills as a circus performer and kept multiple balls in the air, always a useful trick! I met a journalist on Hospodárske Noviny, the daily business paper in Prague, still going, and he told me how in the 1950s, any journalists who fell foul of the regime ended up working in the coal mines.

The so- called Prague Spring was in full spring, but even though there was much talk of liberalisation under the then prime minister, Alexander Dubcek, in practice it meant very little. But there were clear signs that the Soviet Union was deeply unsettled by what was happening. I remember one day in August, 1968, when I went into a jazz club just off Wenceslas Square in Prague. There was a radio on, tuned to a French long wave station and it was clear from the news bulletins, that the USSR and some of its allied were massing their military might close to the borders of Czechoslovakia. I was booked to fly back home, so I thought it sensible to take those flights, rather than stay put in an increasingly dangerous situation. The last night of my stay in Prague, I went to the national opera house just across the street from where I was staying, to see a performance of Janacek's opera, Jenufa. For the cast and the audience, it was a very emotionally charged performance. The next day, I took a Pan Am flight from Prague to Brussels; the flight was extremely turbulent, with the plane bouncing up and down in the stormy weather. At

Brussels, I changed planes and was soon back in Dublin. A couple of days later, when I arrived at work in Business & Finance first thing that morning, Nicholas Leonard, the editor, said to me: "I don't think we'll be doing your supplement- the Russians have just invaded Czechoslovakia." But a couple of months later, it did come out. The only Irish journalist who was in Prague during the invasion, reporting for The Irish Times, was Vincent Browne.

A couple of evenings later, a great protest meeting was held in the old Jury' s Hotel in Dame Street, but it was all rather pointless- what could anyone do? When I met up with Miroslav Hudec, I told him I was very sorry for what had happened to his country, but as a true party man, he said nothing. Soon afterwards, he and his family left Dublin, but I heard years later, in a roundabout way from Kevin Myers, the well- known journalist who these days writes for The Sunday Times, that Miroslav Hudec was alive and well, living in retirement in what is now the Czech Republic.

The following year, 1969, I went back to Prague, with a friend. The city was quiet and sullen, with troops everywhere. In the end, the people of what was then Czechoslovakia had to wait until 1990 for their freedom. But from what I've heard since, one of the prices of that freedom has been a profusion of brothels, sex shows and other so- called 'entertainments' that were once totally forbidden.

Gloria Hunniford

She comes across on screen as a delightfully warm- hearted and empathetic person- that' s the real Gloria, not some artifice of the make- up department. Gloria can also appear to be rather scatty, but in reality, she' s anything but, having built a massive broadcasting career over the past 50 years. She was born in 1940 and now, well into her 70s, she' s still going strong, a remarkable woman.

Brought up in very modest circumstances at Number 94 Armagh Road, Portadown, her father had varied interests and it's obvious that Gloria inherited her showbiz talents from him. By day, her father, a staunch Orangeman, was advertising manager with a couple of local newspapers, the Portadown Times, then the Ulster Star. But he was also a pigeon fancier and a very talented musician. Gloria started as a production assistant with the BBC in Belfast, before moving into radio broadcasting. From the BBC, she moved across town to what was then Ulster Television, where she was the presenter of the main local bulletin in the evenings. Her job with UTV gave her an entrée to cross- channel television and she never looked back. She married her first husband, Don Keating, a local TV director, in 1970 and that marriage lasted until 1992. Subsequently, in 1998, she married her second husband, Stephen Way, a hairdresser, and they are still together.

From the 1980s onwards, right up to the present, she has appeared in a whole host of cross- channel TV shows, everything from Loose Women to Rip Off Britain and Strictly Come Dancing. She also had a daily radio show on BBC Radio 2, which started in 1985 and lasted for 10 years. One of the most traumatic events in Gloria's life came in 2004, when her beloved daughter by her first husband, Caron Keating, died from breast cancer at the age of 39. Gloria subsequently set up a cancer charity in her daughter's name, the Caron Keating Foundation.

Indian connections

On my father's side of the family, there have been long connections with India, for something like 150 years until not long before Indian independence. Distant relatives, long ago, worked at such jobs as being a fireman on the East India Railways. The brother of my paternal grandmother worked as the manager of the Saxo salt factory in what was then

Calcutta, now Kolkota, and in 1940, he was murdered by his manservant.

Both my father Ronald and his brother, my Uncle Richard, were born in India, and amazingly, the family was living in Amritsar at the time of the great massacre there by British militia in 1919. My paternal grandfather worked for long for the old Burmah oil company, and records show that in 1916, he was seconded on temporary loan to Afghanistan, because of his engineering expertise. My oldest step sister, Emma, has been doing lots of research on all these Indian connections and one of the many things she discovered and sent me was a photograph of what was once the family home in Amritsar, now a guest house. It seems that my relatives in India had generally good relations with local people, so good in fact, that it' s now estimated that each one of us in the current family, myself included have about four per cent Indian genes in our genetic make- up. I've long had an interest in India, long before all this came to light, although I've never had the slightest interest in Indian religions. I've always admired Indians for being super smart; during 2015, when I launched my new website, hughoram. com it was no sooner up and running than I got an email from a company in India offering to look after my marketing needs for the new site. Typically Indian!

Dr John de Courcy Ireland

One of the legendary maritime characters produced in Ireland during the past century, he had an immense influence on how we regard the sea. I was lucky to have got to know him quite well; the first time I met him was when I went to his modest house in Dalkey to interview him for copy I was writing for The Irish Times.

John was born in Lucknow in India in 1911, where his Co Kildare born father was serving in the British army.

His father died young and John didn' t get on at all with his stepfather; when he was a teenager, in compensation, he was devouring every book he could get his hands on, including the Encylopedia Brittanica. But he had a public school education in England, then went up to Oxford, where he met his future wife, Beatrice, usually known to everyone as Betty. After they got married, the pair of them spent some weeks in the Aran Islands and Co Donegal so that they could improve their Irish. Just before he turned 30, he managed to get himself sacked from his job in Derry because of his trade union activities.

Not to be deterred, he was awarded a PhD from Trinity College, Dublin, for his thesis on the influence of the sea. He had become a teacher, joining St Patrick' s Grammar School in Dublin in 1949, then in 1951, moving to Drogheda Grammar School, before going on the Bandon Grammar School in Co Cork. Eventually, in 1968, he joined the staff of Kingstown Grammar School in Dún Laoghaire, which eventually became, with mergers, Newtownpark Comprehensive School. He worked there until he was 75.

But always, the sea was calling him. He was closely involved with the RNLI lifeboat in Dún Laoghaire harbour for many years. Her wrote many very knowledgeable books about the sea and he often broadcast on Seascapes on RTÉ Radio 1. On one occasion, he talked about the maritime traditions of Marseilles; a short while later, we arrived by train in that southern French city, walked out to the front of the main railway station and saw the fantastic view over the city exactly as he had described it. I sent him a postcard to say how much we had enjoyed what had been for us, his preview of Marseilles. He was feted and honoured all over the world for his knowledge of maritime affairs and indeed, when he was 91, after his wife had died, he went to Morocco to explore how the world' s first lifeboat service began. When I heard the news, one day in 2006, that John had died in St Michael' s Hospital in Dún Laoghaire, we were devastated, as were his innumerable friends in the maritime sphere. He had indeed been a wonderful advocate of everything to do with the sea, encouraging people to see Ireland as a truly maritime nation. One thing though, always sticks in my mind about Dr de Courcy Ireland; he had dreadful teeth and talking to him for any length of time meant that one had this unnerving distraction, unable to avoid the sight of his bad teeth.

Dermott Jewell

I've known Dermott for years through his long connections with the Consumers Association of Ireland. I met him first when I interviewed him for copy I was writing for The Irish Times and we've remained firm friends ever since. He is the expert on consumer law and the rights of consumers, although those rights get a fraction of the support they get cross- channel, through the Consumers Association in the UK. But against all the odds, Dermott had fought long and hard on behalf of the rights of Irish consumers and whenever I've found some breach or other, and have told Dermott about it, I have always received a most erudite and often witty reply. It' s hardly surprising that his favourite book is Dubliners by James Joyce.

Anthony J. Jordan

I had long heard of Anthony, one of Sandymount' s best-known residents, but I didn't have the privilege of getting to know him until I was researching my book on Sandymount, published in 2016. Anthony was a tremendous help for me when I was putting that book together. From Ballyhaunis, Co Mayo, he trained as a teacher and eventually became the principal of the old cerebral palsy school in Sandymount, which became Enable Ireland in 1996. After he retired, he struck out on a brand new career, as a writer. He has since produced many outstanding biographies of such people was W. T. Cosgrave, John A. Costello, Eamon de Valera and Major John McBride, and he is still busy giving historical lectures. When Daniel Day- Lewis was living temporarily in Sandymount to take part in the production of the 1989 film, My Left Foot, based on the life and times of Christy Brown, the actor, who' s renowned for his efforts to get inside the personalities of the people he plays, spent six weeks at Anthony' s school to acclimatise himself for the part of Christy.

Nell Kane

Nell was a marvellous lady, who celebrated her 98th birthday in January, 2016, but who sadly died in St Vincent' s Hospital in Dublin on Wednesday, March 30, 2016. From time to time, I used to go and visit her at her home in Wicklow town and marvel at her memory and her interest in current affairs. She was born in Wicklow town, but she and her family moved to the Kilmainham district of Dublin when she was three. By the time she was 10, she was enrolled in the Municipal School of Music and after she qualified with her diploma in music from Trinity College of Music in London, she went on to teach in such schools as Mount Mellerary, Muckross Park, Sion Hill, Cross & Passion in Kilcullen, Co Kildare and at the Christian Brothers in Crumlin. She also taught in the School of Music in Chatham Street, Dublin, for 47 years; the school had started in 1890 and is now known as the Conservatory of Music and Drama in the Dublin Institute of Technology. After she retired, she carried on teaching and only gave up music teaching when she was 86.

She also started her own Nell Kane Orchestra in 1949; it had 30 players, including my late father- in- law, Hugh Quinn, who was a violinist and a great friend of Nell. It was through that connection that we came to know Nell so well. The orchestra played at many venues for many years and all the money raised was donated to charity. Nell also toured extensively in the US. She was lucky when she decided to more or less retire 35 years ago; the old family home in Wicklow town, Hillside Cottage, was still owned by her family, so that was where she move to and where she lived up to the time of her death. Her community carers and her many relatives and friends, had great expectations that she would live to be 100, but it was not to be.

Kate, my sister

My sister, Kate Moulin, born five years after me in 1948, had a conventional upbringing first in Birmingham and then in London. She went to university at Warwick and her first job was in London with Wiggins Teape, the paper makers.

In the early 1970s, she shared a flat at Ladbroke Grove in north London; it was a big first floor flat and it seemed to be like Euston station, there were so many comings and goings. Before we were married, and afterwards, we spent many delightful times kipping down in Kate' s flat. She was bridesmaid at our wedding in Peel in the Isle of Man in 1972, and then a couple of years later, Kate got married to Peter Moulin. I well remember the wedding in the registry office in north London, then the reception at Peter's father' s home near Regent' s Park. For many years now, Kate has been living in Scotland, close to Edinburgh, in East Lothian. She worked for Edinburgh city council and even after her retirement, she continued as a local non- elected councillor, standing in for a neighbour. In recent years, Kate and a friend of hers have developed a remarkable business, organising classes in upholstery in their part of Scotland, widely advertised on social media and most successful.

Kate and Peter have two children, Dan, who has two boys, Felix and Douglas, and Jo, who is married to Steve and has a delightful daughter called Martha, three in August this year, 2016, who has a marvellous capacity of learning very fast how to do things. She' s a very smart wee lassie, so bright and eager to learn.

I also have two step sisters. Emma, the oldest, is married to Adnan, a surgeon, and they have two children, Rafii and Amelia. They are in the process of moving to Dubai, where Adnan is working. My younger step sister, Sarah, is passionate about cat welfare. The house just outside Bury St Edmunds in Suffolk, which had been the family home for Emma and Sarah, is in the process of being sold. It was once home to Pat, formerly Pat Roberts, my late step mother, who died four years ago. My father, and her husband, Ronald, died 25 years ago. He had mellowed a lot in his old age and I got on quite well with him, although my visits to England became very intermittent and indeed, non- existent for the past 30 years. My step brother James lives in Cambridge with his German wife, Tania; they co- founded his own financial planning business. Tania also founded and is the chair of the Cambridge European Women' s Society.

Kenneth Kaunda

He was the first president of Zambia, from 1964 until 1991. He was born in 1924 and is now aged 91. He came on official visits to Dublin on a couple of occasions in the 1960s, when the official Irish government policy was to encourage black governments in Africa. He had been in prison during the 1950s for his part in Zambia' s quest for independence. When he came to Dublin, where he got to know Bernadette in the foreign ministry, he was always meticulously dressed and Bernadette remembers that when he was leaving Iveagh House, he was always careful to wave his snow white breast handkerchief in fond farewell. He eventually retired from politics in his own country after he was accused of being involved in a failed coup attempt in 1997. During the 1960s, Irish government policy favoured the emerging nations in Africa, as they found independence after colonialism. In one famous photograph taken at Iveagh House, amid a whole sea of black faces, there are just two white ones, those of Bernadette and the then Minister for External Affairs, Frank Aiken.

Patrick Kavanagh

Now considered a world class poet, much read by the present generation at school in Ireland, he came from a poor farming background in Co Monaghan, where he was born in 1904. In the mid-1930s, he stayed in London for a couple of years, but failed to find major success there. So by 1939, he had decided to settle in Dublin. He went on to live the rest of his life in Dublin 4, living for long in a flat in Pembroke Road.

On one occasion, he was in bed with a local lady of the night, at this flat, when the Archbishop of Dublin, Dr John Charles McQuaid, called in his official car to give him some presents. The Archbishop was always a supporter of his, but on this occasion, not even the bottle of whiskey that was being left in to him, could tempt him to answer the door. Paddy Kavanagh always had a rough and ready reputation and one of his habits was spitting into doorways all along Baggot Street. During his lifetime, Patrick Kavanagh had a dreadful reputation for being rough and crude; the worst story I heard about him concerned the time that he was in McDaid' s pub, off Grafton Street, in Dublin. He was bet a shilling that he wouldn' t shit on the floor. Ever anxious to scrape up any money he could, he promptly let his trousers down and earned his shilling.

The only time that I ever met him, he was his usual unrefined self. I was at a conference in Queen' s University, Belfast, with my friend Professor Alan Warner, who had taught me English at Magee College in Derry. Professor Warner had written several books about Kavanagh, so knew him very well. He said to him on this occasion he wanted to introduce a former student with a strong interest in Irish literature. Kavanagh simply cleared his throat, turned his back on both of us and stalked off. Eventually, Patrick Kavanagh married Katherine Barry Moloney, a piece of Kevin Barry, the young UCD student killed in Dublin after the 1916 Rising. They were married in April, 1967 and seven months later, Kavanagh was dead. Only when he was safely dead and could no longer behave so badly towards his fellow citizens, was he recognised as a great poet.

John B. Keane

Born in 1928, he created some memorable plays, such as Sive, The Field, Big Maggie and the Chastitute, 18 memorable plays in all. He had a unique ear for dialogue and for bringing to life many of the tensions in rural life. A superb writer, he also kept his day job for his whole career, running his pub in the centre of Listowel, Co Kerry, which he ran with his wife Mary O' Connor, whom he had married in 1955. One evening in 1990, when I was in the middle of one of my tours of Ireland for the Michelin Green Guide to Ireland, when we were in Listowel, we dropped into his pub. We introduced ourselves to John B and we went on to spend the whole evening chatting with him He was a quiet, almost shy man, not remotely given to theatrical histrionics and we spent a most hospitable time with him chatting away about this, that and the other, and meeting his wife Mary. John B. Keane died in 2002, aged 73. His nephew is the renowned BBC broadcaster, Fergal Keane.

Molly Keane

Molly was a delightful woman, chronicler of life in the big house. Small and birdlike in stature, she gave the impression of being a very modest woman, perhaps a little scatty, but in reality, she was as sharp as a razor, cutting to the heart of Ascendancy life. Born in Newbridge, Co Kildare, in 1904, she began writing in earnest in 1928, when she was 24. Between then and 1956, she wrote 11 novels under the name of M. J. Farrell. Her first writing career had survived the death of her husband in 1946. But after 1956, she went into a fallow period, when she wrote nothing, only emerging from her self-imposed literary exile in 1981, when she published her new novel, Good Behaviour, under her own name. For the rest of her life, until she died in 1996, she was a literary star. After her husband died, she moved to Ardmore in west Waterford, a delighful seaside village, and lived there for the rest of her life, but kept herself well in tune with what was going on in Dublin and elsewhere in the world. She was buried in the shadow of the Church of Ireland in Ardmore. I well remember, about 10 years before she died, going to Belfast to do an interview with Sean Rafferty of the BBC about one of my tourist books. I sat in the studio, waiting for my turn; Sean was doing a phone interview with Molly, who was at her home in Ardmore, and she sounded so with it about all the errant ways of the old Ascendancy, yet totally up to date with everything that was going on in the world.

Terry Keane

Once, the late lamented Terry was one of the best- known journalists on the Sunday Independent, with her Keane Edge column, which was required reading among the "in" set, yet it wasn' t until 1999 that she revealed, on the Late Late Show, about her affair with Charles Haughey that had lasted alsmost 30 years. Terry, who was born in Guildford in southern England to Irish parents in 1939, pursued her studies at Trinity College, Dublin, but dropped out and married a young barrister called Ronan Keane, who later became Chief Justice. He was seven years older and the marriage lasted until the 1990s, when the couple separated. As a socialite among the high society of Dublin, she had a gilded existence and her column was so popular because everyone considered she had the inside track on Dublin' s social affairs. When I was doing the Paper Tiger series for RTÉ Radio 1 in 1992, one thing she confessed to me was that she thought the most boring star she had ever interviewed was Jerry Hall, the Texan model, for long the partner of Mick Jagger and who in 2016, married the veteran media mogul, Rupert Murdoch.

Michael Keating

Once a leading political figure, I got to know him well when both of us were working at the Creation publishing group in Dublin and I must say I found him always the most charming and helpful of people. Born in Dublin in 1946, he worked as a secondary school teacher before going into journalism. Then politics beckoned. His first run for the old Dublin Corporation, on behalf of Fine Gael, came in 1973 and it was unsuccessful, but when he tried again the following year, he was successful. In 1977, he was elected a TD and four years later, became a junior minister responsible for youth and sport. In 1983/ 84, he was Lord Mayor of Dublin and I quite often met him during official functions, when he was his usual affable self. Then in 1986, he left Fine Gael to join the newly founded Progressive Democrats, where he became deputy leader. But by 1989, he had become disillusioned with politics and left to pursue his business interests.

Much later, he paid the Criminal Assets Bureau £250, 000; in 2002, he sold his house in Castleknock to pay his tax bill. He was also named in a British court case but never charged, over his alleged involvement, which he has always strenuously denied, in a £20 million sterling VAT fraud over the export of non- existent computer parts from the UK. Nowadays, few people remember how Michael Keating was once such a fast rising political star; if he' d stayed with politics he might have had even greater success.

Lorna Kelly

This remarkable Sandymount resident and myself became great friends when I was researching my Sandymount book, published in 2016. Lorna, who is now 91, has been involved with the Sandymount Residents Association since the 1960s and then with its subsequent reincarnation as the Sandymount & Merrion Residents Association, a link that goes back over 50 years. During all that time, whenever a planning objection had to be raised, Lorna was the woman to do it, and still is, a truly remarkable record. I was amazed at her amazing memory of people and events in Sandymount going back all those decades, and even more importantly for the book, by her incredible collection of photographs.

Luke Kelly

I never met Luke, one of the finest folk singers Ireland has ever produced, but Bernadette met him once, at a long defunct art gallery in Dawson Street. They sat chatting for ages, seated on the stairs, and Luke, in recognition of a kindred spirit, planted a big kiss on her cheek. He was truly inspirational and his rendition of Patrick Kavanagh' s poem about Raglan Road is perhaps the best- known and most enduring example of his work. Born in Sherriff Street in Dublin, he had a tough childhood; when he was a young man, he spent much time in the north- east of England, where the folk singing and song writing of Ewan MacColl made a big impact on him. MacColl was a left- wing firebrand, as was Luke. One of MacColl' s children, Kirsty, recorded Fairy Tales of New York with the Pogues in 1987; she was killed by a speedboat while on holiday in Mexico in 2000. Luke became one of the founding members of the Dubliners. In 1967, he had married Deirdre O' Connell, founder of the Focus Theatre, but the marriage only lasted seven years. His next and last partner was a German woman, Madeleine Seiler, whom I got to know quite well. Tragically, Luke died at just 44 from a brain haemorrhage in 1984. Long gone, but who could forget such a colourful personality and such a brilliant entertainer.

John F. Kennedy

This one was Bernadette' s call; she met him during Kennedy' s official visit to Ireland in 1963. One of the nights of his visit was taken up with a State dinner in Iveagh House, home of the Department of Foreign Affairs. She was introduced to him and he took her up the big staircase at Iveagh House by the little finger. He immediately proposed taking her back to Washington- all of us who know her joke about what his real intention was!- but Bernadette' s then boss, Gerry Woods, then chef de protocol, got wind of what was going on and in a very drunken state, marched straight up to Kennedy and said to him: "Begod, Mr President, you are not taking Bernadette back to Washington, she' s mine". A short while later, Bernadette was at a diplomatic event, dressed in a white cocktail gown with long sleeves. A diplomat at the event managed to spill his glass of red wine all down the sleeve of her gown, a tragic portent of what was to happen to Kennedy on November 22, 1963, just less than five months after his Irish visit, when he was gunned down in Dallas.

No- one who was alive at the time can ever forget the moment at which they heard the dreadful news. Bernadette was at home that evening and even though the television was in black and white, Charles Mitchel, the newsreader, came on with an ashen face to announce the news flash. That was seven years before I met Bernadette for the first time, in 1970; on that dreadful night in 1963, I was still a student at Magee College in Derry, hating virtually every minute of my studies. It was a Friday night and when we had concluded the usual Friday night debate, we came out into the main hall and immediately, the rumours about Kennedy' s assassination had started.

Nearly 20 years later, at Easter, 1980, on our only trip to the US, we paid a dutiful visit to the Kennedy homestead in Brookline, Boston, and to the vast Kennedy library. The old Kennedy home was fascinating and so too was the lunch we had immediately afterwards, at a fast food restaurant in Brookline, where the black waitress wore the most eye-popping of costumes; she was bursting out all over and I can remember her, but I haven' t the faintest idea what we had for lunch!

Tom Kennedy

Bernadette knew Tom before I did; in those days, in the 1960s, he was into film making in a big way and often made presentations to the Department Bernadette worked with the aim of getting funding. He married his Dutch wife, Appie Jonker, at the same time we got married, in 1972, so we couldn' t go to their wedding, as we were then ensconced in the Isle of Man. But when a few years later, I suggested to Tom that we do a book all about Bewleys, he jumped at the idea. At the time, he and his family were living in Leixlip and in those far- off days, we thought nothing of jumping on a bus down to Leixlip to go and discuss the book with him.

The book was duly published in December, 1980, and it was launched in Hodges Figgis, the book store, happily still there on Dawson Street, Dublin. Frankie Byrne, the radio agony aunt, made a speech, despite trembling with nerves, while the other star guest was the veteran Dublin actor, Noel Purcell. The windows of Hodges Figgis were well decorated with the book. The coffee cups in the bookshop were a little dusty to say the least, but Appie, in true hippie style, shrugged her shoulders and said "what' s a little dust? ".

Appie worked in the School of Education at Trinity College for many years; she' s now retired. I've always admired her forthright sense of humour. On another occasion, Tom had published a book of poems by a well- known Midlands poet, Leo Daly. The launch was in Mullingar golf club. When we arrived at Mullingar station, there wasn' t a taxi to be had, so one of the local taxi men, who also ran an undertaker' s business, took us there in a hearse. Talk about arriving dead on time! During her speech, Appie made fun of the fact that sometimes, today' s newspaper is tomorrow' s toilet paper.

I also worked with Tom for many years at Enterprise Ireland, when he was the very enlightened editor of Technology Ireland magazine. I became a regular contributor. After that, Tom went on to found Science Spin, but sadly, neither magazine managed to survive in the long term.

Kenny' s bookshop, Galway

Des and Maureen Kenny founded their bookshop in 1940 in what was their family home in High Street, Galway, where I got to know them in later years. Des had worked for Galway Textile Printers and this gave him a lot of business skills that he applied to his literary interests. In 1968, the Kennys opened an art gallery in their home, which by then was in Salthill, and it was considered the first of its kind in the West of Ireland. Subsequently, when more room became available in their High Street shop, the art gallery was moved there. The Kennys had six children and three of them went on to work in the family business. In the late 1990s, the Kenny family's second hand bookshop became the second in the world to have a website and since then, their digital fortunes have expanded exponentially.

Mary Kenny

In recent years, Mary and I have become great friends. She began her press career by working with the Evening Standard in London, from 1966. Then Mary, who was born in 1944, and brought up in Sandymount, became the woman's editor of the Irish Press in the early 1970s. She was more than bit of a hell raiser in those days and it was reputed that on occasions, she'd whip off her bra in the office. She was also very involved in the whole women's liberation movement of those times, including the famous train journey to Belfast to buy condoms. What was abnormal for women to demand in those days is these days, fortunately, accepted by all and sundry, without anyone demurring. How times change! She also gave rise to a famous phrase in 1973, when someone disturbed her in the arms of a former Ugandan cabinet minister. A poet of the time, James Fenton, coined the phrase "Ugandan discussions" to paraphrase illicit sexual intercourse. The phrase gained great longevity and in 2013, the BBC included it in a list of the 10 most used euphemisms in Britain.

In 1974, Mary married an outstanding foreign correspondent called Richard West; in his later years, his health deteriorated markedly and Mary devoted much of her time and energy to looking after him. He died in 2015. Mary has done a complete about turn in recent years and will now praise conventional morality and the positive powers of the Church. She's still busy broadcasting and writing and contributes frequently to the Irish Independent. Mary Kenny has had a media career of astonishing length and variety and all the while, she has managed to preserve her image as one of the most distinctive characters in the Irish media business.

Ben Kiely

Ben Kiely, a decent man and a generous friend for many years, came from Omagh, Co Tyrone, where he was born in 1919. As a young man, he began trying to become a Jesuit priest, without any success, and then tried his luck in journalism, where he was far more successful. In 1945, he began as a leader writer with the Irish Independent, but found it was a job where he had nothing much to do all day. In 1950, he crossed the River Liffey to join the Irish Press, as literary editor. In those days, long boozy lunches were essential in the newspaper business and Ben better than most, enjoyed his time in such long disappeared restaurants as the Red Bank in D' Olier Street.

He was forever a wonderful source of stories, some of them risqué. One he told me on more than one occasion, was about the "Pope" O' Mahony, a familiar figure in post- second world war Dublin. When he was in Dublin, he often stayed in a religious institution off Capel Street; there was a whole ritual attached to the room he occupied being made available to him and on one famous occasion, he sent a telegram to the nun in charge, telling her that he was arriving that night and advising her: "Leave the bedroom door open- Pope". From 1964 to 1968, Ben lived and worked in the US, but he then returned to Dublin. Besides his newspaper work, he was noted for the books he produced and also as a long- time contributor to Sunday Miscellany, where the sound of his distinctive rolling Northern tones still resonates today. Ben was married twice, first in 1944, then not long before he died, he married again to his long time partner, Frances. Ben was a wonderful person to know and on many occasions, he helped out by giving me interviews, even when he wasn' t feeling particularly well. He died in February, 2007. His funeral, in the church at Donnybrook, was packed and I always remember coming out of the church, together with Bernadette, into an absolute downpour that left us drenched to the skin.

Lord Killanin

He was a remarkable man, most closely associated with the Olympic Games, where he was long president of the international Olympics committee. He began as a journalist, in the mid- 1930s, working for the Daily Express and the Daily Sketch before gravitating to the Daily Mail. He was also consul- general in Ireland for Monaco, from 1961 to 1984, which is how and when Bernadette knew him so well. He and his wife lived for years lived in Lansdowne Road in Ballsbridge, Dublin, having moved there from Spiddal in Co Galway, but towards the end of his life, the family home was in Lower Mount Pleasant Avenue in Ranelagh. One of his most celebrated books is the Shell Guide to Ireland, which I've long thought was one of the best travel books ever produced about Ireland. He also had quite a reputation as a film producer.

He and his wife had four children, one of whom is "Mouse" Morris, the horse trainer, who is based at Fethard in Co Tipperary. "Mouse" and his wife had two sons, but one of them, Christopher, died due to carbon monoxide poisoning in Argentina in 2015. The twin brother of "Mouse" is Johnny, a well- known photographer, whom I've also had dealings with; he is married to Thelma Mansfield, once a star of daytime television in Ireland.

The last time that I met Lord Killanin was in Dublin city centre, not long before he died in 1999, aged 85. He had become a shadow of what he was at his peak, physically and mentally battered by illness. But sadly, that's the state into which nearly all of us will decline before we too pass on.

Adele King

The first time I set eyes on Adele King, better known as Twink, was in the 1980s. One evening, we were coming out of a presentation in the RTÉ television centre when all of a sudden, we heard a commotion, caused by a group of women. It was unclear what all the hubbub was about, but at the centre of it was Twink, who was busy turning the night air blue with a string of foul- mouthed invectives. For anyone not of a nervous disposition, it was hilariously filthy. Every word that Twink could extract from the pool of utterly foul language drifted on the wind for all to hear. It must have been a hint of what was to come; in 2004, her marriage to David Agnew, an oboist, ended; he went on to have a baby with a clarinetist called Ruth Hickey. Twink left a message on his answering machine, urging him to "zip up his mickey", which has been a widely quoted expression ever since. A later row with someone else came in 2010, when Twink called her friend of 30 years, the Irish singer Linda Martin, a cunt. Afterwards, they said they had no plans to speak to each other again.

Twink, who was born in 1951, has had a lifetime in the entertainment business, theatre, TV and radio and through thick and thin, she has kept going. Her dog was dognapped in 2014, creating a media sensation; it was eventually recovered. Then in 2016, she suffered a serious burglary at her home in Knocklyon. Somehow or other, Twink always seems to be in the wars, but she always survives. These days, she' s big into baking, a complete change of direction for her.

In her earlier days, in the late 1960s, into the 1970s, she was part of an all- girl ensemble called Maxi, Dick and Twink. In recent years, I got to know Maxi quite well, who in the later part of her career, was a presenter on RTÉ Radio 1.

Billy King

Billy was one of the old- time characters in the advertising and publishing business who became a legend in his lifetime for his constant good humours and old- fashioned good manners. He worked for many years for Independent Newspapers on the advertising side and when I was researching my book on the history of advertising in Ireland, published in 1986, Billy was an absolute fund of information on the old days and the old ways. He had been around long enough to remember a former headquarters of the group, which stood at the corner of D' Olier Street and Burgh Quay, where O' Connell Bridge House was built in the 1960s. After retiring from the Indo, Billy went on to work in the magazine sector, always the consummate gentleman. His wife Von, whom I didn' t know, died in 1987 and Billy died in 2001, but still remembered with great affection by people in the business.

Cecil King

Cecil Harmsworth King, to give him his full name, was an extraordinary newspaper character, related through his mother to the Ist Viscount Northcliffe and the Ist Viscount Rothermere, who had founded the Daily Mail in 1896. Cecil King was immensely influential in British public life and as chairman of Mirror Newspapers, he worked closely with an equally outstanding editor, Hugh Cudlipp. It' s hard to imagine now, but in the 1950s, the Daily Mirror was the biggest selling newspaper in the world, selling well over five million copies a day. But high office got the better of him. In 1968, he was responsible for an editorial that called for the overthrow of then British prime minister Harold Wilson and his replacement by Lord Mountbatten. In quick order, he was sacked by the board of IPC, when then owned the Mirror.

He came to live in Dublin with his second wife, Dame Ruth Railton, founder of the National Youth Orchestra of Great Britain. Cecil King had always regarded Dublin as his home and had been brought up in the city as a child. Standing 6' 4" tall, he was an imposing figure and could often be seen pottering around Donnybrook. One of his good deeds was helping clean up the old cemetery next to the Garda station in Donnybrook. He and his wife lived at Greenfield Road, directly RTÉ, and Bernadette got to know Dame Ruth quite well, as they both went to the same hairdressers, the old Eileen's salon in Donnybrook. Cecil died in 1987, aged 86, while his wife died in 2001, aged 85.

Richard Kingston

Richard and I became great friends, after we had moved to Wellington Lane; he and his family were in Heytesbury Lane. Very often, we'd see him driving past in one of the old cars he had lovingly restored, very often an MG sports car. On one occasion, when he was driving a restored car along Wellington Road, Breda, who was the wife of the late P. J. Mara, shot out of her driveway right into the side of Richard's car, but it was all settled diplomatically. The house that Mara and his wife lived in had belonged to the Kingstons, who had opened an art gallery there; after the sale, the Kingstons moved into the mews at the back of the house. Right opposite his mews house in Heytesbury Lane was his garage, where he could work for endless hours on his beloved cars.

He had been brought up in the hungry 1930s on the family farm in Co Wicklow; he started studying engineering at Trinity College, but the money ran out. After the second world war, Richard worked as a designer in London, before returning home. His last full-time job was as the designer with the old Swastika Laundry in Shelbourne Road. He redesigned all their shops, the staff uniforms and the posters that went on the sides of their vans. In those far- off days, the laundry's vans could travel round Dublin, their sides emblazoned with swastikas, without the slightest trace of embarassment. Richard took early retirement from the laundry and promptly spent his £500 'golden handshake' on a Jaguar.

But besides his old cars, Richard developed a formidable and well- deserved reputation as a landscape painter. He died in 2003 and was survived by his wife, Jennifer, herself an artist, who remains a good friend.

Cor Klassen

He was one of the Dutchmen who came to work in the advertising industry in Dublin in the 1950s and 1960s. None of his fellow Dutch creatives were as ebullient in his approach to life as Cor. When he arrived in Dublin in 1956, his first job was with the old O' Kennedy Brindley ad agency. Digs were organised for him with an upright Catholic lady in the Ballsbridge area. Cor' s early grasp of English was shaky to say the least, but he soon picked it up from his fellow workers. After his first day at work in Dublin, he returned to his digs for dinner; the landlady asked him how he had got on and he replied: "fucking marvellous" at which the landlady went into a blue funk. Years later, I remember another occasion when Bernadette and myself had been to a reception in the cellars of Mitchells the wine merchants, then in Kildare Street. Cor was also there and as we left the function, Cor followed us out and at the top of his voice and referring to Bernadette, shouted out so that all the world could hear "You lucky fucker". He was a great creative spirit, but the renegade lurked deep inside him. He eventually went freelance, designing around 170 book covers as well as 35 LP sleeves between 1958 and 1988. He also taught design. Cor died in 1989, aged 63.

Someone else I got to know well from the Dutch school was Jan de Fouw, who came to Dublin from the Netherlands in 1951. He was the complete opposite of Cor, quietly spoken, almost reserved, and absolutely dedicated to his work. He designed Ireland of the Welcomes for many years and lived in a wonderful house at Glencullen, up in the Dublin mountains. Jan died in 2015, at the age of 85. His son, Remco, born in 1962, became a well- known sculptor; he and his family live in the Blackstairs mountains in Co Carlow.

Gordon Lambert

Gordon, who died in 2005, aged 85, spent a long career at Jacobs Biscuits, which is how I got to know him. Born in south Dublin in 1919, he qualified as a chartered accountant, then joined the biscuit firm, then in Bishop Street, in 1944, as assistant accountant. He was the man in charge of marketing at Jacobs right through the 1960s and it was on his watch that the famous advertising slogan "how do they get the figs into Jacobs fig rolls" came into common currency. It remains in use even today, half a century later. Also, in the early 1960s, he and Frankie Byrne, that renowned pr lady, started the Jacobs radio and television awards in 1962. For years, it was one of the most enjoyable media events of the year and on several occasions, Bernadette and I went along and had a great time, getting gloriously squiffy in company with our many friends in the media.

As for Gordon, he was made managing director at Jacobs in 1971 and during his time running the company, I quite often interviewed him both for the bakery magazine I then edited in Dublin as well as for bakery publications in London. He was a very pleasant person to deal with, always helpful, and never shied away from awkward questions. In the last few years of his life, he wanted me to write his auto biography, but at that stage, he was quite ill and when I saw the huge volume of letters and other material that had yet to be archived, I politely declined.

On a holiday trip to Paris in 1952, he had bought a contemporary painting and this spurred his interest in modern painting; he became an avid collector. He ended up collecting hundreds of works of art by renowned 20th century artists and his collection was invaluable to the Irish Museum of Modern Art at Kilmainham in Dublin. His vast self- acquired knowledge of art led him to close involvements with such organisations as the Museum of Modern Art in New York, the National Gallery of Ireland in Dublin and the Northern Ireland Arts Council. He also found himself nominated to the Seanad in 1977 by Jack Lynch, who was then coming to the end of his political career. As for Gordon himself, he was always the most generous and kind- hearted person, much hampered by the onset of Parkinson' s disease in his 80s, although it never affected his most genial personality. I remember vividly the day I was parking in the main car park in Temple Bar, when I met Gordon, who seemed crestfallen that day and told me why; he had just been diagnosed with Parkinson' s and it could only get worse.

Hugh Lambert

I got to know Hugh Lambert well when he was working in editorial production at The Irish Times, towards the end of his career. I got to know him well and found that we had many interests in common, including an iconoclastic sense of humour. When it came to computers in newspaper production, no- one had a greater knowledge and there was no problem great or small that he couldn' t solve with his usual good humour.

Hugh' s father had been a printer with both the Irish Press and The Irish Times, so it was almost inevitable that his son, born in 1944, should also go into the newspaper business, but on the editorial side. He worked for years at the Irish Press group, where his duties included being film critic on the Sunday Press. In due course, he was promoted to editor of the Irish Press, the morning newspaper, in 1987. It was a very difficult time, as the paper was changed from broadsheet to tabloid, but it didn't have the resources to market the change effectively. When the Irish Press group closed down in 1995, Hugh found himself out of a job.

I was very familiar with the Irish Press group and interviewed many of its protagonists for my two books on Irish newspaper history. For the first book, published in 1983, I went to Burgh Quay one evening to interview Tim Pat Coogan, the then editor of the Irish Press; for some reason I never fathomed, he didn' t want me to take notes, so I had to memorise the whole interview and write it up when I got home. Yet when I' d done that, Tim Pat hadn' t actually said anything that was particularly contentious, so I never knew what all the mystery was about.

But after the Irish Group closed down, Hugh joined a brief attempt at producing a new evening newspaper for Dublin, the Evening News. It was a full colour tabloid that was plagued with technical gremlins and lack of investment and it survived for a mere four months, from May to September, 1996. By the time it closed, it was selling less than 20, 000 copies a night. These days of course, the evening newspaper market in Ireland has almost disappeared. Titles like the Herald in Dublin and the Belfast Telegraph are now all day newspapers and the only true Irish evening newspaper left is the Evening Echo in Cork, which manages on a pretty small circulation.

After the rapid demise of the Evening News, Hugh made a more successful transition to The Irish Times. There, apart from his production work, he also wrote a series about walking trips, which were pleasant to read and follow in person. I had a great rapport with Hugh Lambert and a great admiration for his newspaper skills and for his wonderful urbane, well informed personality. He often said to me that he was worried about how his pension contributions would be funded and whether he' d get a pension when he retired. It was all taken out of his hands. In the autumn of 2005, he and his wife had an extensive trip to the US, which was hugely interesting. Before he went, he had seemed in normal health, but soon after he got back home, he became seriously ill and within a short space of time, ended up in the hospice in Blackrock. He died on St Stephen' s Day, 2005, a devastating shock to his many friends and colleagues. I well remember going to the church in Glasthule, south Co Dublin, for his removal service; the church was absolutely packed. The last thing I' d worked on with Hugh at The Irish Times was a big supplement for UCD in the summer of 2005; he had ben his usual immaculately organised and courteous self. His sudden departure from this life created a big void and even today, I still often remember one of my greatest friends in the newspaper business. We were on so many parallel wavelengths, it was uncanny.

Lausanne

We were in Lausanne in Switzerland a couple of times in the 1980s; the first time, in 1984, we went to the small village of Celigny, between Lausanne and Geneva, to see the grave of Richard Burton, the great Welsh actor, who had died there that year. There was a work motif behind the trip to Lausanne; I'd started working with the Berlitz travel guide publishers, who were much more easy going than Michelin, but still turned out some fine looking and detailed publications.

On the 1984 trip we stayed in the Beau Rivage Hotel in Lausanne. We' d read a big write- up about the place done by a well- known travel writer for the Daily Telegraph, Nigel Buxton. He gave it such a superlative boost that we decided to stay there, despite the expense. The reality turned out to be far different to the pr plug; we hated the place and thought that the one dinner we had there was dreadful. When we got back to Ireland I complained vigorously to the manager of the hotel and I was somewhat surprised to get a letter back from him giving us a full refund. Ever since then, I've been very wary of pr holiday trips written up in the media disguised as independent, fact seeking holidays, when in fact, they are just the words of freeloaders being kind to those who are indulging them with freebies.

The next time we stayed in Lausanne, it was at the much more modest, but infinitely more delightful Chateau d' Ouchy, down by the lakeside. It was a very charming and friendly place and we soon found out why; it had an Irishwoman as manager and she ran the whole place in such a way that one could really enjoy a stay there, feel comfortable and be well fed and watered.

As a city, we very much liked Lausanne, and as I write this, I'm looking at a poster from a splendid Impressionist exhibition we visited at the Fondation de l' Hermitage In Lausanne. Another place we visited near Lausanne, was the little village of Céligny, between Lausanne and Geneva, where Richard Burton, the actor had lived. He died from a heart attack in 1984 and we went to see his new grave that year; I remember vividly writing a piece about it and providing the photograph, for Image magazine, then as now, a first class magazine. But it was in Céligny that we found the worst pub meal we have ever tasted. We' ve never had a pub meal in Ireland that was remotely as bad; this particular lunch consisted of fried chicken with chips. I think builders' rubble would have been tastier!

The other Swiss city we took a great liking to was Lucerne, with its wooden bridge rebuilt since it went on fire. The modest hotel we stayed in, the Drei Konige or Three Kings, was unpretentious but very comfortable. We found

Lucerne a most delightful city to wander around. On the other hand, we never got to like Geneva- all United Nations and big money stuff- or Zurich-where all the drug dealing would put off anyone. However, in Zurich, the one notable thing we did was go and see where James Joyce was buried. There' s a fine statue by the grave and we were very amused to see in the out stretched hand of the statue, a very old Irish florin coin, which had obviously lain there for years. It certainly wouldn' t have lasted the pace in Dublin!

One thing I often thought about Switzerland was how my father was doing a line with a Swiss woman before the second world war and was in Switzerland with her on various occasions. With a little bit of ingenuity, he could easily have spent the war years there, rather than enlist. Why he didn' t, I' ll never know.

Hector Legge

Hector was one of the old school of newspaper editors, one of remarkable longevity in the business; he became editor of the Sunday Independent in 1940 and retired in 1970, an extraordinary 30 years and two months in the editorial chair. That kind of tenure would never happen today. During the second world war 'Emergency' he gave work to that great short story writer, Frank O' Connor, who at the time was in dire need of financial sustenance. O' Connor had a penchant for affairs with married women, something that was very much frowned upon at the time, and for that and other reasons, he found that he couldn' t get work with Radio Éireann and many other media outlets.

However, Hector came to his rescue, giving him a weekly column in 1943, which O' Connor kept going with great élan for the following two years, under the made- up byline of "Ben Mayo". Hector himself was a very astute, well- connected editor, who brought his newspaper to ever higher heights, even after the launch of the rival Sunday Press in 1949. He got his biggest scoop that year, 1949, when he revealed that the External Relations Act was going to be repealed and that the 26 counties of what had been "Eire" would be declared a republic. It was a momentous occasion in 20th century Irish history and Hector's paper revealed it first to the Irish public. When I met him at his house in Ranelagh for my 1983 book on Irish newspaper history, he gave me chapter and verse on how he had got his scoop and the uproar it had created. Hector died in 1994 at the grand old age of 93; in subsequent years, I became friendly with one of his sons, Simon, who runs an art gallery in Ranelagh and is a painter himself.

Hugh Leonard

I got on rather well with Hugh Leonard, although a former colleague in The Irish Times, who used to go on boating holidays with him in France, before they had a big bust- up, used to call him a "little fascist". I always found him willing to be as helpful as he could and on a couple of occasions when I went out to his home at Pilot View, Dalkey, I found myself in the delightful situation of having his various cats trying to clamber all over me while I took my notes or made recordings. His real name was John Joseph Byrne, which has rather less of a ring to it than Hugh Leonard. But in a 50 year career, he had an extraordinary output, including neaely 30 full- length plays, six film screenplays, three novels and two anthologies. He also did many TV adaptations for TV channels in both Ireland and Britain. One of his earliest TV successes was in 1966, with the script for the Insurrection series on Telefís Éireann, to commemorate the 50th anniversary of the 1916 Easter Rising. He also wrote a weekly column for the Sunday Independent for many years and it was always required reading, as he had a go at any sacred cow he could unearth. I well remember when the Fours Seasons, now the

Intercontinental Hotel, opened in Ballsbridge, Dublin, over a decade ago, Hugh Leonard said it print that it looked like an explosion in a Lego factory and that it had all the architectural charm of a gasometer. He kept up his literary vituperations, week in, week out, and few in public life were spared. Yet to me, he was also the most courteous and helpful interviewee. I always remember one of his favourite phrases, l' ésprit de l' escalier, literally the spirit of the staircase, to mean that one thinks of something superbly apposite to say when it's too late.

He was married for 50 years to a Belgian lady called Paule; after she died in 2000, he promptly married an American woman called Katherine Hayes, but that was more short- lived, as Hugh Leonard died in 2009.

Nicholas Leonard

Nicholas Leonard was the editor I had to thank for giving me my first start in the media, back in 1966. At that stage, I was kicking around in Dublin doing all sorts of odd jobs to survive, including selling charity raffle tickets door to door, when I had a bright idea one day when walking through Trinity College' s quadrangle. Business & Finance hadn' t long started, so out of the blue, from a public call box in Trinity, I rang up Nicholas, had a chat with him, told him what I wanted to do. Despite the fact I had no experience and he didn' t know me from Adam, he told me to come in the following Monday morning and they' d find a job for me. It was all quite extraordinary, so I did what he suggested; when I went in, the job they offered was not in editorial, but on the commercial side, liaising with advertisers, such as estate agents. It took me about five years to make the transition from commercial to journalism, but the experience has always stood me in good stead, as it gave me a good grounding of the economics of publishing.

But I did get my first start in feature writing at Creation and I always remember asking the boss, Hugh McLaughlin, if there was any chance of upping the writing fee. A great man for the charm, he turned me down and made it seem like a good offer! But the two or three years I spent at Business & Finance were very educative and my immediate boss, the advertisement manager, was quite a character. He was George Harman, a real Cockney, who had a great way of chatting up advertisers. But one story I always remember about him is the time he went to a pr 'do' in the Gresham Hotel, complete with his wife and dog. By the end of the event, all three were stretched out comatose on the floor, having emptied every Champagne bottle they could lay their hands on. I always remember, too, another occasion, when George came back from lunch one day, very drunk. He had a bone to pick with Nicholas Leonard over some trivial issue; he staggered into the next door office, threw a punch at Nicholas, and promptly went sprawling on the floor!

As for Nicholas, he spent five years with Business & Finance after starting it up; he had left The Irish Times, where he had been a pioneering business editor. In those far off days, newspapers rarely bothered with detailed business coverage. From Business & Finance, in 1969, he became a merchant banker, then teamed up with Tony O' Reilly and Vincent Ferguson in a new wave of 'shell' companies, before going on to join the board of firms like Independent Newspapers and Atlantic Resources. Nicholas, whose father Ralph had been publicity director of Aer Lingus, was always a whirl of new ideas. Some didn' t work, like the novel he wrote, or the technology magazine he launched in the UK, but for many years afterwards, he was the London editor of the Irish Independent. He was indeed a truly inspirational journalist, pioneering business coverage that is taken for granted these days.

June Levine

She was one of Ireland' s pioneering feminists, born in 1931. She came from a Dublin Jewish family and by the time she was in her late teens, she was already writing for The Irish Times. Many stories were told of her having a passionate physical relationship with one of her colleagues there, sometimes in the printing area, so that the noise of the printing press drowned out any noises that the two of them were making. But by the time she was 18, she had got married to a Jewish medical student from Canada; they moved to Ontario and had three children, but the marriage didn' t last. Much later on, in 1999, she married her partner of the previous 30 years, a well-known psychiatrist, Professor Ivor Browne.

June was always sexually advanced and precocious and she was one of the founding members of the Irish Womens' Liberation Movement, along with other feminists such as Nell McCafferty, Mary Kenny and Mary Maher. June was one of the women who created a sensation in 1971 by going to Belfast by train to buy armloads of contraceptives, them bringing them back to Dublin. It was a major media news story of the time.

When she had returned to Dublin from Canada, she continued her work in journalism. June wrote two best selling books, one her personal history of feminism, the other about prostitution. By the late 1960s, I had left the Creation Group, publishers of Business & Finance and had gone to a rather chaotic magazine publishers in Haddington Road, Ballsbridge, where both she and I ended up working. One of their titles was Irishwomens' Journal, an excellent and rather avant garde magazine that had been started by Sean O' Sullivan, an Irish-American journalist. One of its earlier contributors, with some of her poetry, was Bernadette. By the time I arrived on the scene in Haddington Road in the late 60s, June Levine was the editor of this magazine and I'll never forget the day we were having a quick chat about this, that and the other, when she suddenly said to me, as the subject for discussion moved to sex, "I find that sex between two women is far better than sex between a man and a woman". It was a very heretical notion for the time, but not of course these days.

Roy Lillie

One of the most engaging, helpful and with-it newspaper editors I have ever had dealings with. Roy began his career in 1957 with the Larne Times, which was then owned by the Belfast Telegraph. From there, he went to London in 1965, for three years, where he was Westminster lobby correspondent for Thomson regional newspapers. He then returned to work on the Belfast Telegraph as political correspondent, moving up to deputy editor in 1970. In 1974, he was promoted editor, a job he held for 19 years, through some of the worst times of the troubles, including the bombing of the Belfast Telegraph itself in 1976. He ended his career at the Belfast Telegraph with six years as editorial director, retiring at the end of 1998. Roy's approach was completely different to that of earlier editors of the paper, such as Jack Sayers, who were very much old stock, very formal in their approach. Roy was always very hands- on, very efficient, but someone who always kept a cool head through the worst of times. When I was liaising him for various reports I was writing about the media in Northern Ireland, I always found Roy exceptionally easy, yet always meticulous, to deal with.

Walter Love

One of the funniest incidents I ever encountered in broadcasting happened with Walter Love, who is now 81 and seems to have been broadcasting for the BBC for ever, or nearly that. On one occasion, when one of my Ireland travel guides had been published by the Appletree Press in Belfast, an interview was lined up with Walter. He was in the BBC studios in Belfast and I was in the BBC radio studio close to Leinster House. There was just one snag: Walter could hear everything I was saying, but I could only hear at some of what he was saying. As a result, I could only half hear the questions he was asking me, so I had to answer on the basis of what I thought he'd asking me, which must have made for a very peculiar live interview indeed!

Walter's first appearance on the BBC was on Children's Hour in 1946; he joined the BBC in London in 1958 as a studio manager and then he spent a year with the BBC in Edinburgh before returning home to Belfast. For over a decade, from 1960 onwards, he was the main BBC television newsreader in Belfast. In 1978, he went freelance, but has continued to work for the BBC ever since. After Radio Ulster started in 1985, he continued to be a regular presenter on that station, only semi- retiring in 2006. But even after that, he has continued to do programmes on a subject very close to his heart, jazz. His wife, Mary, died in 2011; Walter is now 81. He's a most genial person who's had a near legendary career with the BBC in Belfast, but as as the case with a former BBC Belfast colleague, Sean Rafferty, Walter rather unbelievably started out as an accountant.

Carmel Lynch

When I was doing my original book on newspaper history, published in 1983, one of the many people I interviewed was a charming elderly lady called Carmel Lynch, who had been, if you'll excuse the pun, the linchpin for many years of the old Cork Examiner offices in Grafton Street, Dublin. She was active there during the 1950s and 1960s. What had been the Cork Examiner for many decades became The Examiner in

1996, as it attempted to become a national newspaper rather than the leading daily in Munster. Then in 2000, it changed its name again, to the Irish Examiner. I well remember the Examiner' s old offices in Academy Street off St Patrick Street in central Cork, a real myriad and maze of corridors and offices, but reeking with the atmosphere of the newspaper business. It stayed there until 2004. And for many decades now, one of the Crosbies in particular, Ted, has been the man who has kept the show on the road. Tragically, Ted' s wife Gretchen, died 20 years ago, in October, 1996, when the car she was driving back to Cork from Dublin crashed near Abbeyleix, then a decade ago, their daughter, Suzanne, died. She was in her 40s and worked in the library at 'de paper', where she was always most helpful to me. The Irish Examiner has been through many recent travails, but happily is still going strong and is still producing a lot of very vibrant news and feature coverage. Its annual, the Holly Bough, is still being produced and so too is the Evening Echo, despite its small circulation.

Jack Lynch

Born in 1919, and a Corkman through and through, he began life as a great GAA star, before qualifying for the Bar. But his life' s real work started in 1948, when he was 29, and became a Fianna Fáil TD for the first time. Within less than 20 years, he had risen to become Taoiseach, an office he held on two occasions, firstly from 1966 to 1973 and then from 1977 to 1979. He led the State when the troubles started in the North in 1969 and he was there through the worst of times. Jack Lynch was a remarkable man, quiet and self- effacing and unassuming, a gentle and and a gentleman in his entirety. He married Máirín in 1946; she died in 2004, five years after he died. They had no children. She became as well- known in public as her husband. One story about him illustrates just how much society in Ireland has changed. Even after he became Taoiseach for the first time in 1966, he always insisted, whenever he could, on going home to Rathgar to have his lunch with his wife. I got to know him in his later life, when he contributed to my RTÉ Radio 1 series, Paper Tigers. I found him as everyone else found him, a true gentleman, always willing to help, yet behind that gentle nature was a steely determination to ride out all the challenges and complexities of political life. Bernadette had known the Lynchs for far longer than I did and her estimation of them was exactly the same as my own. These days, I doubt a person of such gentility could find themselves at the top of the political pile.

Joe Lynch

Another remarkable Corkman, from the "real" capital of Ireland. Born in 1925, he was a fine performer on radio and television, both as an actor and as a singer. When the 50th anniversary of the Easter Rising was commemorated in 1966, he was much in demand as an actor by Telefís Éireann, and subsequently, another and later series that he appeared in for years, Glenroe, also brought him widespread fame. He was a most charming person to meet; on one occasion in Iveagh House, at a reception, he told Bernadette that she had the most beautiful pair of hands he had ever seen, and his wife was standing beside him. He spent much of his last years in Spain, whilst at the same time embroiled in contractual disagreements with RTÉ. He died, in Spain, in 2001.

Joe Mac

I only met Joe Mac of the Dixies once, but true to his status, as one of the legendary figures from the show bands of the 1960s, he was exuberant, over the top and full of fizz and sparkle, just as he was on stage. He was born Joseph Terence McCarthy in Cork in 1936, but sensibly picked a far snappier stage name for himself. He served his time as an upholsterer with Cash's department store in Cork, now Brown Thomas, and it was there that he met a fellow employee, Ann Malony, whom he married in 1960. By that stage, the Dixies were well on the road; their first gig had been at UCC in 1954. Much later, in 1968, the group had their biggest ever hit, Little Arrows. By 2004, by which time Joe Mac had clocked up 50 years in show business, he reckoned he had made 12, 500 stage appearances, while he and the band had clocked up 27 hits that were in the Top 20.

Not all his colleagues were so lucky. He mentioned to me the sad case of one fellow musician in the group, Brendan O' Brien, who was seriously injured in 1974 when he touched a microphone that was "live". Brendan survived but the trauma took a huge toll on his health; he died in 2008, aged just 66. Another player with the Dixies, Theo Cahill, who played the saxophone, was playing with the group at a dance on Achill in 1988, when he collapsed and died on stage.

Proinsias Mac Aonghusa

Prionsias was a remarkable film maker and an extraodinary knowledgeable man to chat with. Born in Galway in 1933, he was long involved with the Labour Party, from which he was expelled in 1967. He was also a president of Conradh na Gaeilge, since the Irish language was one of his lifelong passions. He was also a member of the Arts Council of Ireland for many years and in between all that, in 1974 and 1975, worked in southern Africa with Seán McBride, as a UN special representative. But he also made a big name for himself as a television broadcaster and film maker. He also long wrote a commentary column in the old Sunday Press under the byline "Gulliver", in which he often praised his old friend, Charles Haughey.

His wife, Catherine McGuinness, worked in the Labour Party in the 1960s but by 1994, she had been apppointed a Circuit Court judge. Then in 2000, she was appointed to the Supreme Court. Very interested in childrens' rights, she was also president of the Law Reform Commission. Prionsias died comparatively young, aged 70, in 2003.

Eddie McAteer

When I was at college in Derry, I often went to political meetings in the city, including some in the Bogside, and heard some of the noted politicians of the day speaking about all the injustices the Catholic community both in the city and the North generally, were suffering. The most prominent of them was Eddie McAteer, who had been born at Coatbridge in central Scotland in 1914; the family moved to Derry when he was young. Rather improbably, he worked for the Inland Revenue from 1930 until 1944, then became an accountant, before going into politics full time. His brother Hugh was a prominent republican but Eddie chose the nationalist path.

He was first elected to Stormont as an MP in 1945, eventually becoming leader of the Nationalist Party there in 1964. He lost his seat in the 1969 general election in the North to John Hume, whose SDLP party went on to eclipse the Nationalist Party, just as in time, Sinn Féin became the largest party in the North for Catholic voters. Eddie McAteer was quite militant in his earlier political career; he became chairman of the Anti- Partition League of Ireland in 1953. When I saw him in action at political rallies in Derry, he was then the city' s best- known nationalist politician and he was a striking figure, a big, bluff man with prominent eyebrows. He went on to become prominent in the campaign to get the new university planned for the North set up in Derry, with an expansion of Magee, rather than going to Coleraine. In the event, setting up the University of Ulster in Coleraine was a major factor in Derry in creating the discontent that led to the start of the troubles there in 1969. Yet when the troubles did start in the city, Eddie McAteer was the politician who called constantly for moderation.

Within a month of arriving in Derry for the first time in early October, 1962, and without any prior knowledge of the city' s history, it took me exactly a month to suss out what was wrong. In essence, the Catholic population of Derry and the North was being treated in the same way as the blacks in apartheid South Africa, second, third and fourth class citizens with far fewer rights than their Protestant neighbours. In Derry, for instance, Catholics were very restricted in their voting rights for the local council, whereas Protestants, especially business owners, could get multiple votes. I had also gone to places in Derry like Springtown Camp, where evicted Catholic families were living in deplorable conditions in old Nissen huts, to write about their plight for the student newspaper at Magee. I thought the situation was so bad that I sat down and wrote a long missive to The Guardian about the Northern situation. I had thought that The Guardian was one of the few media outlets in Britain that might be sympathetic, but at that stage, even they didn' t want to know about the North. Neither did the political establishment in Britain, which had buried its head deep in the political sand when the Northern Ireland state came into being in 1920 and refused to discuss any aspect of Northern politics until the troubles erupted. But in the end, Eddie McAteer and his Nationalist Party were swept away and few people today remember what a prominent figure he was in Derry politics up until the mid- 1960s.

Michael and Rosa McAuliffe

When I was doing my book on Sandymount published in 2016, I had several meetings with Michael and his wife, who comes from Kilkenny. Michael' s father had worked for a chain of pharmacies in Dublin before being sent to manage the branch in Sandymount in the 1920s. The following decade, he managed to buy it and McAuliffes became a familiar pharmacy name in Sandymount, which it still is, although Michael sold out and retired in 1960. When Michael was starting out as a pharmacist, he worked for a while in an old- fashioned pharmacy in Sandymount called Batts, which had been established in 1875. Eventually, it closed down, more than 30 years ago, and the present Sandymount branch of AIB was built on the site, while the last owner of Batts retired to take up a new profession- pianist on cruise ships. As for Michael himself, besides being a pharmacist, he has long has a big involvement in community affairs in Sandymount, such as the Wren Boys parade staged on St Stephen' s Day.

Desmond McAvock

Desmond, a big, genial man, who died in 2013, aged 95, lived for many years in Heytesbury Lane, the next lane to where we live, and that' s how I got to know him and his wife, Adele. He came from Ballina, Co Mayo and ended up by being chairman of the old Ballina UDC on three occasions. Then he and his family moved to Dublin, where he began an entirely different career, as an art critic for The Irish Times and other publications. When he had been a young man, he had studied art in Paris, so he was very well versed in the subject.

Later, he and his wife ran a language teaching college in Westland Row and lived above the shop, so to speak. Their back garden was Merrion Square and when, in the early 1970s, it seemed possible that a Catholic cathedral could be built on the central garden of the square, the McAvocks moved first to Wellington Road, then to Heytesbury Lane. Desmond was also active for many years in the Upper Leeson Street Residents' Association and helped prevent many architectural monstrosities being built. The McAvocks had two children, Jane, who lives in Paris, and Peter, who lives in Geneva with his family.

Seán MacBride

A remarkable political figure, he was born in Paris in 1904, son of Major John MacBride and Maud Gonne. His first language was French and for the rest of his life, he always talked with a French accent, a little hard to understand at times. He was a one- time chief of staff of the IRA who ended up founding the Clann na Poblachta party in 1945. In the mid- 1920s, after he had been involved in republican politics, he decided it was safer to move to London. There, as he told me himself, he had, rather incongruously, as an old IRA man, found himself a job as a sub- editor with the Daily Telegraph. By the late 1940s, he was well and truly respectable and indeed, from 1948 until 1951, was Minister for External Affairs, and was instrumental in the declaration of the Republic in 1949. Much later still, he did did much work for the UN, including in the field of human rights, and was awarded the Nobel Peace prize in 1974.

His wife was Catherine Bulfin, daughter of William Bulfin, a well-known nationalist and writer; Seán MacBride married Catherine in 1921 and she died in 1976. In his latter years, he returned to live in his mother' s house, Roebuck House in Clonskeagh, and it was there that I met and interviewed him in the late 1970s. He died in 1988.

Jack McCabe

He was a publican and off- licence owner in Portadown, whom I got to know quite well at the start of the 1970s, when I was writing about the drinks trade. Jack McCabe, who was a relative of Senator Feargal Quinn and the McCabes who own the noted off- licence of the same name in Mount Merrion Avenue, south Dublin, was a very convivial man and someone who knew his way all round the intricacies of the wine business. He was an excellent person to interview on the subject.

Tragically, he met a violent death as the troubles escalated around the North in 1972. Ralph Henry, 34, a former RUC officer and a member of the UDA, a loyalist organisation, had been banned from Jack McCabe' s pub for his anti- social behaviour. Then on July 12, 1972, the day that Orangemen parade, a Protestant civilian had been shot dead in Churchill Park in Portadown. Hours later, Henry made his way to McCabe' s pub and shot dead both Jack McCabe, who was 48, and William Cochrane, a 53 year old Protestant customer. Jack McCabe had been one of the most prominent members of the Catholic business community in the Portadown area and his murder came as a shock to many; Ralph Henry was eventually convicted and sentenced to 27 years in prison.

Martha McCarron

I got to know Martha, noted for her huge frizz of purple hair, very distinctive altogether, when she was working in RTÉ. She worked as a senior producer in the features department and she was a great producer to work with, knowing exactly what she wanted and making sure that things turned out exactly as planned. With Martha in charge on the control desk, there was no chance of even the slightest slip of pronunciation getting through, which is as it should be. In 1997, she had won a Prix Italia for a radio documentary she had produced and that's just about the highest international award you can get for radio work. When Eddie MacSweeney, aka Maxwell Sweeney, had died, he was succeeded by Paddy O' Neill, and after Paddy died, a succession of producers worked on Sunday Miscellany. I had done a lot of work with both Eddie and Paddy and went on to work with various other producers, such as the famed Kevin Hough, noted for Theatre Nights. He retired in 2009. Then Martha came on board as long term producer and it was a joy doing pieces for the programme, she was always so precise and knew exactly how to get the effect she intended.

It was there that I met another long- term contributor, Peter Jankowsky. He had been born in Berlin in 1939 and grew up there during the second world war. Later on, he came to live in Dublin; he worked at the Goethe Institute, where he was a teacher. His English was always perfect, but he never got rid of his German accent. Martha always used to say that she would jump for joy when she got a new piece from him, but after she left RTÉ, so too did his contributions to the station dry up. He died, in Dublin, in 2014.

Professor Charles McCarthy

He was professor industrial relations at Trinity College, Dublin, a short man with an abundance of knowledge and always kind and eager to help. On one occasion, when my late brother- in- law, Eamonn Williams, was looking for career guidance, Charlie was only too willing to help.

His wife Muriel is an indefatigible lady. In 1989, she became the first female keeper at Marsh's Library, the remarkable 300 year old library beside St Patrick's Cathedral in Dublin. She only retired in 2011. Charlie had died in 1986, so she never had his companionship during her term at the library. But after she retired, the library and the church authorities graciously arranged for Muriel to remain living in an apartment beside the library she adored so much, a magnanimous gesture.

She has often written about the library and in the 1980s, produced her first book on the subject, for The O' Brien Press. In those days, it was a customary role reversal for an author to take his or her publisher to dinner after the launch, so Muriel duly organised a dinner at a city centre restaurant. The guest list was quite extensive, about 30, and included Bernadette, who told me afterwards that it had been a real fun night, full of literary talk. At the end of the dinner, Charlie was landed with an enormous bill, but in typical fashion, he simply paid up and never said a word in complaint about the massive dent in his bank account.

Colin McClelland

While I was writing my books on newspaper history, I got to know Belfast- born Colin quite well, and found him very amiable, always keen to help. I always found him good company, not at all abrasive, unlike many investigative journalists. He had worked in the Sunday newspaper business in Belfast before coming to settle in Dublin.

The Sunday World was launched in 1973, with Joe Kennedy as editor. He was succeeded by Kevin Marron, who was struck down by a brain haemorrhage but managed to recover and resume as a columnist. Kevin was one of a number of journalists from Independent Newspapers who were killed when the light plane they were in going to the Beaujolais Nouveau wine celebrations in France in 1984, crashed near Eastbourne in the south of England.

A great personal friend of mine was on that plane, John Feeney, who wrote an ascerbic column for the Evening Herald, slating the Catholic church, politicians and the great and the good in Irish society, at a time when it wasn't the done thing at all. A total iconoclast, he crucified the lot of them without fear or favour, and it made for great reading, highly uncomfortable for anyone who was the subject of one of Feeney' s diatribes. These days, when social media has so much vitriol, it' s almost commonplace, but in those days, it took real courage to write like that.

But to get back to Colin McClelland, he was editor and a director of the Sunday World, from 1981 to 1994, a long stint by today' s standards. After he retired, he ran his own media management company and went on to spend eight years as press officer for Horse Sport Ireland and the Equestrian Federation; he retired as press officer of Horse Sport Ireland in 2016.

Malachy McCloskey

Malachy has been involved in food manufacturing and retailing in Drogheda for well over 50 years. He started in his father' s bakery shop in West Street; the McCloskey name is as well known as every for its bakery products. But Malachy became best- known for setting up Boyne Valley Foods, to promote honey as a natural food, while under his Don Carlos brand, had brought many Spanish specialities to Irish tables. Just over a decade ago, in 2005, he was given a lifetime achievement award in Drogheda. He also has an intense devotion to Irish history, something that' s often reflected in the marketing of the brands belonging to his group. Hardly surprisingly, one of his hobbies is restoring old buildings.

Larry McCoubrey

We got to know Larry reasonably well at the BBC in Belfast in the early 1970s, a very genial fellow. He was an engineer by training but his real love was for writing and performing.

He spent years hanging around the BBC in Belfast, including a stint as an announcer, and he was on the point of quitting Belfast and going to live in England that the BBC offered him a role as newsreader on Scene Around Six, the nightly news programme it produced in Belfast.

On one of its first nights, a technical hitch meant a lot of airtime to fill, so Larry adlibbed with jokes. Viewers liked this so much they wrote hundreds of letters, so ever after, at the end of every bulletin, Larry would sign off with a signature joke. In those days, the troubles were at their worst and the nightly news bulletin was an endless catalogue of horror stories, so the joke to end became a much- needed relief. Larry was an all- round broadcaster, who was good at everything, from sports to comedy, but the BBC was very slow to recognise his talents. Sadly, success came late for Larry, who died at the young age of 38, from a brain haemorrhage, and his death was a huge loss to the BBC in Belfast and its viewers.

Kevin McCourt

Born in Tralee, Co Kerry, in 1915, his first job when he left school in 1933, was as a tramways' clerk. He subsequently qualified as a company secretary and as a certified accountant. Between 1958 and 1962, he was joint managing director of a big aluminium company in the Netherlands, then he came home to one of the top jobs in the public service, director-general at RTÉ, a position he held from 1963 to 1968. He had started there the year after the Irish television service had been launched.

He was often involved in controversies. The then Catholic Archbishop of Dublin, Dr John Charles McQuaid, thought that the TV channel should be an instrument of public policy and that it should have a strongly Catholic ethos. McCourt disagreed vehemently, believing that RTÉ should be independent of both Church and State.

From broadcasting, Kevin McCourt went into something totally different, as managing director of United Distilleries of Ireland, which later became Irish Distillers. Under his guidance, the whiskey distilleries of Dublin and Cork were knit into one group. Later still, Irish Distillers was taken over by the big French drinks company, Pernod Ricard, which still owns it. Kevin McCourt lived with his family for many years at Eglinton Road in Donnybrook, Dublin; he died in 2000.

Jim McDaid

Born in Co Donegal in 1949, he practised as a GP before going into Fianna Fáil politics. He was tourism and sports minister from 1997 to 2002, which is when I knew him. Then from 2002 to 2004, he was Minister of State at the Department of Transport. He resigned his Dáil seat in 2010.

I found him an affable person, easy to get on with, but on the lightweight end of the political spectrum. In late 1997, after he had met her at a function in New York, he began a six month long affair with Anne Doyle, then an RTÉ television newsreader. The affair kept a lot of journalists busy and the papers seemed to cover little else at the time. Jim McDaid and his wife Marguerite had stopped living together in 1988. These days, he has a much quieter life, with his partner, Siobhán O' Donnell, a former barmaid, and their son.

As for Anne Doyle, she is in a long term relationship with Dan McGrattan, a former restaurant owner; they live on Lower Leeson Street. I sometimes see her in the area, an impossibly glamorous figure, as always. From Co Wexford, she had worked for the Department of Foreign Affairs before she joined the RTÉ newsroom in 1978. She often read the nine o' clock news on television and was always a big hit with viewers; she retired in 2011. In her private life, she is a great cat lover.

Bob McDonagh

Bob was a diplomat of the old school. Bernadette knew him well during her years at the Department of External Affairs, then the Department of Foreign and I too got to know him well after he retired.

Born in Tralee, Co Kerry, he was the son of a county inspector in the RIC. Bob married a fellow diplomat, Róisín O' Doherty, whose family came from the other side of the fence, very involved in Republican politics from 1916 to 1921. As for Bob, he came into the Department when Seán MacBride was the Minister and altogether, he served under 10 ministers. He was Irish ambassador in several locations, including the old Federal Republic of Germany, Italy and at the UN. He also headed up the Anglo- Irish section in the Department at one stage and became secretary of the Department, a job now known by the grander title of Secretary- General.

Bob's wife Róisín died in 1988, just after Bob had retired, so he spent the rest of his life living in a flat, by himself, at Clyde Court, on the corner of Clyde Road and Wellington Road. But he had a busy family life, with 14 grandchildren and four great- grandchildren. Two of his sons, Bobby and Philip, also became ambassadors. His daughter, Sunniva, is a barrister and I' ve also met her on occasion.

He had a great sense of humour, always understated, very laconic, and never malicious. When Bernadette retired from the Department, just before we got married in 1972, a big presentation was made in the dining club in the Department and Bob, in his speech, said that one of the enormous tables was going to be given to Bernadette as a going away present. She immediately sensed that this was Bob up to his old tricks! He died in May, 2015, at the age of 91.

Major Tom McDowell

Over the years, many characters have been connected with The Irish Times, but none was so eccentric or over the top as Major McDowell, for long chief executive and then chairman. Many people found his presence intimidating, but I always got on well with him and he was always very helpful to me in my newspaper researches. I even saw the insides of the remarkable office he used to have in the old Irish Times building, complete with coal fire.

Major Tom came from a middle class family in the North, where he was born in 1923. When he was 20, he joined the Royal Inniskilling Fusiliers and in 1944, was made a second lieutenant. He had an accident in the gym, which prevented him from going on active service, so instead, he was sent to work for the British Army's judges' advocates office, a military/civil service kind of job. He also qualified as a barrister, at Queen' s University, Belfast, but never practised. In 1953, he left the army and moved to Dublin to take up a job at Great Universal Stores, then owners of Pims department store and Burton's, the mens' tailors.

Shift forward nearly a decade, to 1962, and he joined The Irish Times as chief executive. He certainly dressed for the part, with a pin striped suit, stiff collars and a monocle. He and his family had a fine house in the Rathfarnham district, close to the foothills of the Dublin Mountains and he used a chauffeur- driven Rolls- Royce to get in and out of the office every working day. His house was called "St Thomas", a pun, perhaps, on his first name. In between times, he was also a member of the prestigious Kildare Street Club.

Then in 1974, he played a big part in devising a scheme to make The Irish Times immune to any take- over bid; The Irish Times Trust was set up. Major Tom was one of the five shareholders, who each benefitted to the tune of £325, 000. In time, one of his two daughters, Erwin, a solicitor, was made deputy managing director, but she never succeeded the inscrutable and leonine Louis O' Neill as chief executive when he retired. Major Tom retired from active management in 1997 and from his chairman' s role in 1999, when he was then made president for life.

Fr James McDyer

He was a remarkable priest, who did so much to revive west Co Donegal, ravaged by economic deprivation and emigration. Born in 1910, he was ordained in 1937 and spent the second world war ministering in London. He returned home to Ireland in 1947, when he was made parish priest on Tory Island. Then in 1951, he transferred to Glencolumbkille.

Fr McDyer toiled there for 30 years, helping bring electrication and running water, as well as encouraging the development of fish and vegetable processing factories and encouraging the start- up of knitting and weaving enterprises. In 1967, he founded the local folk museum as a way of encouraging tourists. In those days, the idea of successive governments was to get international firms to set up branches in Ireland and bring new jobs into being that way, but Fr McDyer had a totally different approach. He was a great believer in communities in the West of Ireland being self-sufficient and using their own local skills to bring about better living conditions.

He was keen to put forward his ideas, so he was an ideal candidate for a new magazine, called Scene. This turned out to be my first celebrity interview, so the publisher, an amiable, rather erratic and very corpulent Englishman called Norman Ames, myself, and a recently arrived photographer from Germany, a thin young man called Walter Pfeiffer, set off for west Donegal. The roads were terrible in those days, so it was a two day drive and I have vague memories of spending the night on the floor of a pub in Co Cavan. But we got the interview; I found Fr McDyer very open and approachable and what he had to say made good copy for a spread over several pages in the magazine. Scene itself continued for a few more years, before suffering the almost inevitable fate for that type of publication.

As for Norman Ames, I had met him in his previous existence, when he was organising door- to- door raffle ticket sales for charities. I got a job working for him. I also got to know a young woman who did the same, except that she was having a lot of trouble getting her commission paid. So one afternoon, when she was sitting in his car, discussing the issue, in Tritonville Road, in Sandymount, she thought of a novel way to solve this industrial relations problem. She reached over and unzipped Norman's flies, so quickly that he didn't realise what was happening. She then whipped out his fat todger and proceeded to administer oral sex. And she got the money she was owed! Fr McDyer and I kept in touch from time to time; I had great admiration for the work he was doing. The last time I was talking with him, not long before he died, he was staying in a hotel in Dublin for a couple of days, after his retirement from Glencolumbkille. He died in 1987, a truly remarkable man, whose solutions to so many of the country's problems are considered avant garde even today.

Gerry McGuinness

I got to know Gerry well, first in Creation, then in the Sunday World. When he was 23, he was working as house manager in the Carlton cinema in Dublin's O' Connell Street. He met Hugh McLaughlin, the man who had founded the Creation magazine empire. Gerry was offered a job, which he promptly accepted. Just over 10 years later, in 1973, Gerry and Hugh McLaughlin were the prime movers in the launch of the Sunday World. In 1978, Hugh McLaughlin sold his shares to Independent Newspapers and Gerry did likewise four years later. Creation itself had collapsed under the burden of its debts, in 1975, but Gerry McGuinness and Hugh McLaughlin had managed to emerge as millionaires.

In 1982, Gerry had plans for a new style full colour tabloid in Britain, with the working title of the Daily Globe, but it never happened. In the event, Eddie Shah launched something very similar in 1986, a tabloid called Today.

When I was researching newspaper history, I always found Gerry very helpful and approachable. His wife, Alma Carroll, a singer, was even better known than he was.

As for Hugh McLaughlin, he was quite a character. Born at Killygordon in east Co Donegal in 1918, it was often said that he made his money from cross- border smuggling during the second world war. After the war, he ran Fleet Publishing, which evolved into Creation. His wife Nuala, often seen as an ambitious social climber, founded Creation magazine, a very upmarket fashion magazine of the 1960s. Among its contributors, for her poetry, was Bernadette. In the early 1980s, Hugh McLaughlin started a daily tabloid newspaper in Dublin called the Daily News, which lasted for exactly a fortnight. When it collapsed, many journalists, who had been recruited locally and cross- channel, found themselves left high and dry. But he did also found the Sunday Tribune, which lasted much longer, until 2011.

I had two spells at Creation, the first in Creation Arcade, the second towards the end of the 1960s, by which time the firm had moved to much bigger premises in Botanic Avenue, Glasnevin. But I found the place so unpleasant to work in second time round that I only stayed for a short while, before quitting to take a more pleasant option, on the dole in Belfast until such time as I could get my freelance work organised.

Edward McHugh

In 1971, I "inherited" a small flat in east Belfast, close to the Strandtown district, from two friends who had bought a house a little further along the street, Belmont Avenue.

It was tiny, with a small front room, an even tinier kitchenette, one bedroom and a shared bathroom, all for a couple of quid a week. Most weekends, Bernadette was there with me. We always found the people we met in the district most courteous and friendly and never had any kind of trouble. We also found examples of Belfast humour, as in the time, coming up to one Christmas, when we spotted a large dog turd on the pavement in Belmont Road. It had been sprayed with gold paint and adorned with glitter, in honour of the festive season!

The landlord of that flat in Belfast was a quiet and gentle man called Edward McHugh, who was always most courteous; when we told him that we were going to get married, he was genuinely delighted and offered his best wishes. After we got married, we moved to a larger flat in the district and lost touch with Mr McHugh, as we always called him. We had quit the north during a loyalist strike in 1974, but it was still a huge shock when we heard on the news, on August 30, 1993, that Edward McHugh had been shot dead by a gunman from the loyalist Red Hand Commandos, while he was in the front garden of his house in Dundonald, a largely loyalist district on the eastern side of Belfast.

Aged 65 when he was murdered, Mr McHugh's main interest outside his work was following the fortunes of the GAA in his native Co Tyrone. Being a Catholic and a GAA follower in the area where he lived marked him out and he died, yet another tragic victim of the age-old sectarian conflict in the North. Every year, on his anniversary, we remember our landlord in Belfast, one of the countless victims of hate crimes there.

Michael McInerney

Michael, a gentle and generous soul, was a long- time political correspondent with The Irish Times and I got to know him quite late in his career, when I went to his flat in Pembroke Road, Ballsbridge, Dublin, to interview him on political affairs. Later in his career, I met up again with Michael and his wife, by then living in a chaotic flat off Ailesbury Road.

Born in Limerick in 1906, he spent the second world war in Belfast, where he started working on the railways, as a clerk, before beginning his journalism career. In 1946, he joined the reporting staff of The Irish Times in Dublin; he was promoted to political correspondent in 1951 and stayed in that job for 22 years, until he retired in 1973. He also frequently appeared on television, where he was also renowned for his remarkably astute and well- informed knowledge of politics.

He also had a lifelong concern for workers' rights and was an organiser and negotiator for the National Union of Journalists. Michael became president of the Irish branch and he was given life membership in 1974, the year after he had retired. This year, 2016, I' ve had a similar honour from the same union, after 40 years' membership. He was succeeded by an equally remarkable political writer, Dick Walsh, who carried on regardless, despite a crippling back condition, but he never let that interfere with his day- to- day work. Dick' s wife was equally well- known, Ruth Kelly, a one- time women' s editor of the old Irish Press, then a feature writer with the RTÉ Guide. Dick died in 2003.

Clare McKeon

She was a very forthright radio and TV presenter, always willing to inject something saucy and provocative into her broadcasts. When I launched my book in 1990 on the 50 year history of Dublin airport, she interviewed me on Century

Radio. After the interview, she invited listeners to phone in; one man did so and whatever he said, quite innocently, Claire turned it into something saucy. "You mean you had your first ride at Dublin airport?" she asked the incredulous listener. She had injected a suggestive tone into the conversation where none had existed and it created a good laugh. Century Radio was a short- lived commercial station, with studios near Christchurch cathedral, that went off the air in November, 1991. That night, Clare was just preparing to do her nightly show when the plug was pulled for good. Another casualty of the station' s collapse was Marty Whelan, who fortunately has gone on to make a long and sustained career at RTÉ. As for Clare herself, she went on to front several TV series for RTÉ, but then faded out of broadcast media, as she and her husband, Eamon McLoughlin, founded a beauty business.

John 'twin' McNamara

Long known as 'Mr Achill', he is an absolute authority on the heritage and history of his native Achilll island. When I was doing my book on Old Achill Island, published by Stenlake in 2012, I sat down one day with John to go through all the old photographs for that book. He knows everyone, past and present, on the island, so he was able to tell me exactly who was who and what was what in all the photographs and by the time we' d finished, about four hours later, a lot of my research had been done!

John, who is known as 'twin' to distinguish him from his now deceased twin brother, has always lived in Achill, where he was the principal of a primary school. Now in his early 80s, he and his wife Mary live in Dooagh. Besides being an authority on the history of the island, John is also a renowned musician and he has long been a principal member of Scoil Acla, Ireland' s oldest summer school, dating back over a century.

A typical event in which John was involved was the gathering of 1, 055 people on the beach at Keel in 2010 to play The Dawning of the Day on tin whistles and thereby make the Guinness World Records. John was there, to encourage everyone. It' s hardly surprising that in 2015, John was given a lifetime achievement award for his immense contribution to Achill' s culture and heritage.

Eddie MacSweeney

Eddie, whose stage name was Maxwell Sweeney, was a producer who worked for RTÉ Radio 1.

He was born in England to an Irish father and an English mother; his father, Dominic, worked for the Royal Mint in London and the family returned to Ireland in the late 1920s when Dominic started to work for the new Currency Commission in Dublin. Dominic also had close connections with the Holborn Empire, one of London' s great old variety theatres, and this no doubt inspired Eddie to his lifelong interest in the theatre, something he often wrote and broadcast about.

Eddie started his first job as a junior reporter with The Irish Times in the early 1930s; in 1940, when the old weekly Irish Times was turned into Times Pictorial, Eddie was made art editor. The Times Pictorial had been inspired by the hugely successful Picture Post magazine, launched in Britain in 1938. After the second world war, he went into cinema publicity in Dublin, then for a time in the early 1950s, spent some time working with the Rank film organisation at its studios in Denham, Buckinghamshire, in the era of the Rank starlets.

He then returned to Ireland, for the rest of his working life. He wrote extensively for many magazines, including Ireland of the Welcomes and for such travel guides as the American- published Fodor' s. He also edited a magazine for the Irish hotel trade for many years. By the mid- 1950s, he was freelancing for Radio Éireann, then based in the GPO in central Dublin.

When what had become RTÉ started a programme called Sunday Miscellany in 1968, a brilliant decision was made, to appoint Eddie as its producer. It was often said of him, in RTÉ, that he became a full- time employee at an age when everyone else was thinking of retiring. These days, if someone is on the full- time staff of RTÉ, they have to retire when they reach retiring age, but there were no such restrictions in those days. Eddie was producer for close on 20 years and he introduced many luminaries to the programme, the likes of Dr John Fleetwood, Val Mulkerns, Sam McAughtry from Belfast and Sean McCarthy from Co Kerry, a whole galaxy of talent. The sonorous tones of writer Ben Kiely were frequently heard. I have to declare an interest here, as Eddie gave me my first big break in radio and encouraged me to keep writing scripts and presenting them for the programme, which I did quite often while he was in charge.

Just before he died, he was in hospital. One day, I was in studio at RTÉ recording a piece, when I overheard someone saying that they had just been at the hospital, talking to Eddie, who was continue to revise scripts for the programme from his hospital bed. Eddie had said to this other person "I'm not going to make it this time" and so it proved. He died on June 1, 1991, just before his 82nd birthday.

Eddie had also been well- known as the producer of another very popular programme, Dear Sir or Madam, in which listeners wrote in to air their views and opinions. The programme was presented by a great personality, John O' Donovan, a very literary man who had worked for the old Evening Press, and a good friend of Bernadette' s.

His wife Maura had pre- deceased him by nearly 20 years; Eddie is survived by their two daughters, Anne and Colette, who have long lived in the family home in Sandymount. I vividly remember when Bernadette and I went to Eddie' s removal to the Star of the Sea church in Sandymount, the place was packed with media folk keen to honour someone who had been held in such high esteem.

Ella McSweeney

Ella is a very bubbly, personable presenter whom I' ve always found it a pleasure to work with. Born in Dublin in 1978, she graduated from Trinity College, Dublin, and went to work for a variety of media outlets, including RTÉ, the BBC, The Irish Times and the Irish Examiner. She began working full- time for RTÉ radio in 2000, then went on to spend three years with the BBC in London and Belfast, before returning to RTÉ in 2004. I got to know her quite well when she was working on the radio side, but since 2008, she has been very involved in a popular television series called Ear to the Ground. I must admit, I know little or nothing about farming, to my shame, but I find the programme immensely interesting to watch. Ella is also bringing up her own family; her second child was born in 2013.

Tom McSweeney

Tom and I go back a long way, since soon after he started presenting the Seascapes programme on RTÉ Radio 1, which started 26 years ago. He began his journalistic career with the esteemed Southern Star weekly newspaper in Skibbereen, West Cork. I always remember the story he told me for one of my newspaper books; as a young reporter in Skibbereen, he was keen to show how enthusiastic he was, so when he reported a local court case concerning a publican who was up for serving drink after hours, Tom included in his report the names of every one of the local people who had been "found on". It didn't make Tom too popular in certain quarters! Tom went on to work for RTÉ and in the 1970s, he was made the station' s first regional correspondent, based in Cork. Subsequently, he became marine correspondent and from that developed Seascapes.

He was so devoted to the programme that he never charged an extra fee for presenting it and many of the trips he did for it were paid for out of his own pocket. Tom was also renowned for his very candid opinions on current affairs, which he wasn't short in putting forward. But when he reached retirement age, he had to retire; he was succeeded as presenter by Marcus Connaughton, who had been the producer, and who also continues in that role. But in the five years or so since Tom has retired from RTÉ, he has kept as busy as ever, including writing for such publications as the Evening Echo in Cork, the Marine Times newspaper and Afloat magazine. In 2012, he was awarded an honorary Masters' degree by NUI, Galway, in recognition of his services to maritime affairs over the years. He also has another very important position; he is vice- president of St Vincent de Paul, the society that does such wonderful work across the country helping people who have fallen on hard times.

Brendan McWilliams

Brendan was a renowned writer about science and weather matters; he joined the Irish Met service in 1965 and retired after 40 years service. But what really brought him into the public eye was the Weather Eye column he wrote daily for The Irish Times; he started in 1988 and continued for nearly 20 years. It was very informative, but very readable, and it soon became one of the most popular columns in the newspaper. During the last year of his life, he also did a weekly weather spot on Pat Kenny' s radio show, then on RTÉ Radio 1. On the odd occasion I asked Brendan about some aspect of the weather, he was always most helpful and obliging, a true gentleman. Towards the end of his life, he lived in Wexford, and died there in 2007, at the comparatively young age of 63.

Professor Myra Maguire

Myra was born and brought up in Ayrshire, Scotland, but she lived her adult life in Dublin. However, she never lost her charming Scottish accent. Her father was for many years a manager with the Dunlop tyre company and the family home was at Leinster Road West in Rathmines, where she continued to live for many years. Bernadette got to know her first, through the Department of External Affairs, as Myra penned the letters of credence that new ambassadors needed when they took up their duties in Dublin. God help them if they got any of the details wrong. One of two of them tried it on, asking Myra if she would redo the document correctly, without any extra payment. She had none of that nonsense and made sure that any ambassador who sought her graphic skills paid in full for whatever work she did- proper order! She went on to do lots of genealogical work and in time, became a professor at the National College of Art & Design in Dublin. I met her on a few occasions, a very feisty woman and a very talented artist. After she died in May, 2015, I went to her funeral service in the Presbyterian church in Adelaide Road, Dublin, a new experience for me, as this was the first time I had experienced a Presbyterian funeral, much plainer than its Catholic equivalent, but no less moving, a fine tribute to a remarkable artistic lady.

Peter Malone

I first got to know Peter when he was the chief executive of the old Jurys Hotel group, always very helpful and encouraging when I was interviewing him. From Dundalk, he had gone to London as a young man to train in hotel management. When he returned to Ireland, it was to the Shelbourne. Then came the venture by Pat Quinn, the man who founded what became Quinnsworth supermarkets, now Tesco. He had what he thought was a bright idea, of opening a country club style hotel in Kilternan in the foothills of the Dublin mountains. So Peter found himself helping to open, then close, the new hotel in quick order. But fortunately, his skills were soon in demand at Jurys, and he rose to become chief executive, a job he held for 11 years. At Jurys, he pioneered the concept of Jurys Inns, a budget accommodation brand, which became very successful. From the hotel business, Peter went on to become chairman of Bord na Móna for two years, while he was also long- time chairman at the old National Roads Authority. During his term in office there, many of the country' s motorways were built. He has also had property interests, as chairman of a locally based estate agents. All in all, Peter has had a very varied and successful business career, but he has always been totally down- to- earth. He was particularly interested in one of my local history books, Old Dundalk and Blackrock, published by Stenlake Publishing in 2006, and was immensely helpful in ensuring that I had all the local knowledge absolutely right.

Louis Marcus

Louis is one of the most acclaimed Irish film directors, and rightly so, for a fine body of work. Born in Cork in 1936, he went on to direct such masterpieces as An Tine Bheo, the 1916 documentary released in 1966, and the 1995 TV series on the great 19th century famine. At the 50th Cork Film Festival in 2005, he was given a lifetime achievement award for all his work as a film director and producer. On the one occasion I interviewed him, for an Irish Times supplement, the circumstances were rather unusual. At the time, Louis was suffering from a lot of back pain and he had to spend his time lying down in bed. But despite that affliction, the interview went well and Louis couldn' t have been more helpful or obliging.

Tony Mathews, Drogheda

During the loyalist general strike in the North, in 1974, we thought it very prudent to get out of the place as fast as we could. We packed all our belongings into a rented Mini car; when we were eventually stopped by a Garda on the border near Dundalk and were able to tell him our story, we were never so glad to see one of the boys in blue. To cut a long story short, I still wanted to do some work in Belfast a couple of days a week, even though we no longer lived there. So we decided to live in Drogheda, a kind of half- way house between Dublin and Belfast.

So we set about finding somewhere to live and we soon met up with a fellow scribe, the late Tony Mathews, who lived at Colpe, just outside Drogheda on the Co Meath side. Tony was a journalist who worked for both RTÉ and the old Evening Press. He had a farm but he also owned a rather run-down cottage nearby, which he let to us for a pittance. The only facilities it had was an outdoor loo and a kitchen, with the oven fuelled by bottled gas, and the place was infused with damp, but somehow we managed for a full year. The big field at the back of the cottage was sometimes filled with neighbouring cows that had wandered in and we also got to know some of the local cats and lambs. In those days, Colpe was almost entirely rural, a complete contrast to what it' s like nowadays, a well- built up suburb of Drogheda.

Tony and his wife Mary, who came from the North, were always most hospitable and often had us over to their house in the evening, so that we could have a chat and watch the nine o' clock news on television. Tony was a very decent guy and I always remember when we went on to buy a semi- detached house on a new estate off the North Road in Drogheda, with the help of a £12 per month fixed interest mortgage from the old Drogheda Corporation, Tony came to see us one day. He took one look round all the gardens divided by breeze block walls, and told us: "you won' t stay long here". How right he was; within two years, we had moved back to Dublin. Tony, who had heart trouble, died at a young age and I honestly thought that all the commuting up and down to Dublin, had a very wearing effect on him. His sister Anne was a long time reporter and feature writer in the Drogheda Independent, so the media business was well engrained in the Mathews' family.

Maxi

I got to know Maxi quite well during her latter years with RTÉ Radio 1; she was always supportive of the work I was doing, as I praised the many documentaries she made. She was born in Harold' s Cross, Dublin, in 1950 with a decidedly plain name: Irene McCoubry. It had to go and it did. In the late 1960s, she was part of a female singing group called Maxi, Dick and Twink. The last- named was the saltily tongued Adele King. After the group disbanded, Maxi worked with Danny Doyle, then in the 1973 Eurovision Song Contest, she represented Ireland, which came 10th. In the late 1970s, Maxi became part of another all- girl group, Sheeba, which represented Ireland in the 1981 Eurovision contest, coming fifth. In 1982, the group were involved in a terrible car crash in Co Mayo, which killed the mother and her little daughter in the other car. Maxi was one of the group who had a long fight back to good health, but the following year, 1983, Sheeba was disbanded. Subsequently, Maxi went to work full- time for RTÉ, in both radio and television. From 1999 to 2010, she presented the early morning radio show, Risin' Time, but in time, the very early starts took a toll on her health. But over the subsequent five years, she went on to make many memorable documentaries, retiring from the station in 2015; she plans to carry on working.

Robert Maxwell

One of the most dubious people in political life I have ever met, I came face to face with Robert Maxwell one day in the Shelbourne Hotel, Dublin. He had come over to Dublin to announce a big expansion plan for the company he owned, the European Printing Corporation on the Malahide Road in north Dublin. It produced typesetting for publishers. But the very moment that Maxwell opened his mouth, I sensed someone who was as crooked as a six dollar bill, and so it turned out.

He had been born in what was then Czechoslovakia in 1923. The family was a poor, Yiddish speaking Orthodox Jewish family in a small town in the east of the country. Most of his family died in Auschwitz, but he joined the Czechoslovak Army in exile, in Marseilles, in 1940. Later in the war, he transferred to the British army and was even awarded the Military Cross. In 1945, he married a French Protestant woman called Elizabeth 'Betty' Meynard and they went on to have nine children.

In time, Maxwell started making a name for himself in academic publishing, then in 1984, he acquired Mirror Group newspapers. After his death, it turned out that he had swindled hundreds of millions of pounds from their pension fund. From 1964 until 1970, he was also a Labour MP and it was then British prime minister Harold Wilson who coined the phrase about Maxwell, whom he nicknamed the "bouncing Czech". Maxwell's behaviour was notorious and not just in financial affairs. When he was running the Mirror group, he'd frequently depart or arrive at the newspapers' head office by helicopter. The helicopter used the roof of the high rise office block and on many occasions, Maxwell would decide to relieve himself over the parapet, so that unsuspecting pedestrians walking along the street far below often found themselves being drenched in unexpected yellow rain.

He died in mysterious circumstances, when he either fell off or was pushed off his boat at sea off the Canary Islands, in 1991. After his death, his publishing empire collapsed and it was only then that the scale of his theft became evident.

Bob Milne

In the 1980s, when I was writing a lot about the advertising industry- something I certainly don' t do these days- I became very friendly with Bob Milne, an old- fashioned man in ways but a whizz at the advertising business in Dublin. He came from West Cork and went on to spend many years in the advertising business in London, before returning home to Ireland in 1962. Grosvenor Advertising has been set up at 46 Wellington Road, Ballsbridge, in 1970 and it was eventually taken over by CDP, a London ad agency. Bob and Peter O' Keeffe became joint managing directors and the creative director was the renowned wordsmith, still writing about the industry in Michael Cullen' s Marketing magazine and website, was Brendain Ó Broin. He has written of what joy it was walking to work in CDP in those days; on spring days, all the trees along the road would be in full blossom. At its height, CDP was one of the top five ad agencies in Dublin, with a swathe of top notch accounts. I well remember that on one of the occasions Bernadette and I were staying at the Cashel Palace Hotel in Cashel, Co Tipperary, during its glory years under Ray Carroll' s ownership, we went down to breakfast one morning, only to find Bob Milne and his secretary doing likewise. They were on their way to see a client, Dairygold in Mitchelstown in north Co Cork, and I don' t know who was the more surprised, Bob or myself.

In 2000, the CDP agency was taken over by the Leo Burnett agency from Chicago and it continued to thrive. But the great recession that took hold in 2008 destroyed the Dublin ad agency's chances and it was forced to close in 2013.

Derek Mooney

We've been good friends with Derek Mooney for something like 25 years, ever since the days when we used to go for our newspapers to Furlong's in Donnybrook, run by Gerry Callanan and his family. Gerry was a very kind-hearted man; as a youngster, he had been rescued from the shop in 1947 when it went up in flames when a stock of fireworks went up in flames. Sadly, on that occasion, a woman working in the shop lost her life. The incident led to much stricter controls on the sale of fireworks.

Coming much nearer the present, I always remember our joy when The Independent was launched in London in 1986, a true innovation in the newspaper business. As soon as it started, we always enjoyed walking down to Gerry's to get our daily copy. Then our joy turned to anger when Independent Newspapers took out an injunction to prevent its distribution in Ireland because the brand names of it and the Irish Independent were so similar. How anyone could confuse the two newspapers was an unfathomable secret. Ironically, it was Independent Newspapers in Tony O'Reilly's heyday that went on to own and bankroll The Independent for so long.

It was also at Gerry's shop that we got to know a young guy with big ambitions in broadcasting very well; it was Derek Mooney. He had started off in RTÉ as a runner during the 1984 Olympics in Los Angeles and he soon started to make a name for himself with all his wildlife programmes. He was, and still is, full of enthusiasm for what he does, a natural broadcaster and a decent fellow. Eventually, he became a big time name on television, presenting such programmes as Winning Streak. Until January, 2015, he had presented a daily radio programme on weekday afternoons, but decided to give it up to become executive producer of nature and wildlife programmes on Radio 1. But even today, he has regrets that he stopped doing his daily radio show. He had earlier made another momentous decision in his life, in 2012, when he came out as openly gay.

Jim Morton

Jim Morton was a true pioneer in the newspaper business in Ireland. His father John, a first world war veteran, had started Morton Newspapers in Lurgan when he bought the Lurgan Mail in 1936. But it was Jim who headed the big expansion of the group; by the time he died, the group owned and ran no fewer than 22 local newspaper titles in Northern Ireland. When I was at Magee College in Derry, one of the more interesting activities I got involved in- far more interesting than actually studying- was the newspaper for the annual college rag day. I vividly remember that in 1964, Mortons had become the first newspaper group in Ireland to install a web-offset press, which produced much better quality papers, in colour. Just after the new press had gone in, myself and other students had done a deal through the Londonderry Sentinel, Morton's weekly title in Derry, published from offices on Strand Road, Derry, to produce the 1964 rag newspaper. I remember writing the front page story, headed: "Revolution in Derry", all about the general chaos caused in the city when warring factions came to blows. I still have a copy of that paper and it's hard to imagine that we had forecast, with uncanny accuracy, the troubles that were to break out in Derry in the summer of 1969, the start of the really serious troubles in the North.

On October 5 the previous year, 1968, a civil rights march in the Waterside area of Derry had turned violent when the old RUC tried to disrupt it. An RTÉ cameraman was there to cover it and his film stock went around the world, screened by numerous TV stations. That too was the famous weekend that I was staying with two friends from Magee who had married and were living in Belfast. The husband went on to become a well- known name in the newspaper business in the city. On that Saturday night, we had heard all about the disturbances in the city and had guessed, rightly, how they had boded ill for peace in the North. But as we were halfway through dinner, the three of us, a very pleasant meal, with not too much wine, took a bizarre turn. My friend' s wife, someone I had always been friendly with, was on various medical prescriptions and the interaction with the wine somehow made her lose all inhibitions. While her husband looked on, in a non-interfering way, she started stripping off all her clothes. She took her top off first to reveal a fine pair of breasts, then she took her skirt and panties off, so that she was stark naked, with a nicely trimmed pubic area. Next, she came and sat on my lap; I was astonished, having a lovely looking young woman, and a married woman at that, sitting on my knee, entirely in the nude. I' ll draw an ever so polite veil over what happened next, but suffice to say it turned out to be a truly remarkable Saturday night dinner.

All that has made me sidestep Morton Newspapers and the Derry connection! As for Mortons, after the death of Jim, a great newspaper pioneer, the business passed to Jim' s son, John, who eventually sold out to Scottish Radio Holdings, who subsequently in turn sold out to the Edinburgh- based Johnston Press.

Fernand Moulin

He was the father- in- law of Kate, my sister. Fernand was French but had long connections with the UK, marrying there. During the second world war, he was an aide de camp to General de Gaulle, who headed the Free French in London. Fernand had been in the French Navy before the war and when France fell to the Nazis, his ship was fortunately berthed in Southampton. De Gaulle was arguably the most outstanding French leader during the 20th century, only matched in his complexity and intelligence by François Mitterand, a later Socialist president. After the war, Fernand was responsible for the construction of the memorial, in the shape of the Cross of Lorraine, which has two cross bars, on a hillside at Greenock, overlooking the Firth of Clyde in Scotland. It was built to honour the Free French sailors who had been based on the Clyde during the war. Subsequently, Fernand was very involved as a top executive with British Rail's catering operations and for a long time, he was managing director of the famed Gleneagles Hotel in Scotland. His last job was on the main board of British Rail, based at the old St Pancras station in London. We only met him once; Bernadette and I had got married in 1972 and a couple of years later, my sister Kate married her husband, Peter, a son of Fernand and his wife Joan. The wedding was in a north London registry office and afterwards, the reception was held in the Moulins' apartment just off Regents Park in north London. It was a very elegant apartment and Fernand was the absolute epitome of Gallic charm.

Munster Express, Waterford

I have long known the Walshs of the Munster Express weekly newspaper in Waterford, including the legendary 'Smokey Joe' Walsh, the owner and editor, from the the 1940s until his death in 1992. He was one of the outstanding personalities of the old- style regional newspaper business and many stories were told about him. My favourite is the one about his toupée; it was often said that before he left the office to go to any "do", he would sprinkle salt from a salt cellar on his collar, to make it look as if he had dandruff! However, the equally legendary journalist on the paper, John O' Connor, who made the transition from the show band era of the 1960s to newspaper man, takes the story with, well, a pinch of salt.

Another story about 'Smokey Joe' concerned his negotiations over pay claims at his paper. He fought long and hard to resist them, but eventually, he' d give way. The younger members of staff, in particular, would be delighted they had won a pay rise. But most of them lived in flats in the city owned by 'Smokey Joe' and they had no sooner got their pay rises than they had an equivalent rise in the rents they paid, so it was back to square one.

He was particularly famed for his coverage of the Olympics. He attended the 1936 games in Berlin and always claimed to have looked Hitler in the eye when the great black American athlete, Jesse Owens, was refused the medal that was rightly his. That claim too can be taken with a large dose of salt. But from then until the Olympic Games in Seoul in 1988, 'Smokey Joe' went to every one and sent back voluminous amounts of copy to his paper in Waterford. He was at the 1956 games in Melbourne to see Ronnie Delany win gold for Ireland, but his claim that he was the only Irish journalist there wasn' t quite true. But during the last games he was at, in 1988, a famous picture was taken of him, in truly proprietorial mode, on the Great Wall of China.

I got to know him quite well and he was always good company and very genial with me. On one occasion, he took Bernadette and myself to lunch in the Granville Hotel in Waterford; the amount of talking we had to do was minimal. Once 'Smokey Joe' had started on his reminiscences, there was no stopping him. On a couple of occasions, I went out to interview him at his house, Cliff Grange, in Tramore, a place with fantastic views over Tramore Bay.

I only met his wife Josephine once; when I was doing the Paper Tiger radio series for RTÉ in 1992, one of the episodes was on the "Munster". A lovely man who took part was the late Michael Whelan, for years, the advertisement manager, who when 'Smokey Joe' was away on his world travels, ran the paper in his absence. Josephine said a few words as well; during the second world war, she had worked as a nurse in England. She only lasted three months after her husband died in September, 1992. Some years after his death, Kieran, one of his sons, who took over as managing director and editor, asked me to write his father' s biography. I did just that and was suitably paid for it; we also managed to find an amazing selection of photographs. It would also have covered the many innovations 'Smokey Joe' created for newspaper printing. But sadly, due to internal family wranglings, the book was never published, a great shame. I was never given a direct reason for its non- appearance. But I did contribute to a subsequent book, Waterford Memories, on the newspaper' s history over 150 years and how it was intertwined with that of its native city, edited by Kieran Walsh and published in 2010.

Over the years, I've had many other dealings with Kieran. I also got to know very well one of Kieran' s two sisters, Priscilla, a lovely woman with a keen sense of humour. She worked for a number of years as news editor on the paper, one of the first women in the Irish newspaper business to hold such a title. Eventually, she married Peter Noble and went to live in England; they had a son together. Priscilla, a most charming and good natured woman, was born in 1955 and died in 2015, her young age at her death a great shock to her many friends. But despite living in England for so long, she kept all her Waterford connections and interests alive and her funeral was held in the Holy Cross church in Tramore. Her passing was well commemorated, in The Irish Times, by John O' Connor, who apart from having written for the Munster Express for more than four decades, also did the Friday afternoon slot on RTÉ Radio 1, reviewing the weekly newspapers.

Peadar Murnane

Peadar was one of the most genial and helpful local historians I ever had dealings with. In 2014, Stenlake Publishing in Scotland published my book on the history of County Monaghan, illustrated with many old photographs collected by Martin MacKenna. It was a substantial undertaking, running to nearly 100 pages in A4 format. It needed considerable research and that was how I came to know Peadar, as the expert on the history of Ballybay in Co Monaghan. He could tell me everything I needed to know about Ballybay and district, but there was precious little he didn't know about the whole county.

While I was doing all my research, the emails were flying backwards and forwards between Peadar and myself; he was in his late 80s then, but totally au fait with the latest in modern computer technology. He and his brother Jim had produced a book in 1999 on the history of Ballybay, At the Ford of the Birches. For my own book, Peadar was so helpful on every occasion, to make sure that everything was just right, and he was full of enery and enthusiasm for the project.

Gradually, I came to know more of his own family history, although he himself never told me that his parents had fled the anti- Catholic pogroms in Belfast in the early 1920s and had settled in the peaceful surroundings of Ballybay. His mother went on to run a dressmaking business in the Main Street and Peadar himself went on to develop the business into garment retailing and indeed manufacturing, all the while maintaining his intense interest in local history. He and his wife Eithne went on to have a big family, daughters Mairead, Catherine, Áine, Eithne and Pauline and sons Peter, Joseph and Michael. Peadar died in hospital in Cavan on March 2, 2014, just before the Monaghan book to which he had contributed so much came out. I really miss his tremendous enthusiasm and knowledge of local history.

Christina Murphy

Born in Breaffy, Co Mayo in 1941, she went on to have a remarkable career at The Irish Times, where I got to know her, a woman never shy about voicing her opinions on any given subject. From 1972 until 1975, she was the woman's editor of the paper's Living section, then from 1975 until 1987, she was education correspondent. This interest in education was at the heart of her journalist work. In 1987, she was made assistant editor, and then finally, she became duty editor and education editor. She married Dermot Mullane, who was an RTÉ journalist and they had a son, Eric. Christina died tragically young, in 1996; I remember it well, it was a Sunday afternoon and I was driving down to Waterford to research my contributions to a supplement on the city in The Irish Times when news came through on the car radio about her radio. When I got to Waterford, the first thing I did was find an old fashioned pay telephone box and tell Bernadette in Dublin the sad news. Does anyone at all use one of those old style phone boxes these days? At Christina's funeral, it was said that there are very few people of whom it can be said "they made a difference". She did.

Subsequently, her husband Dermot, married someone else I knew, Kay McGuinness of the Southern Advertising agency in Limerick and they set up home together in Killaloe.

John Murphy

I first met John Murphy, who had founded the legendary Appletree Press in Belfast in 1965, when I was working in Belfast in the early 1970s. I was keen at that stage to get into books and after length discussions with him, he eventually suggested I edit a fishing book, Fishing in Ireland. I had never done serious fishing in my life and have never had the slightest ambition in that direction, but we recruited three superb contributors, to cover coarse angling, game fishing and sea angling, and the book was eventually produced, in 1979. John had many traumatic experiences when the troubles were bad in the North, including the loss of his then premises, close to the City Hall in Belfast. But he never, ever gave up and has kept his company going right up to the present, based on the rather posh Malone Road in Belfast. One of his big successes has been his series of cookery books, which have sold well in many parts of the world. It wasn' t until he asked me to do a book for him on the history of Calor Gas in Ireland, a few years ago, that I did another title with Appletree, but we' ve always kept in touch; he has long been one of the stalwarts and one of the survivors in the Irish book publishing business.

Mary J. Murphy

Mary is a truly remarkable woman whom I first met when she asked me to do the Galway launch of her book on Eva O' Flaherty, in 2012; thankfully, we' ve been great friends ever since. She' s a true inspiration and if I ever feel "down" she' s the down- to- earth writer who will pep me up. I value her company and her expertise immeasurably. She studied at NUI Galway and she has often told me that her sociology lecturer there was a man called Michael D. Higgins who was so brilliant that he always had full classes at nine o' clock on Monday mornings, a remarkable achievement. The same Michael D. Higgins is now President of Ireland.

She describes herself as a sociable hermit, an independent scholar and an author/ historian. When she did her English degree, her thesis was on the life of the Anglo- Irish writer, Elizabeth Bowen. Then in Dublin City University, she did the postgraduate course in journalism, under Professor John Horgan, majoring in radio and libel law.

She' s been living in Caherlistrane, not too far from Tuam in Co Galway, for close on 30 years. In her younger days, she helped set up a news agency in Dublin, as well as working in Iceland, London and New York. Mary has interviewed the likes of Jimmy Carter, a former US president, and Tammy Wynette, the American singer. She spent some time living in Nashville, Tennessee, where she interviewed Jimmy Carter. As she says herself, staying in Nashville enabled her to follow her true calling, country music.

Her husband, Gerard, introduced her to a friend of his, Brendan Gannon, who told her of the woman he once worked for, Eva O' Flaherty. The end result was an amazing book, Achill' s Eva O' Flaherty, forgotten island heroine, 1874- 1963. Thanks to Mary' s diligent research, Eva is no longer forgotten and has been well honoured in retrospect for her contribution to Achill. She would also like to see a film or documentary made about the life and times of Eva. Mary also has a home on Achill where she and her family, husband Gerard and three children, Morgan, Mason and Minette, stay regularly.

Mary has also contributed to such newspapers as The Irish Times, while at the Connacht Tribune, she' s been writing about music for over two decades. An earlier book by her was Viking Summer, the filming of Alfred the Great in Galway in 1968. Then much more recently, at the end of 2015, she produced another stunning book, all about the village where she lives in Co Galway, Caherlistrane. The foreword to this book was written by Eilish, daughter of Maureen O' Carroll, a one- time TD and mother of Brendan O' Carroll, the famous comedian. Currently, Mary is researching the life of Emily Lawless, an Anglo- Irish poet who was highly regarded by Lady Gregory and W. B. Yeats.

Mike Murphy

Mike Murphy, who was born in Dublin in 1941, had a long broadcasting career, to which he has returned very recently. He has that little bit of devilment in him that made him such an outstanding broadcaster and few people can forget the famous TV clip, when Gay Byrne was trying to make a programme in the square at Trinity College, when a foreign student, who turned out to be Mike Murphy in disguise, kept interrupting him. When all is revealed, by which time everyone except Gaybo was in stitches, one felt that Gaybo would really like to tell Mike Murphy to go and fuck himself.

Beginning with an elevated start in the Dublin Shakesperian Society, Mike Murphy's working life began in a drapery shop, before he got into radio with scripts for sponsored programmes. He had a small part in the film based on the Edna O' Brien film, The Girl with Green Eyes; he became a radio announcer with RTÉ in 1965 and his big break on TV came in 1971 when he presented the national song contest as the prelude to Eurovision. Having worked on so many light entertainment shows on both radio and TV, he surprised many people by developing his own arts show on RTÉ Radio 1. He proved himself an astute interviewer even of the most esoteric artistic personalities. Mike Murphy interviewed me live on various occasions and it was always great fun, for the simple reason you never knew what surprises he was going to throw at you.

He retired from radio and TV broadcasting at the start of the 21st century and once again, created another big surprise, by going into the property development business. That lasted until 2011, then once again, he started making forays into broadcasting.

Peter Murphy

Peter, who was born in Clonegal, just on the borders of counties Carlow and Wicklow, in 1923, became one of the leading lights in farming organisations, before transferring to the media.

He was very active in Macra na Feirme in his his 20s and went on to play a leading role in the setting up of the National Farmers Organisation in 1953. His wife, Bridie, whom he married in 1967, also worked for Macra na Feirme. With all his travels round the country, Peter reckoned he knew people in every townland in Ireland. Yet all through his travels and throughout his life, he retained an intense affection for his native village, even though he and has family have lived for many years in Sandymount, Dublin. Then his distinctive speaking voice brought him to work in radio, where between 1961 and 1979, he presented sponsored radio shows for close on a dozen different companies and organisations. From then, he diversified into television, including on the Land Mark television series about farming, in the 1960s. From there, he went on to present for many years, the Cross Country Quiz programme, which was a joint production between RTÉ and BBC Northern Ireland.

Then between 1973 and 1988, Peter compiled well over a dozen quiz books based on this television series. But even after he formally retired in 1992, he continue to compile quizzes and crosswords and up to the time of his death in 2011, he was compiling a weekly crossword for the Sunday Independent. He was a very pleasant, courteous and humorous person to meet and on one occasion, after I had written a profile of him, he told me that it was the best piece that had ever been written about him.

Nicholas Nally

Up to 2000, the Westmeath Examiner newspaper in Mullingar had had just three editors in its long existence. The paper was founded way back in 1882 by a man called John P. Hayden, who was just 18 at the time. He stayed in the editor' s chair right up to the time he died, in 1954, well into his 90s. Then the mantle passed to Nicholas Nally, who had joined the paper in Hayden's latter years. Nicholas held the reins for 55 years, another remarkable record, until he stepped down in 1999, handing over to David O' Riordan. In 2004, the Celtic Media Group paid €20 million for the paper, which was then 90 per cent owned by Martin McNally, son of Nicholas. The paper has another claim to fame, as well; Joe Dolan, the singer, started there as a trainee compositor. But altogether, the Westmeath Examiner has had a remarkable track record; in 2009, it sponsored the press room for journalists at the new council building housing Westmeath County Council.

Eoin Neeson

A remarkable man from a remarkable family; his father, Seán, who died in 1964, had been the director of the Radio Éireann station in Cork from 1927 until 1931, while his mother, Geraldine, was a long- time music critic for The Irish Times. Eoin himself started as a journalist in the regional press, going on to become editor of The Kerryman, as well as managing editor of a long- defunct paper, the Munster Tribune. Then he moved to Dublin and from 1961 until 1967, he worked with RTÉ. Next he became chief press officer at CIE, the national transport company, before becoming director of the Government Information Bureau. Apart from all that, he was the author of 10 plays and 14 books, mostly about 1916 and the civil war of 1922- 23. He also collected antique weapons, including swords and pistols, and this led to a very embarrassing incident in the 1970s, when he was in charge of government press relations. He used to drive an old style Citroën, the car that used to raise itself up when started, using its air suspension. He was driving this Citroën along Lansdowne Road in Ballsbridge one night when he was stopped by a Garda, who found a gun in the car. Fortunately, Eoin had a good explanation for it, but the incident created a lot of intriguing headlines! Eoin Neeson died in 2011.

Ronnie Nesbitt

He was the only managing director that I' ve known in Ireland who was a regular reader of The Guardian, which he preferred to any other daily newspaper. His family had owned Arnotts, the Dublin department store, since the early 20th century, and Ronnie joined the firm in 1937, eventually becoming managing director. He retired in 1979, when his son, Michael, took over. Ronnie married his wife Ella, a great character in her own right, in 1939, and by the time she died, in 2009, she was aged 92 and a great- grandmother. Her death came a decade after that of her husband. I was fortunate in getting to know both of them quite well, as they lived for years near us, in Heytesbury Lane. These days, Arnotts is owned by the group that owns another noted department store in Dublin, Brown Thomas.

Richard Nixon

The 37th president of the United States, it was Bernadette who met him through her work with the Department of Foreign Affairs, when he and his wife Pat paid a three day visit to Ireland in 1970. They were greeted everywhere they went by anti- Vietnam war protestors. Everyone said that Nixon and that visit to Ireland were only a pale shadow of the Kennedy visit seven years previously, in 1963. Nixon' s ancestors were Irish Quakers, and he went to Timahoe in Co Kildare, where they came from. As for Nixon' s career, it ended in 1974 when he resigned, a consequence of the 1972 break- in at the Democratic national committee headquarters in the Watergate complex in Washington. Yet even though Nixon was such a dull character in comparison to Kennedy, he was responsible for some ground- breaking political changes, such as the rapprochement between the US and China.

Jim Nolan

Around 30 years ago, the Institute of Advertising Practitioners in Ireland, which represents advertising agencies, had a man in charge called Jim Nolan. An advertising man through and through, he was the ultimate smoothie, always sunny side up, always relentlessly positive, a very decent guy to do business with. As I was writing a lot in those days about the business, including my 1986 book on the history of advertising in Ireland, I often met up with Jim, unfailing courteous and benign, unlike some of his colleagues in the industry, who would quite happily be nice and polite to your face, but all the while perfectly capable of a quick stab in the back. Jim was one of a number of outstanding advertising characters then, including Frank Fitzpatrick, the print buyer at Aer Lingus, with whom I had some spectacular booze- ups, including at the Publicity Club, and Michael Hayes, a one- time chairman of the Advertising Press Club. Then there was Eddie O' Mahony, who worked in Peter Owens Advertising and who was the brother of RTÉ' s Andy O' Mahony. As for Peter Owens himself, he was known as the "little grey gnome from the west" (of Ireland). He was the best man for sleight of hand in the advertising business; many was the time that rival agencies crowed about winning an account from Peter Owens, only to find that he had been working feverishly behind the scenes to recover it successfully for himself.

Dr David Nowlan

I got to know Dr Nowlan quite well at The Irish Times; whenever there was a group editorial meeting, he was there, as managing editor, a funny and gentle soul, always very pleasant to have dealings with. He had begun as a medical doctor, then gravitated into journalism, having joined the paper as medical correspondent in the 1960s. He went on to spend 30 years as a theatre critic for the paper and he had a great reputation for speed; within half an hour of the final curtain coming down on a first night in one of Dublin' s city centre theatres, he had finished writing his notice, at The Irish Times, ready for the next morning' s paper.

He also had a keen interest in human rights and he was one of the founding members of the Irish Family Planning Association. Yet another of his enthusiasms, and perhaps his greatest, was for the inland waterways of Ireland. David was a man with an enviable spread of interests, a great loss to all his friends and admirers when he died in 2010.

Professor Kevin B. Nowlan

I only met this particular Nowlan a couple of times, but he was a most erudite and learned man, ever willing to take part in any issue he felt strongly about. He died in 2013, aged 91, but I had met him once or twice, in the company of a great friend of his, Ben Kiely. Kevin Nowlan was once professor of Irish history at UCD, a post he had retired from in 1983. Outside teaching, his interests revolved around Dublin' s heritage, for which he was a tireless campaigner. He was a president of the Dublin Civic Trust, a vice- president of the Irish Georgian Society and a past president of An Taisce. In his younger days, he had spent much time in France and Germany. But besides his historical interests, he had a great appetite for socialising and for engaging most directly in the cultural life of Dublin.

Senator David Norris

He is a most extraordinary person to chat with, full of energy, enthusiasm and knowledge, often very funny, delighting in some straight to the point puns, as in the title of his 2012 autobiography, A Kick against the Pricks. He didn' t spell out what kind of pricks he had in mind, but as everyone in Dublin knows, he has long been a campaigner for gay rights, so not hard to guess!

David was born in Kinsasha in what is now the Democratic Republic of Congo, in 1944, but he returned to Ireland when he was a child. For long on the staff of Trinity College, Dublin, he has long had an interest in everything to do with James Joyce. He has also had a long interest in politics and he's a long- time Senator; he was first elected in 1987, on behalf of Trinity College, and has been re- elected on every subsequent occasion. He can be very outspoken in the Seanad, as well as very witty. He was also an unsuccessful candidate in the 2011 presidential election in Ireland, a contest that became very combative for him.

He has also had major health issues; in 1994, when he was in central Europe on political business, he contracted hepatitis; he ended up having a liver transplant in 2014, which fortunately proved very successful. When I wished him well after the transplant, he was most courteous and good-humoured in his replies. A remarkable scholar and an equally remarkable politician, who's more than ready to tell it as it really is, a rare quality among politicians.

Oliver Nulty

Oliver had some wonderful "first nights" at his Oriel Gallery in Clare Street, Dublin, and also some magnificent parties at his home in Pembroke Lane in Ballsbridge. Bernadette and I were frequent guests and often met some most interesting people. One of the people I well remember meeting at the gallery was a young journalist called Emily O' Reilly, who was working for the old Irish Press. We helped her identify some of the people at the launch. She went on to become Ireland's first female Ombudsman, in 2003, and a decade later, she became European Ombudsman, her current position.

Born in 1920, Oliver named the gallery after the ancient province of Ulster, now Co Louth, the county were he was born. The gallery opened in 1968 and soon became a mecca for the promotion of Irish artists, with particular favourites like Percy French, who was an accomplished water colour artist. Markey Robinson from Belfast was a long time artist on the gallery' s books, with his very distinctive 'primitive' style. On one occasion, he got into an argument with Oliver' s partner Maureen, and broke her arm, a savage assault that was hushed up at the time. Oliver died in 2004 and the gallery was taken over by his son, Mark; since then, it has come through some turbulent times, but has thankfully managed to keep going.

Dr Conor Cruise O' Brien

A remarkable man, he was probably the most pugnacious, and cleverest, Irish intellectual since George Bernard Shaw. Born in 1917, he worked for much of his early career in the Department of External Affairs; he also had a spell as managing director of the Irish News Agency, an ill- fated attempt to run a national news agency in and for Ireland. His second wife was Máire MacEntee, or Máire Mhac An tSaoi, who was born in Dublin in 1922, five years later than the man she married in 1962, after a highly controversial meet- up in the Congo. Máire also worked in the same Department as her husband and during the course of her long life, she has become a noted poet.

In 1969, Conor had an entirely new departure, when he was elected as a Labour TD, then in the Fine Gael/ Labour coalition government, 1973- 77, he was the often controversial Minister for Posts & Telegraphs. When I was preparing my 1983 book on Irish newspaper history, I well remember going out to their home at Howth, where I had a long and very informative discussion with Conor about all his work in the newspaper industry. On another occasion, he and his wife took

Bernadette and myself for drinks in a long defunct Dublin pub called Bartley Dunnes, which had a reputation for being a gay pub. We had a jolly, not to say gay, time, in the other meaning of the word, that sunny afternoon. We saw no evidence of a long- standing myth about Bartley Dunne's, that pennies were glued to the floor. The idea was that men would spot them, then bend down to try and pick them up, giving other gays an ideal opportunity to mount a rear-end assault. Bartholomew Dunne,the pub owner,who lived in Blackrock,Co Dublin,died in September,2016.

Later on, Conor was editor in chief of The Observer in London, between 1978 and 1981. Frequently controversial, something he thrived on, especially for his support of the Unionist community in Northern Ireland, he was rarely out of public notice. He died in 2008.

Denis O' Brien

A remarkable entrepreneur, he was born in 1958 in Co Cork, but grew up in Anglesea Road in Dublin. He got his first job at the age of 14, in the Central Hotel in Exchequer Street, central Dublin. Since then, his interests in Ireland and the rest of Europe in radio stations, his interests in mobile communications in the Caribbean, central America and the Pacific region, to name just two, have made him a very rich man. In 2015, he was described as one of the top 200 billionaires in the world, worth US$6. 9 billion. Here at home in Ireland, he is also the largest shareholder in Independent News & Media. I' ve only met him once and it was rather a long time ago, when one of his Dublin radio stations, 98 FM, was based in Upper Mount Street. I was writing a report on the Irish media industry for a London- based publication and on that one occasion, I found Denis very personable, ready to answer all my questions, sometimes with his good sense of humour much in evidence.

Tommy O' Brien

He was one of the old- style presenters on RTÉ radio, once a household name and often mimicked for his his very personalised kind of presentation. From Clonmel, where he was born in 1905, he began a junior reporter with the Clonmel Chronicle, a Protestant- owned paper, in the early 1930s. When that folded, in 1935, he started with the Clonmel Nationalist, where he soon became senior reporter and in time, the editor. He had taught himself shorthand, so successfully that he had another string to his bow, official stenographer to the Tipperary Circuit Court. He could take shorthand notes at 200 words a minute, without the slightest bother.

Tommy was editor of the Nationalist in Clonmel for 13 years, from 1940 to 1953, but another interest beckoned. From a relatively early age, he had started travelling to London, where he was a regular visit to the opera performances in Covent Garden, and from that developed a huge interest in classical music, especially opera. One day, in the late 1940s, he wrote to one of the head people in Radio Éireann and told him about his interest in Covent Garden and the vast collection of gramophone records he had amassed. The end result was a series of six 15 minute slots called "Covent Garden Memories".

Out of that grew a series called "Your Choice and Mine", which ran on the station for 40 years. He' d travel up to Dublin on the train with his box of records and he told me how once, an American on the train saw the box of records and asked him what he did for a living. "Oh, I' m a DJ", Tommy replied. His introduction to his weekly show was always: "Good evenin' listeners", a phrase that was often imitated.

Quite apart from music and newspapers, Tommy had another abiding interest, billiards. He never married and lived with his sister in an old house high above the town of Clonmel. He was a delightful person to know, full of stories in his very distinctive accent, and when I heard, in early 1988, that he was very ill in hospital, it was a bitter blow knowing that at his age, he was unlikely to recover. He died that same year, the death of a true legend on Irish radio.

Diarmuid Ó Broin

For the best part of 30 years, he ran the commercial side of Management magazine, founded in 1967 and published by the Irish Management Institute; it no longer exists, having been closed down 20 years ago. Diarmuid was an an exceptionally talented person, besides being consistently extrovert and often humorous, and his many friends often wondered why he stayed in that particular job for so long and didn' t put his abilities to more demanding use.

Before he made the transition to the magazine, he had worked for Eason' s Advertising, an offshoot of the newsagents' chain, and one of the smaller ad agencies in Dublin. But he also had a keen interest in Irish culture; he was a long time member of Gael Linn, which promotes Irish language and culture. Indeed, I've seen a photograph taken in 1959, of Diarmuid as the compere at a Gael Linn concert in Bundoran. The harpist in the group is Kathleen Watkins, wife of Gay Byrne. Diarmuid had also been the national organiser at Gael Linn for a long time, so he was deeply devoted to the organisation. It was there that he first met Bernadette, my wife, and he had a long time grá for her. Diarmuid' s wife, Colette, is a former principal of Stratford College in Rathgar. Diarmuid died in August, 2003.

Éimear Ó Broin

I had seen him in action during the late 1960s, as a conductor of the RTÉ Orchestras, then when I was researching my book on Bewleys, published in 1980, I discovered an interesting anecdote about him, when he was a student during the second world war. His father Leon was an influential figure, secretary of the Department of Posts and Telegraphs from 1948 to 1967 and deeply involved in the setting up of the Irish television service, which started in 1962. He was also an accomplished author, in both Irish and English, writing nearly 20 books, in both Irish and English, and three plays.

The family home was in Booterstown and Éimear told of how during the second world, he often tuned in on the radio to the marvellous Beethoven concerts that were staged in Germany, even at the height of hostilities. Eventually, he worked for a long time as a conductor with Radio Éireann and then RTÉ, conducting both the symphony orchestra and the concert orchestra. He was short in stature, but that didn' t stop him being a compelling presence on the podium.

When I first saw him conducting, in the late 1960s, it was often at the Francis Xavier Hall just behind the church of the same name in the north inner city. Friday night concerts there were free and it was a regular ritual to collect tickets at the old radio studios at the top of the GPO. The concerts always attracted full houses. The principal conductor of the symphony orchestra was a volatile Hungarian called Tibor Paul, born in Budapest. If someone came in late to one of his concerts, he would stop the orchestra and wait until that person was seated before resuming. He was eventually sacked by RTÉ, a scandal that made front page newspaper headlines.

I well remember having a detailed conversation with Éimear in 2006 when I was writing An Irishman's Diary column for The Irish Times about music making in Dublin in the late 1940s and early 1950s. He recalled almost every note of every concert then. In 1947, Radio Éireann had split its orchestra into two parts, a symphony orchestra and a light orchestra. The public concerts were held in the Phoenix Hall, off Exchequer Street, close to the telephone exchange. The hall had 400 hard wooden benches for audiences to sit on and despite the discomfort, they turned up in their droves, to see such musical legends as the Croatian conductor, Milan Horvat, Hans Schmidt- Isserstedt, the German conductor, and Charles Lynch, the corpulent but brilliant pianist from Cork. Concerts were held there three times a week, until in the early 1960s, they were transferred to the Francis Xavier Hall and then eventually to the National Concert Hall, converted from the old great hall at UCD in Earlsfort Terrace, nearly 40 years ago.

The last time that I was talking with an elderly Éimear, he was plagued by pain from his various ailments and could only read about music and listen to it. He died in 2013, survived by his wife Patricia, who in her heyday was a well- known concert pianist.

Enda O' Coineen

I' ve known Enda, who' s a native of Galway, for years. He' s now close to 60, but when he was in his 20s, he was very involved in maritime affairs, having started Afloat magazine, still going strong. He also sailed the Atlantic single- handedly, from Boston to Galway, a feat that attracted a lot of attention. But then after the Berlin Wall fell in 1989 and the communist regimes behind the Iron Curtain fell like a pack of dominoes, he made a decision that surprised his many friends. He went to what was then Czechoslovakia, to begin a business career in Prague. He started off selling cheap phone calls, which was a real novelty for consumers there, and eventually built up a business empire in what became the Czech Republic.

He has invested, very successfully, in several sectors there, including engineering, property, renewable energy and telecoms and these days is reckoned to be worth around €50 million. In 2015, he was worth €45 million, but the previous year, he had been worth a mere €35 million.

Dave O' Connell

I know Dave O' Connell, the group editor of the Connacht Tribune, quite well. He had started his media career there in 1983 before going on to work at several other regional newspapers and being made editor of the Westmeath Independent in 2001. In between, he had also worked for such titles as the Cork Examiner and the Irish Daily Star, then finally, seven years ago, he returned to where he had started, this time as group editor. The Connacht Tribune is the only paid newspaper in Galway and it' s been going for 104 years. It also has an ever increasing online presence. Dave has always been very helpful to me when I' ve been looking for a quote about the newspaper business; he also sometimes does the Friday afternoon review of the regional newspapers, on RTÉ Radio I.

Dave' s wife is Teresa Mannion, who is a journalist working for RTÉ out of Galway; she often presents news segments from her part of the country. In December, 2015, when she was reporting from Salthill on the Six One television news about the tremendous storm raging at the time in the West of Ireland. She was hardly able to get a word in edgeways, because the wind was so ferocious. The video clip created a sensation on the Internet and made Teresa an instant media star!

Don O' Connell

He was undoubtedly the maddest of the mad men in Dublin' s ad agencies, even though he had a lot of competition; yet no-one could beat him for sheer eccentricity, although he was a talented business person.

Originally a merchant seaman, which was where he had acquired his pronounced limp, when he returned home, he worked for the old Irish Press group selling advertising.

Then in the mid- 1960s, he set up his own agency, Doherty Advertising. His japes there were the stuff of legend. On one occasion, he invited a potential client to his offices for a presentation. As soon as the man walked into his office, Don took his overcoat, and then threw it out of the open window. The man saw his overcoat go sailing down towards the pavement, but Don had stationed someone there to catch it and bring it back. Why did Don perform such an outrageous stunt, especially when he didn' t win the account? The answer was simple; according to Don, the man would never, ever, forget Doherty Advertising. He was also a very inventive copywriter. It was he who created the tagline for Zhivago' s, the old nightclub in Fitzwilliam Lane, "where love stories begin" and he invented the "almost nationwide" tag line for Shaw' s department stores.

On another occasion, when I was writing copy about the advertising business, he took me out to lunch and promptly made a series of extremely derogatory remarks about the anorak I was wearing. Diplomacy and tact were never in his armoury. He did all sorts of other odd things; the family home was in Dalkey, and in the mornings, when he was driving into work, if he saw a complete stranger waiting forlornly at a bus stop, Don would stop and offer the person, male or female, a lift, something no- one would do nowadays.

But he took over a rival ad agency in Lower Baggot Street, Padburys, and when Don reached 70, he sold the enlarged agency for €6 million. He died in 2007, one of the last of the true eccentric characters in the Dublin ad agency business.

Professor Maurice O' Connell

Bernadette and I got to know Prof O' Connell and his wife well; while they were living in the US, they also kept an apartment on the Clonskeagh Road in south Dublin, which they used as their summer base for many years. We lived very close by, from 1977, when we' d given up the house with the low mortgage in Drogheda, because commuting by train to Dublin was then so wearing, until 1988, so we often had chats with them.

He was a very friendly soul, even if he could go on a bit, but then we' re all capable of doing the same, myself included. Maurice was born in Co Tipperary in 1922 and he was the great- great grandson of Daniel O' Connell, the Liberator. Maurice started studying medicine at Trinity College, Dublin, in 1939, but it didn' t really agree with him. He then found an opening for himself in the Bank of Ireland, where he worked for the next 12 years. During the last three of those years, he did a night- time degree at UCD and in 1955, went to the US, to pursue work and study opportunities at the University of Pennsylvania.

In 1964, he joined the staff of Fordham, the Jesuit university in New York, and remained there for the rest of his career, mostly as professor of British and Irish history. He made several attempts to get appointed to a chair in history at an Irish university, but this ambition remained unfulfilled. He eventually retired from Fordham in 1988, after 44 years there, and came back to Ireland for good. His wife was Betty McCan, who worked in the old National Bank in Ireland; they were married in 1962; her uncle had been a founding member of Sinn Féin in 1905. While Maurice was working at Fordham, she had a job as a secretary to a Wall Street brokerage in New York, which is where they were living.

In the last years of his life, Maurice and his wife moved out to Blackrock and they also had a cottage on the O' Connell estate in Derrynane, Co Kerry. Maurice had managed to achieve two of his main ambitions, to see the reputation restored of his ancestor, Daniel O' Connell, and to see O' Connell' s great house and estate at Derrynane fully restored. When I was working on the Michelin Green Guide to Ireland, around 1990, we visited Derrynane, where a substantial part of the restoration had already been carried out.

Maurice was pre- deceased by his wife Betty; he suffered a stroke in 1995, which had debilitating effects, especially on his writing and on his memory. He died in 2005 and was buried at Derrynane Abbey.

Fergal O' Connor

In the mid- 1960s, I decided to try and do something that would rectify my leaving Magee College in Derry without bothering to complete my degree course. I did something that now seems rather bizarre; I enrolled for an evening diploma course in business administration, which needless to remark I never finished. There' s just something about me and academia that doesn't remotely gel! But I distinctly remember the highlight of that course, lectures by that renowned priest, Fergal O' Connor, a true inspiration. He had been born near Causeway in Co Kerry in 1926; from 1961, he lived in Dublin. He lectured in the department of politics at UCD, then in Earlsfort Terrace, from 1962 to 1992.

He had a deep regard for social concerns and what' s more, outside his teaching work, put his beliefs into practical effect. He set up Ally, an organisation that supported single mothers, and he founded Sherrard House, a hostel for homeless girls in Dublin. His commitment to social justice was overwhelming and his passion was at the heart of all his lectures in UCD, truly inspirational. He was often a very provocative guest on the Late Late Show.

Fergal remained a truly inspirational teacher right up to the end of his life; although he officially retired in 1992, he kept on teaching Plato to final year students every year up until 1998. He died in 2005, at the age of 79 and was buried in the plot at Glasnevin belonging to the Dominican Community of St Saviour' s Priory in Dublin.

Moira O' Connor Jenks

She and I became friends when I worked in Business & Finance, in Creation Arcade in Grafton Street, in the mid-1960s. Moira was secretary to Nicholas Leonard, the editor, and even though I was the office junior, and she was much older than me, we hit it off straight away and became friends for the rest of her life, until she died in 2013, aged 90.

Moira was a northsider, brought up in the family home at Griffith Avenue in Dublin, somewhere I visited on several occasions. She was educated in both Dublin and London and then spent 10 years working with the American Newspaper Association in London. Then she returned home to Dublin and promptly started work with Business & Finance when it began in 1964. Her stay there was relatively brief, as she emigrated to the US in 1968 to marry Homer S. Jenks, a journalist living in Boston. Moira became a naturalised American citizen and for decades, she contributed much to arts and culture in that most Irish of all American cities. She wrote many articles, gave frequent talks, did tours of the Massachusetts State House and was a long standing member of Boston University Womens' Guild.

But she frequently came home to Dublin on visits and inevitably, when she was here, she and I would meet up for a little reminiscing; she was always great company and knew everyone and everything. Quite often, she brought Homer with her, so we got to know him as well. He was quite a character, a senior American journalist of the old school. He' d been born in Massachusetts in 1914 and apart from war service during the second world war, had a long career in newspapers. From 1962 to 1964, he was managing editor of the Boston Traveler, a newspaper that no longer exists; he was particularly proud of the issue they produced when President John F. Kennedy was assassinated in Dallas, Texas, on November 22, 1963. That day, they sold an extra 100, 000 copies. From there, he went to work at the Boston Herald, becoming assistant managing editor, and happily, that paper is still going, along with its opposition, the Boston Globe. Homer died in 1995; Moira carried on for nearly 20 more years, although her latter years were spent in a care home and her letters got more and more infrequent. Herself and Homer had one child, a daughter, Jacqueline, but even though Moira often told us of her, we have never met her.

I still have vivid memories of one occasion that Homer and Moira were in Dublin and we took them out to dinner one night in the old Kilmartin's bistro in Upper Baggot Street. It was an excellent meal and everyone was in great company, except that I found it very off- putting that a patron at the next table insisted on blowing cigarette smoke over as wide an area as possible. When I asked him politely to desist, he got most annoyed. I' ve always thought, since then, that the anti-smoking legislation, banning smoking on buses and trains, in restaurants and all other public places, has been one of the most socially advanced pieces of legislation in Ireland over the past few decades. We set a global example and it' s good to see that it has been copied in many other countries, including and especially France, where it long seemed that the idea of a good night out was to "drown" in a fug of blue cigarette smoke.

Frank O' Donoghue

He is one of my more recent friends; he and his wife Anna live in the town of Tramore, a lovely spot, with a superb beach and promenade, and now the biggest town in Co Waterford, outside Waterford city. I didn' t know him when he was running the city' s Chamber of Commerce, but instead got to know him recently when I wrote An Irishman' s Diary in The Irish Times about the old Waterford to Tramore railway. Eeveryone I talked with on the subject said that I must read Frank' s book on the subject. He self- published a book called The 5- Minute Bell the history of the Tramore train, 1853- 1860. Frank knows the whole story inside out and did a fantastic job of research and design with his book. It ended up with the two of us meeting up for coffee and having a good chat on the subject. He brought similar expertise to bear on another book in similar style, Goin' to the Pictures, old style cinema going in Waterford city and county, that he did together with Andy Kelly. Frank' s two books couldn't be bettered by the most professional publishers and I must admit it' s great to see self- publishing like this making such great advances.

Cardinal Tómas Ó Fiaich

I only met the Cardinal on one occasion, at a "do" in the Austrian Embassy in Dublin. But who hadn' t heard of him? He was a national figure of the first importance and a time when the northern troubles at their height, he made no secret of his pro- nationalist and republican views, since he was a native of South Armagh, where he was born in 1923. He had a typical Northern "no nonsense" approach and said explicitly what was on his mind. The British political establishment was very wary of him, to say the least, and that hostility was also evident in parts of the political establishment in Dublin. But many people really appreciated the fact that he spoke his mind on the troubles and the causes of their gestation. He was Catholic Primate of All Ireland from 1977 to 1990, when he died suddenly on a pilgrimage to Lourdes.

The time that I met him, we had a great conversation; he was genuinely friendly and welcoming. I found him very open and approachable. He was familiar with my work and when he said that he had read my first book on Irish newspaper history, published in 1983, alarm bells began to ring. It had some strong stuff, especially in the bad language department, enough to make most clerics dish out the incense! I asked the

Cardinal what he thought and did he have any objection to the bad language. He laughed "not at all, I'm well used to it". Many high officials in the Catholic or indeed other churches, can be timid about expressing opinions or else are extremely conscious of the importance of their high office; Cardinal Ó Fiach was neither and I must admit that after meeting him, I had great admiration for his straight talking.

Martin O' Flaherty

During the time that Eamon de Valera was President of Ireland, his official secretary, and therefore someone of much influence, was Martin O' Flaherty, Máirtín Ó Flaitheartaigh in Irish. He was a mild mannered man but a stickler for getting all the details right. From Co Galway, he always had a great adherence to Irish and used it on every possible occasion.

When Bernadette was working in the Department of External Affairs, Máirtín had a habit of ringing her up at home, early in the morning, long before she was due in the office at 9 am, to discuss the table plans for a dinner that would have planned for that evening that involved the President. Who sits where at these occasions is always an occasion of great diplomatic skill and when Máirtín rang, it was always to ensure that between himself and Bernadette, the table plans were always as perfect they should be. Just to complicate matters, he also insisted on having these conversations in Irish, but fortunately, Bernadette has always had perfect Irish. He and his wife lived for many years in Mount Eden Road in Donnybrook and after his wife died, he continued to live there, although friends were always concerned that he would look after himself properly. I remember clearly the last time that Bernadette and I had a conversation with him, while he was doing the simplest of tasks. He had gone to Donnybrook Fair, near his home, to get some meat for his supper.

Willie O' Hanlon

For years, Willie O' Hanlon was the owner and managing director of the Anglo- Celt newspaper in Cavan. When I was doing my first book on Irish newspaper history, the Anglo- Celt was a fount of information on the history of their newspaper, which was founded in 1846. For nearly 20 years after it was started, it had various breaks in publication, but then managed to settle down. The O' Hanlon family had owned it since the mid- 1860s. Willie was born in 1924 and went on to spend his career running the paper and for many years, he often wrote the main leader in the paper, week by week. Many a local politician was stung in action by what Willie had written. He had become managing director in 1958, when he was 34; eventually, in 2004, the paper was sold to the Celtic Media Group. Even though Willie was a very decent kind of guy, always obliging and willing to help, he was bit of an oul' gasbag and people soon found to their cost that once Willie had been encouraged to start talking on a favourite subject, stopping him was well nigh impossible. On one occasion in RTÉ television, when it was running a middle of the day chat show hosted by Marty Whelan and Mary Kennedy, they did a segment about the newspaper business. They invited two people as guests, Willie and myself. Getting all made up was a hilarious experience and I kept it on for the rest of that day- it must have been an improvement. At one stage, I bumped in Appie Kennedy, Tom Kennedy's wife, and the make- up elicited some typically humorous comments from her. But back to the chat show. Willie was just unstoppable; not even Marty Whelan could get a word in edgeways and what had been meant as a segment on the newspaper industry came across as Willie O' Hanlon waxing endlessly lyrical. He died in 2013.

Fionnuala O' Kelly

Better known as Enda Kenny' s better half, I knew her quite well when she was a press officer in RTÉ. She comes from a Dublin family- her father was brought up on Co Kerry- that' s staunchly Fianna Fáil and through the 1980s and into the early 1990s, she was press officer for that party, official spokesperson for Charlie Haughey. Later, she headed up the Government Information Service. She never put up with any nonsense and on one occasion, she threw a file at Charlie after one of his outbursts; afterwards, he did something very rare, he apologised. After doing a line for a decade, Fionnuala and Enda got married in 1992. Since 1997, the family home has been in Castlebar, Co Mayo.

While I' ve met her, I' ve never met him. Enda seems decent, genial and well- meaning, but a lot of what happened when he was taoiseach between 2011 and 2016 was more bluster and blarney than anything else. Many vital issues, like homelessness, were simply ignored, while vital sectors in Irish life, such as the public health service, were left in a semi-ruined state. He was re-elected Taoiseach in May, 2016 – will we have more of the same or will there be even more chaos? A friend of mine, who' s into politics in a big way, compiled a list of all the promises made by Fine Gael and Labour before they formed the government in 2011 and then noted all the promises that had been broken. It turned out to be an email of extraordinary length, which my friend duly fired off to every member of the two houses of the Oireachtas.

Andy O' Mahony

A very bookish but very affable man (the two aren' t incompatible), I only ever took part in one radio broadcast with Andy, but got to know him well on the shopping circuit! Since he lived near the Merrion Centre in Dublin 4, I often bumped into him there and we' d have a little chat about the state of the world and in particular, the Irish media, although sadly, I haven' t seen him there for quite some time now.

From Clonmel, Co Tipperary, where he was born in 1934, he got a variety of academic honours, including a PhD in Psychology from Trinity College, Dublin, while he was also a Visiting Fellow in the Department of Philosophy at Harvard. In his working career, he began as a clerk in a food company in Clonmel, in 1952/ 3, "'graduating" to the Bank of Ireland, where he worked until 1961. During his last year with the bank, he also did part- time announcing and news reading work with Radio Éireann. He joined the national broadcaster full- time in 1961 and during his first decade there, was a television as well as a radio newsreader. He left the newsroom in 1972 to concentrate on feature programmes. In the decades that followed, he presented several television series, as well as a host of radio shows. Probably the best- known radio show that he presented was Off the Shelf. He also worked for the BBC in Belfast, on radio and television shows about well- known writers.

Andy retired as a contributor to RTÉ at the end of 2013, when he was 79. In 2015, he donated his personal library of over 7, 000 books to the Glucksman Library in the University of Limerick.

Des O' Malley

He was a Limerick solicitor who came to political prominence in the 1970s and 1980s; he left the Fianna Fáil party and was a key figure in the founding of the Progressive Democrats in 1985, a notable shift to the right in Irish politics and succour for the money making classes. The first time I saw him in action was in the late 1960s, when I was attending a press reception in the old Royal Hibernian Hotel in Dawson Street, Dublin, when most of those attending, including in an official capacity, had been busy enjoying what was on offer at the bar with some considerable zest. Personally, I never put too much credence in the Progressive Democrats who eventually fizzled out. In 2014, O' Malley published his autobiography, Conduct Unbecoming: A Memoir. Reviewing it in The Irish Times, historian Diarmaid Ferriter gave it a monumental put- down, saying it was "an infuriatingly bad and poorly written book". O' Malley, born in 1939, has long since retired from politics.

Liam Ó Murchú

Liam, who died in June, 2015, aged 86, was an unfailingly genial personality both on and off screen; he was exactly the same person onscreen as off it, and Bernadette and I used to meet him quite regularly in the Roundwood Inn at Roundwood in Co Wicklow, run for well over 30 years by a delightful couple, Jürgen and Áine Schwalm. Jurgen comes from what was Konigsberg, now the Russian Baltic enclave of Kaliningrad, while his wife is Irish.

Their Roundwood Inn was the ideal setting for cosy chats over lunch or dinner, such as we had with Liam, a most convivial person. Born in Cork, after he graduated from UCC, he eventually joined RTÉ in 1964 as editor of Irish language programmes and later became assistant controller of programmes and assistant to the Director- General. But he was also an excellent broadcaster and many people remember vividly such shows that he presented as Trom agus Éadrom. Liam left RTÉ in 1988 to set up his own production company, but still returned to television screens from time to time as a presenter.

Paddy O' Neill

Paddy was a long- time radio producer with RTÉ; he had previously been in the Army and he never lost his military bearing. During the 1980s, the station was very involved in community radio throughout the country and he was the person who organised this new broadcasting stream. Into the 1980s and 1990s, Radio 1 had an especially gifted man at the helm, Michael Littleton, who was head of features and current affairs. I always remember that in 1992, I had made a proposal to Radio 1 to do a series on the regional and national newspaper industry. One day, I got a phone call from Michael Littleton to say that he had decided to go ahead with the series; I was a little gobsmacked, to say the least, but then he summoned me to go and meet him at the Radio Centre. He dreamed up the very apposite title for the series, Paper Tigers.

But back to Paddy; after Eddie MacSweeney, aka Maxwell Sweeney, died in 1991, Paddy took over as producer of Sunday Miscellany, inheriting all the contributors. He continued to use my contributions to the programme but I got the distinct impression at first that he didn't quite know what to make of me. But in time, as we got to know each other better, he relaxed a lot. He died in 1995; Bernadette and I went to his funeral in the Catholic church at Foxrock, south Dublin. I remember one person who was then very well known in RTÉ venting his displeasure at us being there; after all, I was a mere freelance, not a highly paid super star! I thought it was a very odd and un- Christian attitude to have at a funeral.

Alpho O' Reilly

Bernadette knew Alpho for much longer than I did; he came from Westport, Co Mayo, and spent all his working life in theatrical and television design. He began by working for a number of years at the Gate Theatre in Dublin, where he not only designed many of the productions, but helped make many of the sets himself, as well as acting in some of those productions. Then when the new Irish television service, Telefís Éireann, was about to start in 1961, Alpho was made head of design. Subsequently, in 1972, he was promoted to director of design and held that position until he retired; in his long years in television design, he ensured many striking set designs. He was also a very affable person to know, but then towards the end of his life, he was involved in a strange mystery that has never been solved.

In his latter years, his health declined and he often seemed confused. At the start of the new year in 1996, Bernadette and I bumped into him on Sandymount Green, when he seemed very confused, unwell and unsure of what he was doing. He lived nearby, on Strand Road, by himself; he had never married. Then on January 4, 1996, he disappeared. The last sighting of him was at a petrol station in Ashford, Co Wicklow, at 3 am, when he was filling up his car with petrol. He was never seen again and neither was his almost brand new car ever discovered.

Alpho, who was 74, had disappeared into thin air. He is still on the Garda missing persons file and from that day to this, there has never been the slightest hint of what happened to either him or his car. Some people believed that he was on his way to catch a ferry at Rosslare and that he might have taken a ferry to either Britain or mainland Europe to start a new life there, but his state of health at the time was so poor that this explanation seems highly unlikely.

Sir Anthony O' Reilly

Born in 1936 and brought up in relatively modest circumstances on Dublin' s northside, he first came to fame as an international rugby star. Then in the 1960s, when he worked for the Irish Dairy Board, he had the first of his many marketing triumphs with the creation of the Kerrygold butter brand, which quickly became an international success. From there, it was across the Atlantic, to the Heinz corporation in Philadelphia, where he ran that vast food processing company with great aplomb. It was he was at Heinz that I sought to interview him for the grocery trade magazine I was then editing in Belfast. I was rather surprised to get back a quick affirmative, with an invitation to visit him at his Castlemartin estate in Co Kildare.

He was the genial host, only too ready to answer all my questions without hesitation; it was an engaging interview and when it appeared in print, I was happy with the outcome. His great sense of humour was evident and when I was leaving, he said to me: "I have a little going away present for you". He went into the kitchen and fetched out a tin of Heinz baked beans; it was what you might call payola on a minute scale!

While Anthony O' Reilly was still deeply involved in the running of Heinz, he also engineered his takeover of Independent Newspapers from the Murphy family, who' d owned it since the start of the 20th century. The 1973 takeover was a dramatic moment in Irish newspaper history, but by today' s standards, it was a comparatively modest affair and cost little over £1 million. While Independent Newspapers was under O' Reilly' s control, it never suffered from proprietorial interference. He also saw the Independent group expand enormously, in markets far beyond Ireland, while here, it bought up many regional newspapers. The group later became the owners of the Independent, which had been launched in London in 1986. The London Independent was little more than a burden, financially, to Independent Newspapers, but it was a good calling card for Tony O' Reilly. He also took a British knighthood, becoming Sir Anthony O' Reilly, something that didn' t always go down well at home in Ireland.

Tony O' Reilly stepped down as ceo of Independent Newspapers, which had become Independent News & Media, in 2009, to be succeeded by one of his sons, Gavin. I got to know Gavin far better than his father, from the time he was deputy managing director. Quite often, when he was running the group, he' d invite me out to the group headquarters in Citywest for a chat about the latest media developments, which I'd turn into copy for one of the publications for which I was then working. Gavin has followed his father in being someone of immense charm and ability; Gavin also took over the time consuming role of president of the World Association of Newspapers. When I first got to know Gavin, he was still married to Alison Doody, a former Bond girl, whom he had married in 1994, and Gavin often talked about his two daughters. Gavin and Alison were divorced in 2006 and six years later, Gavin remarried, this time to Danish woman Christina Grimm.

In the end, Independent News & Media went belly up for the O' Reillys. A long takeover battle by Denis O' Brien resulted in the O' Reillys being ousted and O' Brien becoming the largest shareholder, although not the controlling shareholder.

Tony O' Reilly had an equal disaster with the Waterford Glass company, which merged with Wedgwood, the English pottery firm. The joint firm that was created managed to lose hundreds of millions of euro and it went bust in 2009. O' Reilly has often been described as Ireland' s first billionaire, but in recent years, his financial fortunes have waned dramatically, from his halcyon days of unlimited wealth. One of the properties he disposed of was Castlemartin, where he had given me a present of a can of Heinz baked beans all those years previously.

P. P. O' Reilly

P. P. was one of the stars of RTÉ for many years; he could do no wrong. He was born in Liverpool in 1915, to Irish parents, and during the second world war, he served in the Irish Army, from 1940 to 1946. Not long after, he began his broadcasting career with Radio Éireann and when Telefís Éireann came along in 1962, he soon found plenty to do there, including presenting Broadsheet, the station' s first current affairs programme. It was hugely successful and ran for 393 episodes, with P. P. in charge. When it ended, it was replaced by Newsbeat, but P. P. went on to present all kinds of other TV programmes. For long, he was a personality at Montrose who could do no wrong, with a vast office to match his standing at the station. But then all of a sudden, in one of those whirlwinds that can blow up in an instant in broadcasting, he suddenly found himself out of favour.

But despite that, in the latter part of his broadcasting career, one of his regular slots was What it says in the Papers, broadcast after the early morning news. He often did these reviews from Monday to Friday and of him it was often said that he was the best presenter of its daily newspaper reviews that Radio 1 has ever had. Everything was pronounced perfectly, whatever language was involved. Even the names of remote cities and countries far from Ireland, if they were mentioned by him, were always pronounced with absolute precision.

Bernadette knew P. P. for years before I did, and when I got to know him, he and I became firm friends, always a most agreeable and knowledgeable person to have a discussion with. For many years, P. P. and his wife lived in Bray, then they moved to Naas, Co Kildare, where his wife Antoinette' s family owned a pub in the centre of the town. Sadly, P. P.' s wife had a long running battle with alcohol addiction, but she recovered and managed to well outlast her husband. I always remember that the last time I met P.

P., it was in the family pub in Naas, and he was suffering from such serious lung trouble that he spent the whole time coughing and spluttering. He died in 1995; after his death, Antoinette asked my advice about getting a book together about P. P.' s life and times in broadcasting, but sadly, it never materialised. He had a fascinating career in radio and television that had run for nearly 50 years and this was one potentially good book that never came to fruition. Antoinette herself died in 2012.

Peadar Ó Riada

I never knew his father, Seán, although his father' s music, especially in the 1960s was so standout as to be unforgettable, such as his score for the film Mise Éire. His blend of Irish traditional music and classical music was outstanding, but Seán died young, in 1971, aged 40, from cirrhosis of the liver. He loved the 'wedge', two generous glasses of whiskey separated by a pint of Guinness! But the mantle has long since passed to his son, Peadar, whom I do know, renowned as a composer, musican and choir director. He also has a dazzling mix of other interests, including film making, beekeeping, painting, writing, radio presentation, on Lyric FM, alternative medicine, and different cultures and traditions from around the world. In the sheer variety of his interests, he is definitely his father's son. Peadar' s discography alone is very impressive, quite apart from his other numerous creations.

Mary O' Rourke

She was long one of the most charasmatic Fianna Fáil politicians, always ready to call a spade a spade. From Athlone, she comes from a family of politicians; her brother was the late Brian Lenihan senior. Mary was minister for a number of departments, probably most memorably education, where she was in charge from 1987 to 1991. I well remember meeting her at a presentation in the now disgraced and abolished Fás organisation in Upper Baggot Street, just as I once had a chat with her brother Brian, who told me that if he had his choice of career over again, it would have been as a journalist.

Mary moved on to become a senator, from 2002 to 2007; she has an uncanny knack of hitting the headlines, in no more spectacular fashion than when she admitted taking Ministerial phone calls while she was having her morning bath. It was a revelation that she has never managed to live down.

Cathal O' Shannon

Of all the media personalities I' ve known over the years, Cathal was one of my favourites. It was always a joy to have a conversation with him about the media, because the way he told his stories, and the often astonishing claims he made, created marvellous fables. He became a journalist with The Irish Times and many of his best stories dated from the period he spent with that newspaper.

When I was doing the Paper Tigers radio series in 1992, Cathal told me some priceless stories, which I dutifully recorded in the lovely house he and his wife Patsy had on Anglesea Road in south Dublin. He told me for instance, that on one occasion, the Church of Ireland correspondent came into the paper one night with his notes for the following week. One of the sub- editors was ffing and blinding like no- one' s business, a stellar performance of bad language. The Church of Ireland correspondent heard all this and sounded quite shocked, at which someone piped up: "You'll have to excuse so and so, he' s our arts editor".

One story he told for that programme was absolutely hilarious, but we decided not to air it; today, of course, we would have and no- one would have taken any notice. It concerned a very argumentative sub- editor at The Irish Times; he came from Belfast and typically, would always speak his mind. One night, he was having his dinner off a plate on his desk, when his boss came by and asked him to do something extra, which he thought unreasonable. The sub- editor simply stood up, unzipped himself and plonked his genitals on his dinner plate, asking his boss "Do ye want these as well?"

Cathal was born in Dublin in 1928, the son of Cathal O' Shannon senior, who came from the North, a well- known socialist and republican. Cathal senior died in 1969. Young Cathal was brought up in the Fairview district of Dublin and when he was 16, joined the RAF, serving in Burma. On returning home, he became a journalist in quick order, eventually being sent to work in The Irish Times' London office. There, he met Patsy Dyke, her real name, an English magazine journalist.

Patsy became a well- known journalist in Dublin, writing gossip columns for the old Sunday Review and Sunday Press newspapers. I well remember, in the mid- 1960s, that in Dublin city centre on a Saturday night, people would clamour for the first editions of the Sunday Press to see what Patsy had been writing about. She told me one hilarious story about the time she went to meet Patrick Lenihan, a TD from 1965 until 1973, and father of Brian Lenihan senior and Mary O' Rourke. Patrick suggested they form a little group and go and see some of the tourist sights of the Midlands. It turned into a four day bender and when Patsy got back to Dublin, she was still so sozzled she could scarcely remember a moment of the trip, but somehow, she managed to bang out her copy.

For much of the 1980s, Cathal and Patsy lived in Limerick, as Cathal was in charge of public relations at Alcan, the aluminium processing plant on the Shannon estuary.

He made no bones about it; he took the job for the money, as it paid five times the going rate in RTÉ. Before he went to Limerick, he already made some of the most memorable TV programmes of his career, including his interview with Muhammed Ali in 1972 and a 1972 documentary, Even the Olives are Bleeding about the Spanish civil war. Much later in his career, in 2007, he made a programme about the Nazis who came to live in Ireland, a highly controversial subject.

Patsy, to whom he was married for over 50 years, died in 2006. Subsequently, he confessed that he had been unfaithful on many occasions, as a serial shagger, and hinting that Patsy might well have been equally promiscuous. Cathal died in 2011, aged 83.

John O' Sullivan

At the height of the crazy property boom in Ireland, before it all came crashing down in 2008, I was writing lots of copy for a magazine called Shopping Centre Ireland. At that stage, shopping centres were opening all over the place and the magazine did well by covering them all, before itself collapsing and disappearing. I remember being at a dinner of shopping centre managers and developers, in the Conrad Hotel in Dublin, one night in 2008 and thinking to myself that the whole property bubble is about to burst, there' ll never be another occasion like this.

One of the property developers I got to know well, and like, was John O' Sullivan. From south Kerry, he had graduated from the Dublin Institute of Technology and started off teaching engineering and technical drawing. Then he got into small scale development in Dublin, before deciding to move to Athlone, the home town of his wife. Eventually, he came to own the Hodson Bay Hotel near Athlone and the Galway Bay Hotel in Salthill and he was also responsible for developing the Athlone Town Centre, which cost €500 million and which started trading in 2007. Getting the centre built was quite a saga, and I went through every step of it, as I reported on the latest stage. Then came the crash. The centre was taken over by AIB in 2013.

Michael O' Toole

Michael was the very gifted journalist from Hospital, Co Limerick who wrote Dubliner' s Diary in the old Evening Press. He had met his wife Maureen Browne when she too was working in newspapers in Limerick, then they graduated to Dublin. Michael was just 26 when he joined the Irish Press group. For night after night, year after year, he kept the diary going in the Evening Press. Going to one function after another, always coming up with an interesting angle and fresh copy was always a mighty challenge. I remember vividly on one occasion interviewing Michael in Mulligan' s, the pub that was so popular with Irish Press workers. He described what it was like being an employee of the Irish Press: "like living and working on the San Andreas fault in California" was his instant and memorable reply. Michael came to a sad end; he was found dead one day in 2000 on the beach at Portmarnock in north Co Dublin, close to the family home. He was only 61.

Our only film appearance

We' ve managed to appear in just one movie. One day in 1976, we were flying to Vienna via Heathrow- in those days, there were no direct flights from Dublin to Vienna. As we were in the middle of changing planes at Heathrow, a production assistant approached us and asked if we could spare a few minutes to be unpaid extras in a film scene. The film in question was a Hammer Films production and was called To the Devil a Daughter. It starred Christopher Lee and among the other stars was Nastasha Kinski. The film was duly released and was shown at the old Ambassador cinema in Dublin city centre; we hadn' t ended up on the cutting room floor, but our unpaid appearance was slight, to say the least!

Dr Gerry Owens

He was a brilliant dentist and also a brilliant sportsman. Bernadette had been going to him for years, since the late 1940s. In those days, a ridiculous protocol existed, that if someone wanted to go to a new dentist or other health specialist, you had to get an introduction from an existing patient. Much later, when I launched my 1986 book on Irish advertising history, Dr Owens was there, thoroughly enjoying himself, knocking back the pints. This was of some concern to Bernadette, as she had an appointment with him the following morning, but needless to remark, Dr Owens was on top of his form.

Gerry was born in 1914 and always had close connections with Skerries in north Co Dublin, where he went on to captain the local golf club on three occasions, as well as being president. After finishing his secondary education at Belvedere College, he qualified in dentistry in 1943 and went on to have his own dental practice for 46 years. His son, also Gerry, and his grandson, Roger, continue the practice, which started in Fitzwilliam Square, but which has been at Merrion Court, near the Merrion Centre, in Dublin 4, for many years.

He played international golf for Ireland before and after the second world war and in 1939, when he won the Irish Close championship at Rosses Point, Co Sligo, it was very big news indeed in the world of golf in Ireland. Gerry also went on to become a president of the Golfing Union of Ireland and was very interested in promoting junior golf.

Gerry was also a member of the legendary Royal and Ancient St Andrews golf club in Scotland, a rare honour.

On one occasion, he was advising the people behind of the then new course about to be laid out in Killarney. Dr Owens gave the entire design of the hotel over the phone, from St Andrews, to the team in Killarney, who followed his design details completely, ending up with a superbly designed course. He also had a keen interest in sailing.

His first wife, Noël Conroy, with whom he had two children, died when she was just 37, but Gerry married again, to Mary Raftery and had five children with her. Described as someone who loved life and loved people, Gerry died in August, 1997, at the age of 83 and is resting with his first wife, in Holmpatrick cemetery in his beloved Skerries.

Rev Ian Paisley

For years, many people regarded him as the eminence gris behind the troubles in the North. In the mid 1960s, when he was known for being the founder of the Free Prebysterian church, his religious/ political meetings where he poured scorn on the nationalist and republican communities in the North did much to sow discord. There's no doubt that his sectarian rantings and ravings did much to create inter- community instability and worse; how many Catholics were murdered by people who had been inspired by Paisley' s heated words? In later life, when he seemed more mature and benign, people often saw him as merely a great character and a teller of jokes; he became First Minister in the power sharing executive and he and Martin McGuinness, the deputy First Minister, became known as the "Chuckle Brothers". But there was much of dubious distinction behind that façade of genial bonhomie. By the time that Paisley died, in 2014, at the age of 88, he had contributed much to the general unrest in the North that had started in the mid- 1960s, but towards the end of his life, had also contributed much to bringing stability and peaceful joint government.

On one infamous occasion in the early 1970s, when we were living in Belfast, we decided to go to the main church that Paisley ran, on the Ravenhill Road in Belfast. He was beyond doubt a captivating speaker, able to exercise great power over his congregation. He was so persuasive that I became slightly worried that Bernadette would stand up and say: "I'm Bernadette, I want to be converted". With a good Catholic name like that, undoubtedly pandemonium would have ensued.

David Palmer

When Independent Newspapers installed a new managing director, 20 years ago, it came as something of a shock to hear the cutglass English tones of David Palmer echoing round their old headquarters in Middle Abbey Street, Dublin. He had spent much of his career with the Financial Times in London and had been recruited to Dublin to bring Independent Newspapers' new printing plant on stream. He made the move to Dublin in 1994 and soon settled in at his new home in St John's Road, Sandymount. Independent Newspapers had been very slow to install new print technology and were still relying on letterpress 15 years after The Irish Times had made the big change, and even longer after the Cork Examiner had converted. But in due course, the highly impressive and very expensive web offset plant at Citywest, on the outskirts of Dublin, was topped out in 2000. Palmer was made chairman of the company in 1998, before retiring as an executive director in 2002. By the time he had completed his stint in Dublin, the company had done what he had been hired to do, make the transition to full colour web offset printing. Under Palmer, the deputy managing director was Gavin O' Reilly, a son of Tony, who I got to know much better when he eventually took over the running of the company.

Peel

When Bernadette and I decided to get married, we wanted to do it far from the madding crowd in Dublin, so we explored various options, before discovering that we could more or less turn up on the Isle of Man, give the minimum of notice, then have a church ceremony, so that's precisely what we did, in June, 1972. We went to Peel, a small fishing town on the west coast of the island, having attended to the brief bits of documentation that had to be submitted in Douglas. The charming vicar of St German's, the Anglican church in Peel, which is now a cathedral, Rev H. A. McCullough, said we could do the wedding ceremony the next day, so we did that precisely, with my sister Kate as bridesmaid, and Bob Shimmin (a good Manx name) the people's churchwarden (one of two wardens in the church) as best man and that was that. It was all done and dusted in half an hour flat, very plain and simple but very memorable. My sister has often said since that it's the best wedding she's ever been to. The three of us had afternoon drinks at the lodgings where we were staying. We had discovered that a terraced house in Victoria Terrace, Peel, did b & b; it was run by Arthur Davies, one of the local postmen, and his wife Ruth. When we told them why we were in Peel, they couldn't have been nicer. On the afternoon of the wedding, Ruth served drinks in her upstairs front room and told us all about her sister who had recently died. In the evening, the three of us, Bernadette, Kate and myself, went for a Chinese meal in a local restaurant.

We became great friends with the Davies and remained so until they died. They were a lovely couple. On our 15th wedding anniversary, they went to get trouble to get a specially painted plate done as a memento. Even today, all those years later, we still keep in touch from time to time with the Davies' daughter, Vivienne, who still lives in Peel with her husband. We also kept in touch with the vicar, who had been to Trinity

College, Dublin, until he passed on. After that, his widow lived in Co Wicklow, until she too died.

Bernadette and I paid several subsequent visits to the Isle of Man, which we have always found a delightful place, and a wonderful place for cycling, although Douglas, the capital, is too much like an English seaside town for comfort. But it does have a wonderful cattery, where all the cats are Manx, in other words, without tails. On one occasion, we took Bernadette's parents to the island and they loved making a return visit, having spent their honeymoon there in the late 1920s.

Richard Pine

I got to know Richard Pine quite well when he was working in RTÉ. Born in London in 1949, he completed his studies at Trinity College, Dublin. He stayed on in Dublin and started to work for RTÉ, first as concerts manager and then as a senior editor; always classical music was at the forefront of his interests. In 2001, he made a big move, away from Ireland, going to settle in Corfu in Greece, where he has been ever since. He founded the Durrell School of Corfu as soon as he arrived.

Years later, in 2014, he admitted that he had been drinking himself to death, having had a massive haemorrhage; but by 2014, his mainstays were his two daughters and his writing. He has long written a regular column on Greek affairs for The Irish Times and in 2015, published a book called Greece through Irish Eyes, based on the columns he has written for the Dublin paper. To Richard, Greece and Ireland are remarkably similar in so many ways and he writes memorably about Greece from his eyrie in Corfu; from the end of the main street in the village where he lives, you can see very clearly across the channel to Albania.

Poland

In 1974, we made one of our most daring trips, which took some organising. It was to Poland, then still a communist country. We had to organise the holiday through a travel agency in London and getting all that done, through the post, as well as getting visas from London, was quite onerous. The plan was to spend a fortnight touring Poland by coach, which was one of the few ways westerners could get into the country in those days.

It started off in dramatic fashion. We took the ferry from Dún Laoghaire to Holyhead, which was all very straightforward. We thought the train journey from Holyhead to London would be simple, too, giving us plenty of time to get to Heathrow. At some point on the journey, the loco on the train broke down and we were stuck for hours until a replacement loco arrived; we eventually arrived into Euston, hours late. But by a stroke of luck, Bernadette's sister, Gloria, and her late husband, Eamonn, were on holiday in London and they had their car, a VW Beetle, with them. They went to Euston station to meet us and when they heard what had happened to the train, they waited for our arrival. When we eventually turned up, Eamonn drove like the clappers to Heathrow, where we just made our flight. We owed them a great debt of gratitude, as without their help, we would have missed the flight and forfeited what we had spent on booking the holiday. I have always had a strong fear of flying and I had taken some pills to calm me down during the long flight to Krakow. They also had the effect of making me zombie- like (no comment!). We also had a ridiculous amount of luggage with us; I wasn't capable of carrying it, so once again, Eamonn stepped into the breach. Eamonn,a most lovable person with a great sense of humour,died a decade ago.

We had left Heathrow about 10 pm that night and arrived at Krakow airport in the middle of the night. By the time we got to our hotel in the city centre, it was about four in the morning. Later on that morning, we went down for a late breakfast. I had left my suitcase, complete with US currency, unlocked and in our room. When we returned, we found that one of hotel staff had been in the room and had opened the case, but had taken just one of the dollar bills, a very clever move to ensure we didn' t raise the alarm. That night, we found something else very strange. The room we had in the hotel was huge, with a bathroom of equal size. The bedroom was decorated with very large mirrors and in the middle of the night, we felt deeply uneasy about the sinister ghostly presences that seemed to swirl around the mirrors. It was only much later that we discovered that during the Nazi occupation of Poland during the second world war, the hotel had been the Krakow headquarters for the local Nazis and that they had interrogated many prisoners there in the most brutal fashion. So our imaginings weren' t so wild after all.

We toured all the main sights in Krakow, including Wawel castle, the cathedral and the great square, before moving on swiftly to western Poland. En route, we stopped at Czestochowa, to see the famous Black Lady and we stopped at Chopin' s old house to hear an open air piano recital, then we ended up in the western Polish city of Wroclaw. It was while we were there that we went on an open air ride, during which I managed to sprain my thumb badly. It swelled up so much that a hospital visit became urgent. We found the treatment in the local hospital very effective and efficient and it all cost something like the equivalent of 10 p; my one and only experience of hospital treatment in communist Poland was quite an experience, especially when you compare conditions in accident and emergency in present day public hospitals in Ireland. We also found that our guide on the tour, a young woman called Eva, who came from Gdansk, was most helpful and she did everything possible to get me back to normal health.

We also spent a couple of nights in Warsaw, where we had an experience that was common in the then communist countries. As we finished dinner in our hotel one night, we hid a fistful of dollars on a plate, which the waiter took into the kitchen, returning with a positive mountain of zlotys, the Polish currency. We had noticed on our travels round Poland, that the supermarkets usually seemed to be half-empty of goods and in Warsaw we also noticed another then common phenomenon, flash crowds, who would appear at the mere whisper of some new stocks being available. It didn' t matter what was coming into stock, people just queued, in case it might be something useful. Also in Warsaw, we had a strange invitation, which we didn' t take up. One of the other passengers on the coach was a young man from the east end of London, who liked to cultivate an air of bravado and secrecy around him, as if he was on some secret mission, which he probably wasn' t. He took a great shine to Bernadette and offered me an enormous amount in US dollars if Bernadette would spend a few hours with him in the Hotel Bristol. We were pretty hard up in those days, but we weren' t remotely tempted to give in. Also in Warsaw, we marvelled at how the old town had been completely rebuilt, with complete authenticity, after being destroyed at the end of the second world war.

The most harrowing part of the whole trip when we went to Lublin, a city in eastern Poland, not far from the border with Ukraine. There, we visited a second world war Nazi concentration camp, which had been left exactly as it was. Touring the camp was a deeply harrowing experience, one we will never forget, and equally, we never forgot the effect it had on a couple of Jewish brothers from London who were on the trip. At the entrance to the camp, there was a tourist desk and very bizarrely, a collection of picture postcards. I turned to Bernadette and said: "What are you supposed to do, send these to people you really dislike and say to them- wish you were here".

Yet another strange experience came when we were booked to stay the night in a brand new skyscraper hotel. When we arrived, it was quite clear the building was far from finished, but we were all allocated our rooms. We took the lift up 10 floors, in search of our room, only to find that when we got out of the lift, only the landing had been built. What was supposed to have been our room was a mere hole in the wall!

At the end of the holiday, we ended up in Novy Sacs, in the far south of Poland, enjoying the Tatra mountains and a boat trip down the river. But in the end, we were glad to get away from the continual company of everyone else on the coach and return to London. Little did we, or anyone else, know that within a few short years, the unrest that began in the Gdansk shipyards ended up with the overthrow of the Communist regime in Poland. But when we were there, it wasn' t completed restricted; I found that in Warsaw, there was no problem at all in getting copies of up- to- date western newspapers, such as The Guardian.

In those far- off days, we had plenty of energy, so as soon as we arrived in London, we got a train down to Shepton Mallet in Somerset to visit Showerings, the cider people. In those days, I was writing a lot about the drinks industry; its hospitality was always exceptional, as was the case at Showerings, and later, with another West Country drinks firm we visited on a couple of occasions, Harveys the sherry people in Bristol.

Enoch Powell

The public school in Birmingham I had the misfortune to go to for six years, a time in my past that I do my best to forgot, produced one public figure of note, Enoch Powell. He was a pupil there before the second world war, when King Edward

VI school was still in Birmingham city centre. Powell was in many respects a right-wing extremist, very opposed to immigration into the UK, yet he was a very clever man, who could speak a dozen languages. When the UK held a referendum on EEC membership in 1975, Powell could quite happily deliver speeches in French, German and Italian, as well as English. But in another odd aspect to his career, he spent some years as a unionist MP at Westminster for a Northern Ireland constituency. After his death in 1998, he remained most notorious for his "rivers of blood" speeches on what he saw as the perils of unfettered immigration.

Brenda Power

I've known Brenda for the best part of 20 years, a formidable writer and broadcaster, who' s also a barrister. She got her journalistic training on the old Irish Press, where surviving amid the general mayhem was a very good induction to working in the media. She went on to do a lot of radio work, especially for RTÉ, and it was there that I first got to know her. In the late 1990s, RTÉ Radio 1 ran a series that investigated many aspects of the newspaper business; I did all the research and got all the contributors lined up although I didn' t take part on air. I well remember that one episode turned out to be quite contentious, the influence that advertisers have on newspapers. Quite a number of people chickened out when I asked them to take part, but my good friend Paul Drury was well up for the challenge and gave a typically trenchant performance. Most of the series was presented by Brenda Power and I contributed to another series she presented, the Media Show. She has also done a lot of television work, co- presenting such high profile shows as Crimecall. In recent years, she has become better known for her columns in the Irish Daily Mail and The Sunday Times; Brenda is never shy about expressing her own candid opinions, which are often at odds with the bland sentiments expressed by the establishment. Her forthright stances on numerous issues are among her many endearing characteristics.

Terry Prone

One of the best, and the best- known, public relations practitioners in Dublin. She is so well connected that not so long ago, someone tweeted that Terry "had a finger in every hole in Dublin". I first got to know her in the 1980s, when she was working for Bunny Carr' s pr company, based in Dundrum. In 1988, she had a dreadful car accident near Moyvalley, on the road to the west from Dublin. As a result, she had multiple fractures of her left arm, her legs were crushed to pieces, she suffered from aphasia, she had a broken jaw, her teeth were smashed and her cheekbones caved in. She made a remarkable recovery from these injuries and is now in her mid- 60s, working away in her present day company, the Communications Clinic, and turning out numerous newspaper columns without a bother. I' ve always had great admiration for the way in which she refused to give in to her terrible injuries after that car crash. But ever since that car crash, she' s had a penchant for plastic surgery.

She and her husband, Tom Savage, a former chair of the RTÉ Authority, lived in a converted Martello Tower in north Co Dublin, and just to further differentiate Terry from everyone else, she has a habit of getting up at 4 am to start working, long before the phone calls start.

Noel Purcell

A great character actor, who appeared in many films, I only met Noel Purcell once, when he was an elderly bearded gentleman. He was a special guest when I launched my book on Bewleys at Hodges Figgis bookstore in Dawson Street, Dublin, in December, 1980. He was most interested in the book and great company at the launch; he was just coming up to his 80th birthday.

He had been born in 1900 and began his working life as a carpenter, although he had made his first stage appearance at the age of 12 at the Gaiety Theatre in Dublin. But it was when he was making stage sets that he really became hooked on the idea of acting. After more than a decade as a stage actor, he made his debut on the silver screen in 1934 and went on to appear in numerous films, including Captain Boycott (1947) and Moby Dick (1956). He was also a singer, best noted for his rendition of The Dublin Saunter, written for him by his friend Leo Maguire, who compered the Waltons music shop programme on radio for many years. In the song, there's reference to the fact that "Dublin can be heaven, with coffee at eleven" and it was for that reason I'd sent Noel an invitation to the launch.

Noel married Eileen Marmion, also in the acting profession, in 1940 and they went on to have four children. For much of Noel's life, the family home was in Sandymount. He died in 1985.

Laurence Pyman

Around 25 years ago, on Saturdays, we would quite often go for lunch to a delightful restaurant called Harveys, just beside the Fly Fishers' shop in Newtownmountkennedy. It was a very friendly place, with lovely staff, led by the owner, Helen Fox. The meals were excellent, so lunches were always very pleasant occasions. It was also a great place to meet people and we became very friendly with a lovely retired gentleman called Laurence Pyman, who was living in Delgany. Born in 1910, which would have made him about 80 when we got to know him, he had a long career in the British diplomatic service- no wonder he knew how to be so charming. He had begun his career abroad in 1952, when he was made counsellor at the British Embassy in Rio de Janeiro, Brazil. After that, he served in a variety of capitals and countries, including Morocco, Zagreb and Somaliland. His last overseas posting was in San Francisco, where he was the British consul- general from 1963 to 1965. But it was there he got into a spat, which turned into a big legal confrontation, with neighbours, over a fence and that seems to have put a stop to his diplomatic travels. But when we got to know him, long after he retired, he was wise, serene and delightful company. When he died in 1996, aged 86, we were sad to have lost such a companionable friend.

Feargal Quinn

I' ve long known Feargal Quinn and his customer- friendly approach to retailing. Born in 1936, his father Eamon was a born entrepreneur and started such 'institutions' as Red Island Holiday Camp in Skerries, north Co Dublin. It did very well for 25 years, until the early 1970s, when it closed down, due to all the competition from then new package holidays. When Feargal was a youngster, he got his first taste of organising good customer service at the holiday camp and subsequently brought it to the Superquinn group of supermarkets, where I frequently met him. Superquinn began as a single shop, in Dundalk, in 1960, Superquinn has long since ceased to exist, sold off in 2005 and subsequently subsumed into the SuperValu chain, but Feargal battles on, now well into his vintage years, close to 80. He' s still dishing out loads of very sensible advice on how business people can keep customers happy; keeping customers happy has always been very much more than a mere mantra to him. He became a senator in 1993, but has now left the upper house. However, he continues to dish out very sensible advice on a wide range of issues.

Hugh Quinn

My late father- in- law was born in 1902; his family connections went back to Thurles, Co Tipperary, but he lived all his life in Dublin. He spent his entire working life on the railways, a subject he was devoted to. In his younger days, he was offered promotion to an indoor job at the railway company' s head office, but declined. He also had a lifelong love of music and told us an incredible story about the Black and Tans, the British recruits who terrorised many communities in Ireland during the war of independence, 1919- 1921.

One night during this period, he was walking home in the Kilmainham district of Dublin. He had his violin in his case with him. All of a sudden, a big lorry pulled up alongside him and some Black and Tans jumped out. He thought he was a goner, but they had something else in mind; they were having a party at their barracks that night and they wanted him to play for them. Hugh' s love of music stayed with him all his life and for long, he played in the Nell Kane Orchestra (qv). When his wife May was a young woman, before they were married (May was four years younger than her husband), she worked at the gramophone shop that once stood in Johnson' s Court off Grafton Street in the centre of Dublin.

What happened in their families sums up perfectly the dichotomy in Irish society. Hugh' s father eventually died from injuries he had received as a rebel Volunteer in the 1916 Easter Rising, while May' s father, one of the Touhy family from Limerick, a member of one of that city' s well- known families in the bacon processing industry, served in the British army during the first world war. He was killed on the front, in Belgium, and interred there. May' s mother lived with the Quinn family until her demise in 1947. Bernadette, although young at the time, still has vivid memories of her grandmother' s funeral taking place during the dreadful snow in the winter of 1947.

After they were married, they lived for a while at the Crescent in Marino, but Hugh never took to the northside and couldn' t wait until they returned to the southside. For many years, the family home was in Upper Camden Street, then from the early 1950s, in Rialto. Hugh and May produced two daughters, Bernadette, the first, and Gloria, the second. Bernadette spent all her working career in the Department of External Affairs, now Foreign Affairs, while Gloria worked in the old Dublin Corporation, in the civil defence office. Gloria' s late husband, Eamonn, lectured in physics at the Dublin Institute of Technology in Kevin Street. Eamonn' s brother, Kevin, came to a sad end in the 1960s; He was mad about boats and had bought a new boat at a show in the RDS; he was so keen to try it out that it took it straight to Skerries. He and his companions ignored the warnings of local fishermen that the weather going to be so bad they shouldn' t put to sea. They did and the boat, with all its crew, including Kevin, were lost, their bodies never retrieved.

I met Bernadette purely by chance. One day in August, 1970, I was working on a feature about the mining industry for a Belfast newspaper. I decided to take a day trip down to Dublin to find out what was happening there. My last call of the day was to the Department of Foreign Affairs. The woman in the press office who should have come down to meet me and answer my query couldn' t, so Bernadette came down in her place. I think the kipper tie I was wearing caught her eye! Within a week, we were doing a line and less than two years later, married. By the time we were married, in 1972, the civil service marriage bar was still in place, a ridiculously antiquated rule that meant when any woman working in the public service got married, she lost her job. The marriage bar was repealed the following year, not before time, but it was too late for us, we weren' t even living in Dublin at that stage.

Apart from her diplomatic work, I soon found out that Bernadette was a poet of note and a winner of a prestigious Guinness award for poetry. She wrote a weekly poem for years for the old Weekly Cork Examiner and when we were clearing her parents' house, after the death of her mother, one of the items in her former bedroom was a metre high stack of the Weekly Cork Examiner. Each of the issues there had one of her poems. She also published in such magazines as Creation and An Irishwoman's Journal, as well as in The Irish Times.

I soon got to know her parents very well; they were the most welcoming and hospitable people one could ever meet and they became almost surrogate parents for me. I got on incredibly well with them, in a way that I never did with my own parents; I was so happy to have had this wonderful relationship with my in-laws. Hugh Quinn died in 1988 and May lingered on until 1997; every year, on their anniversaries, I make a point of going out to St Fintan's cemetery in Sutton to pay my respects and to remember some truly wonderful times in their home. Sunday lunches were among the occasions that were always memorable, for the good-natured craic and cabbage; no-one else could do cabbage the way Bernadette's mother did it. No-one could ever have asked for better parents-in-law.

Sean Rafferty

I only met Sean Rafferty once, in the early 1980s, when I went to Belfast to be interviewed by him at the BBC for the radio show he was then doing in Northern Ireland. I always remember sitting in the studio, at the top of Broadcasting House in Belfast, with an excellent view of a sunlit City Hall, waiting for the interview to begin. The interview subject was routine enough, about one of my newly published touring guides for Appletree Press. I also remember vividly that before I came on air, Sean interviewed, by phone, that remarkable writer, Molly Keane, who talked to him from her home at Ardmore, Co Waterford.

Sean' s background was interesting; he had graduated in law from Queen' s University, Belfast, but then had gone into accountancy. One day, at a function, he happened to meet the then head of the BBC in Northern Ireland and before he knew it, he found himself working as a newsreader at the BBC. He became a frequent presenter on Scene around Six and he also started Rafferty, the first chat show produced by BBC television in Belfast.

But Belfast couldn' t hold this man of many talents, once described as being like a brown bear, outwardly cuddly, but deadly as an interviewer. In 1997, he moved to London to work for Radio 3 and ever since then, has been the presenter of the In Tune programme, interviewing countless classical music celebrities over nearly 20 years.

Albert Reynolds

Out of all the politicians I've known over the years, Albert was one of my favourites, because he was so down to earth and ready to roll up his sleeves and get on with the job. But he could also be stubbornly wilful a quality that saw the curtain come down on his partnership with the Labour Party in 1994 and the end of his time in government. He had begun his career as a railway clerk with CIE. His first involvement in business came with show bands, when he ran a formidable entreprise during the show band era in the 1960s, building and running dance halls. Then came a foray into the newspaper business, when he took over the Longford News newspaper in the early 1970s, he inherited a remarkable editor, Vincent Gill. He took many remarkable short cuts running his paper, such as making up copy about weddings in the travelling community where the guests included everyone up to the President. At one stage, the BBC sent a film crew to

Longford to make a profile of him, but they never caught up with Vincent Gill and his van full of cats and dogs; he was always six pubs ahead. Vincent Gill was pure gold in terms of anecdotes about newspapers and Albert's foray into newspapers seemed to whet his appetite for stories about Vincent Gill, who died in 1976.

The first time I met Albert was in 1982, when he was a government minister. I found him very approachable and friendly, always willing to help for the book I was then compiling on newspaper history, published in 1983. When that book was published, Albert did the honours in the Guinness brewery, when a great time was had by all. The book launch got such great coverage that I found my photograph on the front page of The Irish Times the next morning.

I always found Albert totally down- to- earth, with no side to him at all, and he told me that when he started his pet food business, he worked on the production line, stuffing the meat into cans for dog food. Then in 1992, when I did the Paper Tiger series for RTÉ Radio 1, the interview with Albert was much more formal, because he was Taoiseach. RTÉ insisted on sending the works, including a sound engineer, whereas for the rest of that series, I interviewed everyone using a portable tape recorder. But as we all sat in Government Buildings for the interview, and I started asking questions, Albert started telling some of his yarns about the newspaper business. They were so funny that everyone on the production team including Dick Warner, the producer, and myself, were reduced to helpless laughter, so much so that we had to stop recording until such time as we had all regained our composure. Albert was only Taoiseach for a short time, from 1992 to 1994, but he made a considerable impact on the country's fortunes, including this work on the Northern peace process, the latter done in conjunction with his great friend, John Major, now Sir John, who was then the UK prime minister.

Albert's life came to a sad end; in his last few years, his dementia was so severe that he no longer knew the various members of his family who came to visit him when he was in care. He died in 2014 and one of those who attended his funeral in Dublin was Sir John Major.

W. Vaughan Reynolds

I got to know him quite well when we lived in Birmingham; I would have been in my early teens at the time. knew his son well at school and we became quite close friends; I then discovered that his esteemed father was a newspaper editor, in an age when a newspaper editor was one of the key figures in the local elite and the local newspaper was a pillar of the establishment. W. Vaughan Reynolds was the editor of the Birmingham Post, a morning paper, through the 1950s and into the 1960s. It had been founded in 1857 and went on to become one of the main regional papers in England, although in recent years, it has been reduced to a small circulation weekly edition and a daily tablet edition. But way back in the late 1950s, it was a powerhouse of the media and on the couple of occasions when I saw inside the newsroom, I was impressed by the scale and solidity of the operation. But in some ways, Vaughan Reynolds was ahead of his time; by the early 1950s, he was also busy contributing to BBC television programmes in Birmingham.

Rod, my brother

Rod, my brother, chose the same career path as myself, journalism, although he took a totally different trajectory. Educated in the UK and the US, when he was in the US, the Vietnam war was raging and I remember the endless side steps he had to take to avoid being drafted into the US Army, to fight in a war that few people believed in. One of my other abiding memories of Rod in the US came from his motor cycling days; he had a spectacular crash with an enormous truck and managed to survive unscathed, by sliding his bike underneath the lorry and emerging on the far side. Much of his education was in the US, at a time when the draft for the Vietnam war, and how to avoid it, was on the minds of countless young men.

For many years, he worked on the Financial Times, in both New York and London. Then close on 20 years ago, he ended up as business editor of the New Zealand Herald in Auckland, New Zealand. The paper had been bought by Tony O' Reilly in 1996 and one of the things he wanted to do was boost the then very weak business section. Rod heard from a friend of his from the Financial Times, who had gone on to work for Tony O' Reilly in South Africa, about the job vacancy coming up in Auckland. Rod came top of the short list, was offered the job, met Tony O' Reilly, and then in March, 1997, arrived in Auckland to start his new job. Lynn, his wife, and Celeste, their daughter, followed in early July.

He stayed at the New Zealand Herald as business editor until 2000 and in keeping with the best traditions of family nepotism, I made several contributions from Ireland. After a change of editor, his stint at the New Zealand Herald came to an unpleasant end, when the new editor made a hash of trying to get rid of him. He and Rod had clashed over editorial policy. Rod left and took a successful lawsuit against the company, winning a year' s salary in compensation. The new editor only lasted for three years; his tenure ended because of his sexual harassment of staff.

Since then Rod has continued to work assiduously and happily as a freelancer in the media, including newspapers and radio, and in academia and has long been at the forefront of the environmental movement in New Zealand. He has become one of the best- known media journalists in New Zealand. He loves cycling and the outdoor life, for which New Zealand is perfect. He is also much more technically proficient than I am; on his most recent visit to Dublin, about three years ago, he was able to keep contributing to his regular radio show in New Zealand via his laptop.

I' ve always been slightly amazed at the marathon plane journeys he often does; he' ll quite happily hop on a plane to China or anywhere else in Asia, as easily as I' d get the bus into town here in Dublin. Lynn' s father, who is now in his 90s, a retired general in the US Army, lives in Little Rock, Arkansas, and Rod and Lynn often pop over to see how he' s getting on. Recently, he wrote and got published in record time, his memoirs of an exciting life. Lynn herself is a very dedicated and experienced actor and fortunately, she has found plenty of work in New Zealand. As for their daughter, Celeste, she is brilliant at music; at one stage in New Zealand she had her own rock band, while she has conducted classical orchestras and is perfectly capable of sitting down and composing a symphony in one session. She' s currently doing post- graduate studies with the University of California in the US.

Basil Rodgers

Basil was my uncle in Plymouth, a much loved character; he came from a Jamaican family that had long settled in south Devon. He was very proud of his West Indian background. When he was a young man, he was very much into performing jazz and after the BBC started its television service in London in 1936, Basil was one of the first artistes to appear on the "box" ; he soon became a familiar performer, a jazz singer, long before jazz had permeated the popular conscience. Indeed, during the 1930s here in Ireland, the Catholic hierarchy did its best to prevent people getting any enjoyment from jazz; they considered it far too decadent. Basil also knew and was very friendly with many of the African freedom fighters, who eventually led their countries to independence; among his close friends was Jomo Kenyatta, the father figure of modern day Kenya.

But while he was still young, in the early days of the second world war, something happened to Basil; he suddenly found that he no longer had to work for a living, so he didn' t, for the rest of his life. This sudden change in his fortunes remained unexplained and never mentioned. When I was a young kid being brought up in Plymouth, I made frequent trips to the wonderful pebble dashed house, Great Berry, that Basil and his wife, my aunt Sheila, and their daughter, Susan, had in Crownhill. The house was wonderfully luxurious and was a delightful contrast to the utilitarian Blind Institution. As a young boy, I always remember something that attracted my attention in the loo; when you pulled out sheets of toilet paper, the holder would play a tune! In those days, such a novelty was way ahead of its time! The district is on the northern side of Plymouth and in those days, it was in semi-open country. We often used to pop across the road to the local dairy to get milk and cream; Basil was always addicted to jam and cream for tea and so it was for the rest of his life. He was a big, affable, kind hearted man and I'm told that when I was young, I would quite happily chat for hours with him about every subject on the sun, while I could hardly string two words together talking to my own father. Basil also had a very fine car, a roomy Austin, in which he loved to take us for drives. For many years, he spent much time as a director of Plymouth Argyle soccer club, while he also loved golf and was very active in his local golf club.

That fine house they lived in at Crownhill is still there, although the pebble dash on its façade has long gone and its magnificent long front garden has been truncated to make way for the widening of the main road to Crownhill. But when I saw it on Google Street View the other day, I recognised it instantly, after all these years!

He died over 30 years ago, in 1982, and I well remember that not long after he died, the whole back garden of their then house, in Plymstock, was absolutely filled with floral tributes, from friends and neighbours, who all appreciated his affability and his wonderful sense of humour. His wife and my aunt, Sheila, is still going strong at 95, going on 96, and we still keep in close touch with her and Susan.

Michael Rooney

I only met Michael Rooney, a former editor of the Irish Independent, once, when I was researching my book on Irish newspaper history (1983). He invited me to his house in Clontarf and we spent the whole afternoon in fascinating reminiscence. He had an extraordinary career transition; during the war of independence, he was active with the rebels in Belfast and got jailed for his involvement. Then as the Irish Free State came into being, he moved down to Dublin and began a long career with the Irish Independent, which lasted until his retirement at the end of the 1960s. He had been made editor upon the retirement of Frank Geary in 1961, so effectively he was editor during most of the 1960s, until 1968. He had spent a total of 37 years with the newspaper. In his earlier days, he was described as "a fiery little bundle of turbulence from Ardglass in Co Down".

That decade, the 1960s, was a game changer in England, but with all the changes in the Irish economy suggested by Dr Ken Whitaker in the Department of Finance, this part of Ireland was finally emerging from its decades long economic through. After Michael Rooney, subsequent editors of the Irish Independent included Aidan Pender and Louis McRedmond, while the man who was probably the greatest editor of the paper in recent times, Vinnie Doyle, became editor in 1981.

Andy Ryan

I' ve long known Andy Ryan, who used to own the Waterloo Bar in Upper Baggot Street; he ran it for 41 years, from 1961 until 2002, when he sold it to the Quinns, who own the Lansdowne Hotel and the 51 Bar in Haddington Road, among other properties. In many ways, Andy, who' s from Co Tipperary, was the traditional publican. He always had a galaxy of a cast as customers in his bar, including literary and journalistic greats like Paddy Kavanagh and Con Houlihan. I always liked one story he told me about Paddy Kavanagh, who had to wait until he was into his early 60s before he could get a bank account. When he did, he tried to pay by cheque, but sensibly, Andy was having none of it.

Annie Ryan

I've got to know Annie Ryan quite well, as a near neighbour, living in Heytesbury Lane. She' s Irish- American, a native of Chicago, and she started training as an actor when she was 12. She moved to Dublin in 1992 to work with Michael West, a writer, who is now her husband; they have two sons. In 1995, Annie founded the Corn Exchange theatre company in Dublin, where she continues as artistic director; she is regarded as one of the best theatre directors working in present day Ireland.

Eamon Ryan

I got to know Eamon Ryan, the leader of the Green Party, when he launched my first book on Dundrum, the place in south Dublin where he was brought up. At the end of 2014, he launched The Little Book of Dundrum and was most complimentary about the book. Eamon, who' s 20 years younger than me, was a Green Party TD from 2002 to 2011. In the 2007 to 2011 government, he was the Minister for Communications, Energy and Natural Resources, but lost his seat in the 2011 general election. When the general election was held at the end of February, 2016, he was re- elected to the Dáil for Dublin Bay South, the first TD elected for this new constituency. In an earlier life, back in 1989, he had founded Cycling Safaris, a company that organises cycling holidays in Ireland and the rest of Europe. In 1998, he married Victoria White, then an Irish Times journalist; they have four children.

My second Dundrum book, Dundrum Then & Now, was launched in 2015, and this time, the honours were done by Catherine Martin, deputy leader of the Green Party. She too was elected to the Dáil in the February, 2016 general election; she had long been a councillor for Dún Laoghaire- Rathdown county council. By profession, she's an English and music teacher at St Tiernan's community school in south Dublin and she has three young children, so she's remarkably busy lady. Both she and her husband, Francis, who is deputy mayor of South Dublin County Council, come from Carrickmacross, Co Monaghan.

The man who took all the new photographs for the book,Vincent Clarke,was a most genial person.Until he retired,he had been for many years the director of lighting for RTÉ television.After retiring,he returned to his first love,photography.He died in August,2016.

Gerry Ryan

The man who took all the new photographs for the book,Vincent Clarke,was a most genial person.Until he retired,he had been for many years the director of lighting in RTÉ television.After retiring,he returned to his first love,photography.He died in August,2016.

Gerry Ryan was a famous, not so say, notorious presenter, on 2FM, from 1988 until his untimely death in 2010. I remember well that when we took a Concorde flight from Dublin to Paris in September, 1988, Gerry was one of the fellow passengers, a thin young man with his hair tied in a kind of ponytail. As the years progressed, Gerry got progressively less thin. He also lived just round the corner from us, in a flat in Upper Leeson Street; he had been going with Melanie Verwoerd, a former South African ambassador to Ireland, after he had split up with his wife. I will never forget the absolute pandemonium on the airwwaves and in the media generally, when Gerry was found dead in his flat, that day in 2010. He was undoubtedly a very talented broadcaster, always willing to push the envelope, but these days, the hulabaloo of 2010 has been consigned to history.

Catherine Rynne

I met Catherine in the early 1960s through my great friend in Derry, Margot Fleming, who knew her and one of Catherine's friends, Sheila Walsh, very well. Catherine had been born in Prosperous, Co Kildare, in 1937 and by the time she was 30, she was well established as a feature writer on the old Evening Press in Dublin. She was the first journalist I got to know well in Dublin. Much later, she wrote a book on Mother Mary Aikenhead, one of the most famous of 19th century Irish nuns; that was in 1980. Before that, she had done a 1973 book on how to enjoy your retirement, then in 1979, a book on that great holy place in the West of Ireland, Knock. Catherine died in January, 2014, aged 77 and her funeral service was at Prosperous, the place of her birth.

John E. Sayers

He was the first person who interviewed me for a job in the media and I didn' t get it. He was the editor of the Belfast Telegraph in the 1950s and 1960s, in the days when it had a huge circulation, close to 250, 000 a night. He belonged very much to the old school of journalism in the North, when so much of it was aligned to the unionist cause. In his earlier days, during the second world war, he had been on Churchill' s personal staff. But when I met him, in the 1960s, I was looking for a job on the Belfast Telegraph and in that capacity, was interviewed by Sayers. We weren' t remotely on the same wavelength and I didn' t get on at all with him, although he was perfectly polite. So it came as no surprise when I found I' d had no luck. Strangely enough, in more recent times, I've had better luck with the paper and have often contributed freelance pieces to over more than 20 years now, although it' s a long time since I was other than a very occasional contributor.

But in John Sayers' time, the Belfast Telegraph was a paper with a mighty influence and reach in the North. It also then had a sports paper of much substance, the now defunct Ireland' s Saturday Night. But even though John Sayers was so well established as a newspaper editor and the paper had such enormous circulation then, he was very over- optimistic about Captain Terence O' Neill' s chances of reform in the North and very much misjudged the influence that O' Neill would have. Ironically, John Sayers' life ended in 1969, just as the Northern troubles were getting under way; he was only 58 when he died, but funnily enough, when I met him, he seemed years older than he actually was.

Anne Sexton

Anne has been writing the Sexed Up column in Hot Press, a remarkable achievement in a magazine that has done extraordinarily well, with one man in charge since it started, 40 years ago, Niall Stokes. He has been editing and publishing Hot Press since 1977, a great achievement in longevity. As for Anne, she has a day job as a graphic artist, but in 2003, when Durex sponsored a competition to find a sex columnist for Hot Press, she won and started work the following year. She's Irish but was brought up in South Africa, where she lived for many years. She has an honours degree in English, so writing the column every fortnight comes naturally to her, and as she says herself, she has always had an abiding and uninhibited attitude towards sex. She makes it all seem so natural and it's a welcome improvement on bygone attitudes that she can write so candidly on the subject without attracting any unfavourable criticism.

Bernard Share

Once a copywriter and a stalwart of the Irish advertising industry, he graduated into magazine editing and book production in his own name, a most learned man with a great sense of humour. He also had a spell as a lecturer in modern literature in both Ireland and Australia.

When he worked in the advertising business, he often wore Mickey Mouse ears for effect! He also ran a long tie creative consultancy with his good friend, Bill Bolger, a designer of renown. When Bernard and Bill both worked for the old Janus ad agency in Parnell Square, they dreamed up a little trick that they knew would perplex Denis Garvey, the owner and managing director. They tied a bra onto a length of string and dangled it out of a top window so that it would dance up and down in the breeze right outside the window of the office occupied by Denis Garvey, to his puzzlement!

As for Bernard, he left CLÉ, the then book publishers' organisation, in 1976, to become editor of a new magazine called Books Ireland, where he stayed until 1988. From 1975 until 1999, he edited Cara, the inflight magazine of Aer Lingus, where I found him a very amiable and understanding editor to work with. He also did a book on the history of Aer Lingus, in 1988. He also produced quite a collection of books on a wide variety of topics. In 1987, he published a book on The Emergency in Ireland during the second world war, a meticulous compendium of the shortages and mend- and-make- do of the second world war, while in 1997, he produced Slanguage, a dictionary of colloquial and slang English in Ireland. A much earlier book, in 1964, had a most unusual title, The bed that went woosh! It was meant for children. His 1966 comedy, Inish, was described by Spike Milligan as the funniest book he had ever read. Bernard was a great character, very erudite, but with a very sly sideways look on life; he died in 2013, aged 83.

Omar Sharif

We nearly met Omar Sharif one day in Paris. It was a lovely sunny day in the 1980s, in the days when we made frequent trips to Paris. We' d decided to have an open air lunch at an excellent restaurant in the Tuileries; as we enjoyed our lunch, the decibels from the next table grew ever louder, so we turned round to see who was making all the noise. It was Omar Sharif, the Eygptian film actor, who was having a whale of a time with some of his drinking buddies. He turned to wink at us, but that was the closest we got to meeting him! Born in Alexandria, Egypt, in 1932, to parents of Lebanese descent, he went on to have a prodigious career in films and television; his best- known films are Lawrence of Arabia (1962) and Doctor Zhivago (1965). In later life, after his marriage broke up, he lived in hotel rooms around Europe, but mainly in Paris. He loved horse racing and was one of the world' s best contract bridge players. Yet sadly, in his latter years, Alzheimer' s overtook him and he could remember little of his film roles.

He made his last film in 2015, the year that he died in his native country.

John Sheeran

John, who lives in Attanagh, near Durrow in Co Laois, has long had a great interest in music, besides being the possessor of a fine singing voice. Around 20 years ago, when the old CKR commercial radio station was going strong, John ran a Sunday evening request programme for listeners who wanted to hear favourite classical pieces, with a strong emphasis on sung pieces. It was a very informal and a very popular programme and John used to have banter with Bernadette and myself on the airwaves on Sunday evenings.

The CKR station lost its franchise in 2002, giving way to KCLR and KFM. In recent years, John hasn' t had the best of health but on the occasions very recently when I've been in touch, he' s been in great form. His wife Kathleen retired recently from night work at An Post in Portlaoise; when we tuned in to John, he and his wife had two young children, one of whom is now a teacher, the other a barrister.

Brian Siggins

I got to know Brian well when I started doing serious research on the history of Ballsbridge and Sandymount and have always found him most generous and extraordinary knowledgeable on local history. Many' s the time I' ve been to the home of Brian and his wife Maureen. There' s nothing he doesn' t know, or no photograph he hasn' t seen. For years, Brian was a technical asssistant in the Tech in Ringsend and after he retired nearly 20 years ago, he was able to devote all his time to his historical work. The Siggins' son Gerard is a well- acknowledged writer on many sports topics.

John Skehan

He was another ex- Army man who came into broadcasting and had a remarkable second career. He was a captain in the Army during the Emergency, but after the war, went into broadcasting, working for RTÉ for four decades. He began his career as a presenter on the Broadsheet television programme in the early 1960s, later moving into radio. In the late 1980s and early 1990s, he presented a very popular radio programme called Words and Music, where he interviewed well- known personalities and played some of their favourite music. John was a very droll character, with a laconic sense of humour. Towards the end of his life, he returned to television, as a snooker commentator, where the pace of the game suited his personality perfectly. He died in 1992, aged 70; his funeral was a very poignant occasion for his many friends in broadcasting, who missed his easy going but well organised personality.

Michael Smurfit

I found Michael Smurfit a rather difficult person to interview; he was excellent on facts and figures, but it was harder to persuade him to relate the human interest side on how his renowned group had grown to such monumental proportions from the small box factory his father had set up in Rathmines, Dublin, in the 1930s. Five years after the K Club had been launched, Michael Smurfit' s pride and joy, in 1991, after three years renovation on the old big house and estate at Straffan, Co Kildare, the first book on the project was prepared. I was commissioned to research and write it. I must admit I found the whole history of the house and estate quite fascinating, as were some of the people working in the K Club, such as Sean McManamon, its resident fishing expert. Ray Carroll, who had owned and run the Cashel Palace Hotel in Co Tipperary, had been very involved in the development of the K Club and became its first chief executive. But strangely enough, although I interviewed far and wide to get all the source material and photographs needed for the book, I never interviewed Michael Smurfit for it, indeed such an interview was never even suggested.

When Michael Smurfit was 27, he had married his first wife, Norma, who was a hairdresser in London. When Michael told Norma in 1985, that he wanted a divorce, when they were out to dinner in a restaurant, she promptly threw a glass of wine over him. He married his second wife, Birgitta, in 1988, but it lasted just for 10 years. Norma has in the years since her divorce, been involved in many charitable good works; also at one stage, she ran the old Soup Bowl restaurant in Molesworth Lane off Molesworth Street in Dublin and it was somewhere where we always enjoyed dining.

Southern Star

I've long had a great interest in the fortunes of the Southern Star, produced and published in Skibbereen since 1889. The very name of the town, Skibbereen, produces much recall even today, for the phrase about the Skibbereen Eagle keeping its eye on the Czar of Russia. The rival Skibbereen Eagle co- existed with the Southern Star for 33 years, until the Southern Star absorbed it in 1929. Around 1907, the Skibbereen Eagle, which was a Protestant owned paper that supported British imperialism and regularly attacked the Catholic church, ran a leader in which it said it was keeping an eye on the Czar of Russia. For such a small paper, on the very edge of Europe, the notion of it having such pretentious ideas soon caught the public imagination, not only in Ireland but far beyond. The phrase became a byword for ludicrous aspirations in politics and resonates even today.

The Southern Star, on the other hand, was a very nationalistic newspaper and was frequently suppressed between 1916 and 1920. The paper had been taken over by Joe O' Regan in 1919 and his son, Liam, spent 50 years as the controlling editor and editor, until his death in January, 2009, aged 72. I got to know Liam well, someone who ran his newspaper in a most efficient fashion. Yet he was a very shy man and when I was doing the Paper Tiger series on RTÉ Radio 1 in the autumn of 1992, we devoted one episode to the Skibbereen Eagle and the Southern Star. That renowned actor, the late Conor Farrington, read blood curdling passages from leaders in the Skibbereen Eagle, to great and humorous effect. Also in the programme, I included recordings of Liam O' Regan, although because he wasn' t a very forthcoming person, had to be persuaded to take part in the recordings.

Dick Spring

Long in the political limelight, Dick, who was born in 1950, was first elected a TD in 1981, then from 1982 to 1997, was leader of the Labour Party. When I launched my Little Book of Ballsbridge in the RDS Library in October, 2014, Dick did the honours at the launch and was most complimentary about the contents. Although from Co Kerry, he has long had connections with Dublin and when I was compiling that book, he was most candid with his recollections. One of his amusing anecdotes concerned the time he was a student and sharing accommodation in Ballsbridge with a woman who was a fellow student, although it was purely a business arrangement, since there was no romantic liaison involved. But the landlord still insisted on the two of them moving out- it didn' t look good to have a man and a woman sharing a flat even if they weren' t an item. In this respect, how much times have changed for the better in Ireland, now that such antiquated views have been rightly consigned to the rubbish bin of history.

George Stacpoole

I've long known George, as I used to write extensively about the antiques trade, something I've given up in recent years. George used to be an estate manager, but he's been running his antiques business in Adare, Co Limerick, for well over 40 years; he has long headed the association of Irish antique dealers and no- one knows more than him all the historical intricacies of the antiques trade. George also found a second career, as a television presenter, something he got enormous enjoyment out of. He is married to Michelina, who is Italian and who is renowed for her fashion designs. George himself is related to Thomas Johnson Westropp, active in the late 19th century and regarded as one of the greatest of Irish antiquarians.

When my book on Bygone Limerick was published by the Mercier Press in Cork in 2010, a most interesting book to compile, based on old photographs of Limerick city and county, the launch was held in George's shop in Adare; it turned out to be a most agreeable occasion, packed to the gills. A great time was had by all, on a beautiful April evening in Adare, long considered the prettiest village in Ireland, with all its thatched cottages. Over the years, I've also got to know well the two sons of George and Michelina, Sebastian, who works in the shop in Adare and Hassard, who has long worked in London and who is as much of an authority on the workings of Irish railways as his father is on the subject of antiques.

Nicola Sturgeon

She's been First Minister of Scotland since 2014, as well as leader of the Scottish National Party. Born in 1970, she came from a humble background; her father was an electrician, her mother a nurse. Nicola herself is a graduate in law from Glasgow University. She first came to wide notice outside

Scotland when the Scottish referendum on independence was staged in 2014. One of the key questions in that debate was whether Scotland would be able to retain the pound sterling in the event of independence. I told her of the Irish experience, that for many years after this part of Ireland gained partial independence, it used Irish currency that was linked to sterling for many years. She acknowledged my interest in the subject and was most cordial. After the referendum was defeated, by a comparatively narrow margin, interest in and support for the Scottish National Party, of which her husband Peter is chief executive, soared. Now in 2016, although politicians in London had hoped the issue had been put to bed for a few generations, the question of another referendum on Scottish independence is fast gaining traction.

John Swift

He was a giant among trade union leaders. He led the bakers' union for many years; even though it wasn' t one of the big mainstream unions, John Swift always had much influence and was much respected in the trade union movement. Born in Dundalk in 1986, he was born into a family of bakers, but when family fortunes declined, he camed to Dublin in 1912. He promptly joined the Irish Volunteers, then in 1927, became an active member of the Labour Party. He also became the first Irishman to be give a Soviet decoration for friendship between peoples; he was long an admirer of the old Soviet Union. John was also very involved with the Ireland- USSR Society in the 1930s. But apart from his long time work on behalf of bakery workers' rights, he also became known for his monumental book, published in 1948, on the history of the Irish bakery industry and its best- known bakeries. John Swift died in 1990, aged 94. I also got to know his son, also John, well, who for several years, ran a café in Ranelagh, Dublin.

Joan Tighe

Joan was a lovely lady of the press, who died in 2014 at the age of 91. After she died, there were many tributes to her and her long career with the Evening Herald, now The Herald, where she began in 1966 and from which she retired in 2002, a remarkable 36 year span in which she wrote, as women's editor, about fashion and countless other topics of interest to mainly female readers. Before the Evening Herald, she had worked for the Tatler & Sketch, but what all her obituaries failed to mention was that she had started off in Wilson Hartnell public relations, and had gravitated towards journalism. She also had a keen interest in local history and was long involved with the Old Dublin Society, much involved in its many publications. As my old and sadly lamented friend, Paul Drury of the Irish Daily Mail and a former editor of the Evening Herald, said at the time of Joan's passing, she was a true journalistic institution, one of a kind.

John Trew

I got to know John Trew in the early 1970s when he was features editor of the Newsletter newspaper in Belfast. I was a young journalist just starting out then, but he gave me plenty of opportunities and encouragement. Although the Newsletter has always been a Unionist newspaper in its long existence, the oldest English language newspaper in the world, going back to 1737, there was never the slightest interference with what I wrote and never any censorship if any story I did had a cross- border angle to it. In short, my time working as a freelance for the newspaper for two or three years while we lived in Belfast, gave me a lot of journalistic confidence and opportunities to hone my skills. Another journalist I knew well in Belfast was Ronnie Hoffmann, who wrote extensively for the Newsletter before gravitating to The Irish Times; he subsequently emigrated to Australia.

But John Trew was quite a character, built like a rugby forward, which indeed he was at school. Then at Queen' s University in Belfast, he edited The Gown, the student newspaper there. After a few years as features editor in the Newsletter, he was promoted to editor in 1974 and stayed there until 1984. After the Newsletter, he went into travel writing, founding Northern Ireland Travel News.

There' s always been a lot of interchange between the various Belfast papers; I' ve written quite a few pieces for the Irish News and I' ve always found them extremely helpful when I' ve been writing about newspaper history. It' s been great to see over the last few years, how the Irish News has more than managed to hold its own and surpass other Belfast papers, like the Newsletter, in terms of circulation. It was at the Irish News, about a decade ago, that I first got to know Margaret Canning when she wrote up one of my local history books. One particular photograph we hadn' t been able to identify, so the Irish News ran a competition. They got deluged with entries and we discovered that the photograph was of Dingle, Co Kerry. Since then, Margaret has moved on to become business editor of the Belfast Telegraph and I'm glad to say we still keep in touch.

Joan Trimble

She was a well- known composer and pianist especially in the North and in musical circles in London, but I came to know her because of her involvement with the Impartial Reporter newspaper in Enniskillen When I was researching my 1983 Irish newspaper book, she was very helpful in providing information and photographs about her newspaper, especially the years that her father, Bertie Trimble, owned and ran it. After his death, she took over the running of the paper. What she never mentioned was that her husband had been severely ill for decades, so she was in fact his carer for many years. Within a few weeks of her dying in 2000 at the age of 85, he too passed away.

Tom Tobin

Tom was an old friend of mine, whom I got to know well when I was a trade magazine editor, and was commissioning copy. He could always be relied to deliver interesting material on time. Tom had a very interesting career, although at one stage, he managed to capsize himself because of drink.

He came from Abbeyside in Dungarvan, west Waterford, where he was born in 1926. When he was starting out, he managed to work for both newspapers in that town, the Dungarvan Leader and the Dungarvan Express. Then he opened a bookshop in the town, before developing his skills as a photographer. After he died, a considerable collection of the photographs he took, many of historical interest, found a home in the Waterford County Museum.

In 1953, he started a newspaper of his own, the Waterford County Gazette, but it only lasted a short while. His later career was spent, not in Dungarvan, but in Limerick, where from 1965 to 1970, he was editor of both the Limerick Leader and the Limerick Chronicle, which had been Protestant owned until it was taken over by the Leader. But one night, he made a fatal mistake. He was drinking heavily in a hotel in Kilkee, Co Clare, when he noticed a female member of the Buckley family, who then owned and ran the paper, walk in. He gave her a very candid opinion of their ownership and their management style; next morning, after he had sobered up, Tom found himself out of a job. But he managed to survive, subsequently, doing a lot of work for organisations like Shannon Development. He also did a long running column in the old Weekly Cork Examiner called Rambling through Munster.

He was a feisty character, who always told it like it was, but he was always very friendly and easy to like; on the several occasions that Bernadette was with me in the Mid- West, Tom was always most hospitable. He was a great character, who had a long and interesting career, despite having been the architect of his own downfall on one occasion. He died in Limerick in 1989, aged 63.

Dr Pat Wallace

I' ve long been friends with Pat, the now retired director of the National Museum of Ireland. From Limerick, he studied archaeology and history at NUI, Galway and joined the National Museum in 1971. Three years later, he was put in charge of excavations at the Viking site at Wood Quay and Fishamble Street in Dublin, where the headquarters of Dublin City Council was subsequently built. In 1988, he was made director of the National Museum, and oversaw its expansion to Collins Barracks in Dublin and Turlough Park near Castlebar in Co Mayo. He has written extensively on Irish cultural heritage and his recently published book on the excavations at the Viking site in Dublin in the 1970s is an extraordinary publication, both in sheer content and size.

Sheila Walsh

A remarkable journalist of the old school, Sheila worked for the old Irish Press for years and became known for her wedding columns. Sheila knew everyone who was anyone, including President Kennedy and Princess Grace of Monaco. As she was such a well- known figure on the social scene in Dublin, Bernadette got to know her quite well, while after we came to live in Dublin 4, I too got to know her well, as she lived in a flat in Pembroke Road, close to the junction with Waterloo Road, and would frequently bump into her in the locality. Subsequently, she left Pembroke Road and went to live in a nursing home in Co Donegal, where she died in 2014 at the grand old age of 96.

Bill Walshe

The late Bill Walshe was one of those characters in the advertising business who had a habit of telling wonderful stories, each layer more extravagant than the one before, so that in the end, the whole concoction became so fanciful as to be compelling. He was long known as the biggest spoofer in the advertising business and that' s saying something! The competition is strong. I had first met him when his agency was in the Kevin Street area, but after he founded the Innovation Group in 1988, it was located in a more upmarket area, Trinity House, a converted church, in Charleston Road, Ranelagh.

Alan Warner

He was my professor of English at Magee in Derry and I got to know him very well, a very compassionate, non- judgmental man. He had been born in Warwickshire, England, to Irish parents, who had emigrated to England. His great grandfather was a saddle maker in Skibbereen, Co Cork. Alan, who was educated at Cambridge, went on to teach at universities in east and southern Africa. He was the first professor of English at Makerere University College in Uganda. In 1961, he took up the job in Magee, but always lived at Fahan, just across the border in Co Donegal. After the decision was made to set up the University of Ulster, based in Coleraine, he became professor of English both there as well as continuing in Derry.

I was often invited to his house at Fahan, a marvellous place with great views out across Lough Swilly. I well remember one day there, when we were discussing cars, and I said that one day, I' d like to have enough money to own a Mercedes- Benz. He gently chided me for having such ridiculous notions; years later, I can see that he was exactly right!

At Magee, he edited Acorn, a literary magazine, to which I contributed. His speciality was Anglo- Irish literature and he wrote several books about the legendary poet, Paddy Kavanagh. I remember vividly the time he tried unsuccessfully to introduce me to Kavanagh (qv), who was characteristically rude.

After Alan retired, his most famous book was the one he had published on walking the Ulster Way, in 1983. He died in 1998, aged 86; I remember him as a kindly and gentle soul, who did much to help me keep going during my very difficult and unenjoyable time at Magee.

Dick Warner

Dick is slightly younger than me, born in 1946, and I got to know him first when I was working on my first book production, the 1979 Fishing in Ireland volume, which I edited. Dick was one of the contributors. A graduate of Trinity College, he worked as a programme producer for RTÉ radio for many years and always managed to maintain his hippy style, at one stage, living with his family on a canal boat. He produced many wildlife programmes, presented by Derek Mooney, who was then at the start of his career in broadcasting. When I presented the Paper Tiger series in the autumn of 1992, on the Irish newspaper industry, Dick was my producer and he did much to create precisely the right format for the programmes. I was taping all the interviews, except the one with Albert Reynolds (qv) and it was Dick who taught me what to me was then the complex art of editing tape, now of course, a long forgotten skill. In 1991, Dick' s first television series about the inland waterways, Waterways, was produced and he went on to have great success with it. Since leaving RTÉ, he has continued to be very busy, covering environmental and wildlife affairs, including regular contributions to the Irish Examiner. The last project we had considered doing together was a guide to Ireland' s best-known pubs, but perhaps it was just as well it never came to anything, as so many pubs, especially in rural Ireland, were wiped out during the recession that lasted from 2008 for six and more years.

Lord Weidenfeld

I met Lord Weidenfeld, one of the big names in British book publishing, on just one occasion, when he came to the National Gallery of Ireland in Dublin to launch one of Molly Keane' s novels. Born into a Jewish family in Vienna, he came to London in 1939, just before the start of the second world war; his monetary possessions amounted to a postal order worth 6 s 9 d. When he was 29, he started his award winning firm, Weidenfeld & Nicolson with his friend Nigel Nicholson. They published such ground- breaking books as Vladimir Nabokov' s Lolita and James Watson' s The Double Helix. The firm was renowned for having such authors as Henry Kissinger and Pope John Paul II on its books. He was also an avid lover of the fair sex and was married four times; he died in January, 2016, at the age of 96, after a tempestuous life at the heart of British book publishing.

Dermot Weld

One of the greatest of all Irish horse trainers, I interviewed Dermot Weld on one occasion at his stables at Rosewell House at the Curragh, right in the heart of Ireland's racing industry. Dermot's father, Charlie, was also a successful horse trainer; Dermot was born in 1948 and eventually took over his father's yard, in 1972. Since then, he has held the record for Ireland's most successful trainer, having trained 2, 578 winners in Ireland, and that record was set back in 2000. He has also been named Ireland's champion trainer on 21 occasions and has won countless big races on four continents, besides winning every possible prize in Ireland. Yet despite being such an outstanding figure in the world of horse racing, I found him a modest, straightforward man, almost a little reluctant to talk about his string of successes.

Garfield Weston

Garfield Weston was one of the best- known Canadians in Britain, apart from Lord Beaverbrook, one- time owner of the Daily and Sunday Express. Moving with his family to England in 1935, Garfield built up a vast empire of bakeries in Britain, as well as a chain of supermarkets, owned by Associated British Foods, which at one stage, owned what is now the Tesco chain of supermarkets in both parts of Ireland. Garfield had also been an MP in England during the second world war.

In the early 1970s, I had the slightly unusual job of editor of a magazine for the grocery trade in Northern Ireland and I thought it' d be a great idea to interview him about his group' s Allied Bakeries in Belfast and Stewarts' supermarkets in the North. I was a little surprised to get back an almost immediate reply saying that he' d be delighted to meet me and do the suggested interview. So in due course, I found myself at his head office, in Berkeley Square in London, sitting in this enormous boardroom, interviewing one of the then leading businesspeople in the UK, who couldn' t have been more friendly or informal.

While I met Garfield on one occasion, I' ve never met his youngest son, Galen, who was born in 1940. In 1966, he married a Dublin model called Hilary Frayne. Although Galen and Hilary have long lived in Canada, she and her family are reckoned to be the richest Irish people, worth around €9 billion. Galen controls such assets as Arnotts and Brown Thomas, the department stores.

Marty Whelan

I' ve only met Marty Whelan once, when he was presenting a daytime TV show with that other great TV broadcaster, Mary Kennedy. The two of them have a great way with words. Marty has been in the broadcasting business for years and he left RTÉ to go to Century Radio, but when the latter collapsed, he found it much more difficult to get back into radio than TV. The story of his life, his autobiography published in 2015, was very interesting reading, if a little on the lightweight side, but it's great that one of the shows he does now is an early morning one on Lyric FM.

David Whitfield

When I was 14 and still at school in Birmingham, I did something very audacious and no- one was more surprised than myself when it all worked out. I had heard that the Birmingham Hippodrome was planning a real pantomime extravaganza that Christmas, centred around a singing star of the time, David Whitfield. So one night beforehand, I went down to the theatre' s stage door, and despite a complete absence of any work experience of any kind and no knowledge of the theatre, I managed to talk myself into a job as an assistant stagehand. It was all very informal, cash in hand; I was merely told to present myself at 7pm the following evening for the dress rehearsal and that was that.

It was a very complex show and in the wings, one of my jobs was to help work the dry ice machine that produced clouds of "smoke" to drift across the stage. For the first time in my life, I became closely acquainted with the girls in the chorus and I' ve been fans of them ever since. Their costumes were incredibly exotic, while they were filled with great zest for life and tremendous enthusiasm for their work. Their language was very colourful and I heard many words for the first time, so their acquaintance enriched my vocabulary no end. In those far- off days, people just didn' t utter profanities, even the mildest, least of all on radio or television. Neither was sex mentioned, except occasionally, as something that happened on another planet, but it became clear from their conversations, that the chorus girls were having fun- filled and exciting personal lives. It was a delight to be in their company and soak in their joie de vivre.

About 20 years later, I was sad to hear about the passing of David Whitfield, the star of that show. He died on tour in Australia in 1980, aged 54. Despite the huge hits he had in the charts, he died almost penniless; his many women friends had been only too keen to help him spend the vast fortunes he was earning.

The best part of a decade after that experience in the Christmas panto, when I was living for a time in Birmingham, after I' d given Magee College in Derry a two fingered salute, another life changing experience happened in another Birmingham theatre, the Alexandra. That noted Irish actor, Micheál MacLiammóir, was giving a performance of his one man show dedicated to Oscar Wilde. I was so moved by that performance that I decided there and then that I was living in the wrong country and decided to quit England and settle permanently in Ireland.

As for MacLiammóir, at that time, he was considered Cork born and bred, a Corkman to his fingertips, and no- one doubted the authenticity of his pedigree. Yet in time, it all turned out to be an edifice with an entirely false front. He had no connections whatsoever with Cork and was in fact a true son of London' s East End, a real Cockney. He also had an amazing gift for learning languages and one of several languages he became absolutely perfect in was written and spoken Irish.

Dr T. K. Whitaker

A most remarkable man, I' ve had the privilege of knowing him in recent years. Bernadette has known him for far longer than I have, through her diplomatic career. He was born in Rostrevor, Co Down in December, 1916, the year of the Easter Rising, but soon afterwards, his father' s work brought him to Drogheda, where the young Ken Whitaker was brought up. He joined the civil service at an early age and made swift progress through the ranks. By 1956, when he was just 39, he was secretary of the Department of Finance, a very young age, even now, for such a high ranking appointment. Two years later, in 1958, he published his plan for economic reform, to get the country out of its decades long doldrums. He helped instigate an amazing transformation in the Irish economy and as a result of its restructuring, the 1960s saw the start of substantial foreign investment in Ireland. Ken retired from the Department in 1969 and went on to other exulted jobs, such as governor of the Central Bank, Chancellor of the National University of Ireland, and president of the Royal Irish Academy. When the troubles erupted in the North, he was able to give politicians in Dublin, including his great friend Jack Lynch, who became Taoiseach when the Northern troubles started in the late 1960s, genuine insights into what the troubles in the North were all about.

Ken has been married twice. His first wife was Nora Fogarty, whom he married in 1941; she died in 1994. In 2005, he married Mary Moore, who worked at St James' s Hospital, but sadly, she died three years later, in 2008. But despite these personal tragedies, Ken has carried on with a very active life. The first time I got to know him well was when I was researching my book on Drogheda published in 2011. I sat down with Ken for an afternoon' s chat, in his house in south Dublin; he remembered everything from Drogheda in the 1920s in absolute detail and total clarity. He also told me on that occasions of his other interests, including fly fishing in the West of Ireland. Altogether a remarkable man; if one person can be said to have changed the fortunes of this part of Ireland over the past half century, it is Ken.

Anne Yeats

I knew Anne Yeats, a daughter of W. B. Yeats, quite well, although I' ve never met her brother, Michael, who had a long political career. Anne was a noted designer, who designed many of the books published by a renowned Irish language publisher, Sáirséal agus Dill, for a period of over 20 years from 1958. Her paintings are to be found in such collections as the National Gallery of Ireland; the municipal gallery, the Dublin City Gallery, named after Sir Hugh Lane, Trinity College and the Ulster Museum. Coincidentally, we also knew another member of the Yeats family, who for a time was our landlady in Belfast, but sadly, and to be polite about it, came from a less enlightened branch of the family.

Lightning Source UK Ltd.
Milton Keynes UK
UKOW01f1441011216
288932UK00001B/7/P